Labor Disorders in Neoliberal Italy

NEW ANTHROPOLOGIES OF EUROPE

Daphne Berdahl, Matti Bunzl, and Michael Herzfeld, founding editors

NOELLE J. MOLÉ

Labor Disorders in Neoliberal Italy

Mobbing, Well-Being, and the Workplace

INDIANA UNIVERSITY PRESS
Bloomington and Indianapolis

This book is a publication of

Indiana University Press
601 North Morton Street
Bloomington, Indiana 47404–3797 USA

www.iupress.indiana.edu

Telephone orders   800-842-6796
Fax orders   812-855-7931

♾ The paper used in this publication meets the minimum requirements of the American National Standard for Information Sciences—Permanence of Paper for Printed Library Materials, ANSI Z39.48-1992.

Manufactured in the United States of America

Library of Congress Cataloging-in-Publication Data

Molé, Noelle J.
   Labor disorders in neoliberal Italy : mobbing, well-being, and the workplace / Noelle J. Molé.
      p. cm. — (New anthropologies of Europe)
   Includes bibliographical references and index.
   ISBN 978-0-253-35639-0 (cloth : alk. paper) — ISBN 978-0-253-22319-7 (pbk. : alk. paper) —
ISBN 978-0-253-00197-9 (e-book) 1. Neoliberalism—Italy. 2. Harassment—Italy. 3. Sex discrimination—
Italy. 4. Bullying—Italy. I. Title.
   HC303.M65 2011
   331.13′30945—dc23   2011025280

1 2 3 4 5 17 16 15 14 13 12

To my mom and sisters, for your integrity, courage, and defiance

Contents

Preface

For Russian linguist and literary philosopher Mikhail Bakhtin, the word "lies on the borderline between oneself and the other. The word in language is half someone else's" (Bakhtin 1981: 293). Eloquently, he asks us to imagine a single word connected on a great invisible chain to every time it has been spoken before, with its precise inflection and saturated with its historical context. "[Any utterance] is but one link in a continuous chain of speech performances" (Vološinov 1973: 72). Words, then, belong in part to everyone along the chain; our own sense of what words mean only approximate these visible and invisible past usages.

My ethnography is about a single word: mobbing. I attend to it as a set of practices, images, discourses, fantasies, mechanisms of control, forms of embodied experiences, nodes of affect. Broadly conceived, my task has been to uncover how individuals came to strongly identify with the word mobbing, and how, given certain historical situations, this word became a crucial way for them to make sense of their experience and the world. This is a big story about a little word.

Acknowledgments

Mirroring its object of study, this book is the product of multiple kinds of labor. My mentor, Laura Ahearn, tirelessly listened, read, suggested, clarified, motivated, encouraged, and cheered for me beginning with the first funding proposal for this book. I thank Angelique Haugerud for her energy, enthusiasm, and clever suggestions in our many chats, and Louisa Schein for helping me to push the envelope and for encouraging my thinking to be "supple." I am indebted to Don Kulick, who has always made so many ideas, from social theories to academia, amazingly lucid for me.

I have benefited greatly over the years from conversations with many scholars whose insights, even if they were brief critical interventions, provided clarity and illumination. I am grateful to Jane Schneider, Michael Blim, Ethel Brooks, Judith Farquhar, Uli Linke, Vince Parrillo, Ana Ramos-Zayas, David Valentine, Lochlann Jain, Dorothy Hodgson, Fran Mascia-Lees, David Hughes, and Parker Shipton. For chapter 5 in particular, I am indebted to the participants at the Rutgers University Institute for Research on Women's Seminar on Health and Bodies, especially to Ann Jurecic and Ed Cohen. My graduate experience at Rutgers leaned heavily on shared conversations, laughter, and lamentations with Andy Bickford, Kathryn Kluegel, Nia Parson, Rebecca Etz, Dillon Mahoney, Chelsea Booth, Debarati Sen, Sarasij Majumder, Arpita Chakrabarti, Darine Zaatari, Nell Quest, and Emily McDonald. For our especially spirited debates and her friendship, I thank Mona Bhan. I'm also indebted to colleagues and friends at Princeton University: João Biehl, Carolyn Rouse, Carol Greenhouse, Rena Lederman, John Borneman, Larry Rosen, Jim Boon, Elizabeth Davis, Kerry Walk, Doug Goldstein, Leo Coleman, Peter Locke, Natasha Zaretsky, and George Laufenberg. For his transformative insight and hyperbolic support, I am grateful to Mark Robinson. And for her exceptional engagement with my work, her spectacular anthropological talents, and her wonderful friendship, I thank Andrea Muehlebach.

I am enormously appreciative of the support I have been given by numerous funding institutions and agencies, including the Council of European Studies, Society for Anthropology of Europe, the Fulbright IIE program, the German Marshall Fund program, the Bevier dissertation fellowship, and special research awards and travel awards from the Rutgers Graduate School in New Brunswick, the Rutgers Institute for Research on Women, and the Rutgers Department of Anthropology.

I have been most fortunate to have had excellent editing and critiques from Donald Donham and Tom Boellstorff. I am also grateful to the editors and staff at Indiana University Press, including Rebecca Tolen, Chandra Mevis, Angela Burton, and Merryl Sloane.

Without the trust and care of a great many friends, colleagues, and participants in Italy, I could not have carried out this project; thanks especially to Grazia, Diego, Barbara, Francesca, Riccardo, Chiara, Margherita, George, Sadi, and William. I owe an immense debt of gratitude to everyone in Italy who entrusted me with their stories, ideas, experiences, and reflections. I am extraordinarily honored and grateful to you for letting me into your worlds. Especially during my years of traveling back and forth to Italy, I was truly fortunate to have the encouragement and generous support of Paride Morello and his family.

The people who surround me every day are nourishing to me in so many ways. Tanya Goldsmith's indefatigable optimism and enduring friendship have been precious gifts in my life. Since our first dialogues in high school, Neha Dixit has played a tremendous role in forming my worldview, pushing my intellectual development, and making my path gentler and warmer in countless ways. My partner, Lane Franklin Liston, has seen me through the tough end stages of this book, and his generosity, positive spirit, wit, and love have made all of my days brighter.

My accomplishments are inseparable from my family. I thank my grandparents Carmel and Vincent Altomare for being lighthouses, beaming and bedrocked no matter where I am. I have infinite gratitude for my sisters: Marissa, who has been a lifelong navigation system that keeps me in calmer waters; she anticipates my thoughts before I can even fully form them; and Dana, who has abundantly encouraged me and infused joy into things big and small. Finally, I am profoundly grateful to my mother, Maureen Molé, for teaching me how to question social conventions—an invaluable gift and, I've come to recognize, a truly anthropological blessing.

Labor Disorders in Neoliberal Italy

Introduction

Mobbing attacks "sick" workplaces, where people are considered tools and not precious resources.

— Flavia Fiorii (2006)

For some people, everything is mobbing. It's not objective, it's just what they've lived [*il loro vissuto*].

—Camilla, mobbing clinic volunteer

In a world of turmoil, who doesn't fear precariousness?

—*La Stampa* (2004a)

"She said, 'Everyone has a cross to bear,'" Cinzia uttered in a quivering voice. Her remarkably large brown eyes met mine briefly before she resettled her gaze downward, twisting her thumb across her palm. Three of us sat in close proximity around a glossy wooden desk positioned near a window, which offset the cold institutional illumination with sunlight. The view was less than comforting: a large parking lot. After a moment of silence, Cinzia was prompted gently by Fiore, a woman in her fifties with shoulder-length gray hair and clear-framed glasses: "What did she mean?" Cinzia began to cry and tremble, and then responded, almost exasperated: "That *I'm* her cross. That *I'm* difficult."

Likening someone to cross-bearing carries a particular set of meanings in contemporary Catholic Italy. Hardly an innocuous remark, invoking the cross and thus the crucifixion of Jesus implies a burden of immeasurable weight: part duty and hardship, part affliction and suffering. Even colloquially, it connotes a highly undesirable encumbrance. In this context, it had been deployed by Jessica, Cinzia's colleague in the sales branch of one of Italy's largest and oldest textile companies. The two women were at nearly the same level, though Cinzia had more years of accounting experience while Jessica had a predominantly administrative background. Cinzia described Jessica, who had been actively harassing her for four years, as someone who was "always first in line," always "had her peace flag," and went to many political demonstrations. Fumbling nervously Cinzia added: "But that's her public face. Then she drops comments like, 'Whoever isn't part of the union is a parasite.'" Jessica rarely spoke directly to Cinzia but rather insulted her via carefully targeted conversations with others. According to Cinzia, Jessica was adept at amplifying her hostile comments in the close office quarters in order to maximize Cinzia's intensifying isolation and humiliation. Their dispute had been further exacerbated, Cinzia explained, because the company had recently closed one of its factories in the Italian region of Umbria, and this had left many at work worried about their own jobs and economic security. She said: "Now it's very slippery, no one even knows what they're supposed to do. Everything's changing so fast." She added that the managers were always off-site: either in Umbria, managing the closure, or in New York, managing a newly acquired firm.

In the midst of capitalist corporate turmoil, this dispute among colleagues might seem commonplace; it might perhaps be interpreted as predictable hostility between women or a tiresome labor conflict in a country where union membership remains important. But Cinzia, like millions of other Italians, named this event in a particular and new way: as an act of mobbing (il mobbing), which suggests, in its most simplified meaning, psychological and emotional workplace harassment. In the fall of 2004, when I met Cinzia, mobbing was a word moving across Italy and spiraling its way into highly visible spaces: it was in scholarly literatures, on the news, in Italian government and European Union documents, even at the cinema.

During another visit, Cinzia discussed the film *Mi Piace Lavorare: Mobbing* (*I Like to Work: Mobbing*; BIM Productions, 2004). In the film, managers and co-workers mob a middle-aged, single mother, Anna, played by acclaimed Italian actress Nicoletta Braschi. For Anna, a seemingly content worker in the accounting department, things begin to change rapidly following her company's corporate merger and the arrival of new managers. One day, her ledger is missing; a few days later, her computer crashes; soon after, her desk is taken over by a colleague. In the meantime, her colleagues begin to ignore her or treat her nastily, while the managers demand that she completes impossible tasks, such as locating a single misplaced file in a labyrinthine archive. To her boss, she claims: "I like to work," adding, "*Not* working tires me much more than working." She continuously strives to accomplish every new task set before her, whether it is counting photocopies or timing the tasks of factory workers. At times Anna is left without anything to do at all and wanders the halls looking increasingly pale and weak. The mounting stress results in a sharp decline in Anna's health, and ultimately she suffers a physical and mental collapse. Upon her return, her boss criticizes her for not "adapting" to the new "rhythm" of the company and urges her to resign. Anna, refusing to quit, successfully sues the company for mobbing her.

The practice of mobbing in the film may be bewildering to American viewers, who might wonder why Anna isn't simply fired or why her colleagues turn on her. From the perspective of the company's executives, we see that mobbing Anna takes a great deal of time, planning, and energy. And it comes at a great cost: health, legal action, capital, resources, energy. For Italian audiences, however, the film gives shape to how victims of workplace harassment might understand their own experiences. Cinzia said she was upset when her friends criticized the female protagonist for not having done enough to defend herself:

"They don't realize how much mobbing makes people suffer," she said quietly. And by suffering it was clear that Cinzia meant multiple levels of human suffering: psychological stress, physical debilitation, and even a sense of despair, chaos, meaninglessness.

Mobbing seems to defy the supposed economic logics of capitalism, with its values of temporal and financial efficiency: it is circuitous, indirect, paradoxical. For no apparent reason, Anna's work experience was suddenly governed by fear, suspicion, and doubt. Indeed these quotidian affective disorderings emerged as the most salient elements in narratives of Italians who believed that they were being mobbed. I met a professional chef who was asked to prepare elaborate meals, only to find the cafeteria refrigerator empty. An engineer told me that he was viciously faulted by managers and colleagues for a company-wide computer virus because he had forgotten to reinstall antivirus software. A woman who worked to counsel victims of mobbing believed that her files were being photocopied at night by managers plotting her removal. An elderly police officer reported to me that the stress of mobbing had led to the loss of six teeth after months of being left alone in a room with just the penal code to read. A hotel worker's visits to the restroom were meticulously timed by her supervisors. There were also people, often men, who described what seemed to fit the prevailing definition of mobbing, but they would either describe it as an instance of the "precariousness" (*precarietà*) of labor or avoid any label whatsoever. For Cinzia, mobbing provoked physical symptoms, including hand rashes and sleeplessness, in addition to anxiety and depression. Mobbing was also why and how she had found Fiore, who ran a clinic for victims of mobbing. The new concept of mobbing had deeply shaped Cinzia's life: socially, in the way she encountered her colleagues' actions; politically, in the way she navigated clinics and contemplated actions related to her employment; and intimately, in her psychic turmoil and ill health.

This book is a study of the complex array of practices, affect, and bodily states, and the cultural assumptions and discourses about gender, sexuality, class, global economics, and labor that have accrued around a single term: mobbing. In a brief span of time, a little more than ten years, mobbing has become a deeply resonant cultural concept and a new way of identifying oneself and others: mobbers (*mobbizzatori*) and mobbees (*mobbizzati*), victims of mobbing. Why the pervasive suspicion and doubt in the workplace? Is mobbing a perverse strategy to bypass Italy's famously rigid labor protections? Why did mobbing become critical just as Italy and other industrialized nations were reforming their labor markets, leading scholars to announce "the end of work" (Rifkin 1995)? How have Italian ideas about social difference, particularly differences of gender and class, reemerged or become obscured within the discourse of mobbing? Through the ethnographic study of mobbing, broad economic, social, and historical structures are made visible in the day-to-day injustices, frustrations, and suffering of workers. At the same time, we see how economic and social alienation and uncertainty can make us, quite literally, ill;

how workers fashion and are fashioned by the state; and how certain cultural narratives help social actors to grapple with immense transformation (Molé 2007b, 2008, 2010).

Mobbing is one symptomatic eruption, one emergent bubble, one dynamic node of what I see as a millennial dialectic between safeguards and uncertainty, security and insecurity, keeping safe and being subject to risk. Mobbing emerged at a particular historical moment when the workplace was characterized by two opposing forms of employment: stable and precarious. The former, similar to other welfare states, was "based on high degrees of standardization in all its essential dimensions: the labor contract, the work site and working hours" (Beck 1992: 142), and the latter was characteristic of the current workings of global capital, "a risk-fraught system of flexible, pluralized, decentralized underemployment" (ibid.: 154). Italy is famous for its elaborate apparatus of labor protections, which allows Italians to keep long-term job positions. For example, in 2005, 45.8 percent of Italians had held the same jobs for over ten years, compared with the 8.2 percent European average (ANSA Notiziaro Generale in Italiano 2005a; hereafter, ANSA). Certain standard employment contracts, such as what I dub the "lifelong" or, more literally, the "indefinite" time contract" (*contratto a tempo indeterminato*), have been likened to being enclosed in a barrel of steel (*botta di ferro*)—nothing can get through it (Williams 2004). In other words, it has been both legally challenging and costly for companies to dismiss workers with such contracts. Since the 1990s, the Italian welfare state has upheld most labor contract protections, while at the same time promoting new policies that legalize nonstandard (e.g., short-term, temporary) job contracts to create greater market flexibility (Di Matteo and Piacentini 2003)—part labor protectionism and part casualization of labor. For the first time, employers in the 1990s and 2000s had a wide assortment of legal ways to hire short-term workers as viable alternatives to lifelong contracts. Many Italian workers suddenly found that their "barrel-of-steel" contracts were less than sound and, for those hoping to find work, the possibility of getting such a contract was reduced to an unlikely aspiration.

Italians use the term "precarious" (*precario*) for this new assortment of what social scientists, notably economists, refer to as "flexible" short-term or self-employed job contracts, and "precarious-ization" (*precarizzazione*) for the process of rendering economic, political, and social arenas precarious—unstable, uncertain, high risk. Further intensifying this sense of everyday precariousness, Italian demographics are in flux: Italy has one of the lowest fertility rates in the world, averaging around 1.2 births per woman since 1993, which has engendered a national debate about the diminishing population (Ginsborg 2003: 69; Krause 2001). There has also been a sharp rise in immigration coupled with increasing xenophobic sentiments, especially in the Veneto region (Colatrella 2001; Tossutti 2001; Grillo 2002).[1] The immigrant "crisis" is often explicitly linked to Italy's low birth rate, and news media portray a shrinking Italian population in contrast to the apparently infiltrating *extracomunitari* (non-EU immigrants) (Krause 2001). Precariousness thus entails both economic and existential risk and uncertainty. Take, for example, a news article that discusses the state of "pseudo-mobbing." It warns workers: "Be careful, however, not to mix up the true and real persecution with a subjective state of mind. In mobbing, these two components are connected, but they shouldn't be confused" (La Repubblica 2001). "Pseudo-mobbing" is an example of existential precariousness: a particular kind of subjectivity and affective state in which persecution of various kinds seems imminent.

Mobbing unfolds as a series of practices, ethics, and ideologies that fluctuate and shift between protection and precariousness. The "cultural biography" (Kopytoff 1986) of mobbing begins at a critical historical moment in Italy when labor rights, good health, and job protections have come vividly into direct opposition with a set of social, economic, and political risks. Mobbing uncovers an Italian state composed of multiple social, political, and economic orders, including a welfare state able to maintain and renew legal protections that safeguard job stability and occupational health; a socialist state keen on upholding the rights of labor; a post-fascist state that tips protection into paternalism; and a neoliberal state that privileges the expansion of corporate power and risk control. This study provides a lens to reexamine debates about the state, neoliberalism, and the regulation of capital. Mobbing also highlights how the configuration of labor under neoliberal conditions creates and shapes particular kinds of gendered and classed subjectivities, somatic effects, and affective registers. Protection and precariousness are not mutually impenetrable categories. Rather, certain labor and state protections actually intensify the precariousness of workers, while within social and economic precariousness worker-citizens find new pathways for protection. It is precisely the volatile simultaneity of protection and precariousness—fueled by social and affective displacement arising from the growing risk-bearing work regime—that has produced mobbing as a culturally urgent issue in Italy.

The Birth of Mobbing

In 2002, surveys estimated as many as 40 million Europeans were victims of mobbing (Corriere della Sera 2002b); in 2005, reports suggested that from 4 to 18 percent of workers in Italy were mobbed (ANSA 2005f); and in 2008, over 1.5 million cases of mobbing were reported for Italy (Craighero 2008). Sixty-five percent of cases occurred in the North (Corriere della Sera 2003) and as many as 100,000 in northeastern Italy alone (Bignotti 2005). But what is it? *Mobbing* is an English word, yet it is an unfamiliar term to most English speakers, due to its particular social history.[2] Alternative terms for mobbing in English include workplace bullying, emotional abuse, generalized workplace harassment, and status-blind harassment. In Italy, common glosses include "psychological pressures, mistreatment, verbal aggression" (La Repubblica 1999b); "moral harassment" (*molestie morale*; Nistico 2003); and "psychological terrorism" (*terrorismo psicologico*). Other terms associated with mobbing include vertical mobbing (*mobbing verticale*), suggesting harassment between workers of two different corporate levels; horizontal mobbing (*mobbing orrizzontale*), which occurs between same-level colleagues; and double mobbing (*doppio mobbing*), referring to the impact on family members and, occasionally, bullying among children (Bignotti 2005). Here is one common definition from an Italian court:

> From the English *to mob* (group assault) and from the Latin *mobile vulgus* (riotous crowd), aggression or violence or persecution in the workplace perpetuated with a certain systematic and repetitive manner by one's manager or . . . colleagues, using behaviors able to harm, discriminate, or progressively marginalize a determined worker in order to estrange him, marginalize him, and eventually induce him to resign. . . . in extreme cases, [this could result in a] propensity for suicide from the absence of self-realization in work and the lack of normal gratification in social relationships at work. (Meucci 2006: 39)

From this definition, it is evident that mobbing manifests not merely as a labor problem, but as a profound form of psychological trauma. Mobbing is highly familiar to most Italians and to many other Europeans; it spans Germany, Sweden, France, Austria, and the United Kingdom (Di Martino and De Santis 2003). In 2001, the European Union encouraged states to pass legislation to prohibit mobbing (Mobbing in the Workplace, A5-0283/2001). In Europe, the Germans and Scandinavians use the term "mobbing," the French use the term "moral harassment" (harcélment moral), and in Holland the term is "pesting" (pesten).

Originally, the idea of mobbing as unpredictable and sometimes unprovoked collective harassment was borrowed from literature on animal behavior, specifically avian mobbing: "The behavior known as 'mobbing' has been defined as a demonstration made by a bird against a potential or supposed enemy belonging to another and more powerful species; it is initiated by the member of the weaker species, and it is not a reaction to an attack upon the person, mate, nest, eggs or young" (Hartley 1950: 315). Despite its origins in the victory riots of smaller animals, mobbing among humans primarily refers to the elimination of the weaker individual, not the superior, though the notion of coordinated group action remains salient. In the 1980s, Swedish psychologist Heinz Leymann redeployed the term to the human realm, using it to describe group harassment in the workplace (Di Martino and De Santis 2003).

What consolidated this meaning in Italy was the work of occupational psychologists. Expanding his research into Italy in the mid-1990s, German psychologist Harald Ege (1996, 1997, 1998) focused on the destructive psychological and social effects of mobbing and codified mobbing into six discrete phases, progressing from isolation to harassment to illness. Ege is one of the leading mobbing specialists in Italy and the president of Prima: The Italian Association against Mobbing and Psychosocial Stress (Associazione Italiana contro Mobbing e Stress Psicosociale; Prima 2005).

Various private and public health organizations have been founded in Italy to address the problem of mobbing, including the Bologna group Mobby and psychiatrist Renato Gilioli's Work Clinic in Milan for research, therapy, and rehabilitation related to mobbing (La Repubblica 1999b). The first mobbing clinic (sportello di mobbing) dedicated to helping victims of mobbing was opened in the northwestern urban center of Turin in 1999 (La Repubblica 1999b).

In 2000, the Italian Movement of Associated Mobbees was created. Its founder recounts: "I have been an executive of the State Railway and for three years I was a classic victim of mobbing: isolated, disqualified, professionally devalued. I began to connect myself to other workers in my situation, and we decided not to be passive subjects, but to create an association, a movement that represented all mobbees" (La Repubblica 2000a). A movement is an appropriate term for the hundreds, if not thousands, of mobbing hotlines, clinics, research groups, and counseling centers in Italy and the rest of Europe. The study of mobbing has become a continually expanding area of specialized knowledge production and includes public discourses, academic and popular literatures, and new educational tracks.

Mobbing and the "New Economy"

In the mid-2000s, mobbing was considered by most Italians to be new and related specifically to the growing instability of the labor market. "Mobbing Prospers in the New Economy," cried the headline of an Italian newspaper (La Repubblica 2001). Of the many tropes within the discourse of mobbing in Italy, one of the most consistent and powerful situates mobbing as a brutal and dehumanizing aspect of work:

> [Workers are] stressed by computers and as if that weren't enough, oppressed by bosses. [It is a] hard life, that of the workers of a technologically advanced society, of the corporations that have adopted the new canon of the "new economy" to the letter. And it is between the desks of the most technologized offices, in fact, that mobbing finds its most fertile terrain: here, the hierarchy is ruthless, exploiting the frustrations of employees. (La Repubblica 2001)

The "new economy," in public rhetoric, describes the state's campaign to advance economic reform of the labor market in order to create fast, flexible, and technologically innovative business organizations (Thrift 2000), and it signifies a new social, political, and economic order of "scientific institutions with techno-elite[s], [a] consumer society, [and] professional communities with social capital and intangible resources" (Carboni 2005: 45–47). Put simply, the "new economy" refers directly to the rise of neoliberalism (Sassen 1998; Edelman and Haugerud 2005; Harvey 2005; Robinson 2007b).[3] David Harvey theorizes neoliberalism as an ideology which "proposes that human well-being can best be advanced by the maximization of entrepreneurial freedoms within an institutional framework characterized by private property rights, individual liberty, free markets and free trade" (Harvey 2006: 145). In addition to political and economic strategies to commodify labor, privatize welfare provisions and ownership, and deregulate global markets (ibid.: 153; Barry et al. 1996; Collins 2005), neoliberalism is marked by "social polarization and pervasive insecurity" (Gledhill 2006: 323; Goldstein 2004, 2005); the acute expansion of inequality (Held and McGrew 2003; Graeber 2005; Sassen 2005); social injustice; and the commodification of bodies, cultural forms, and lifestyles (Comaroff and Comaroff 2001; Scheper-Hughes 2000; Ong 2006b). The current debate about the "free market" and the state recalls concerns that social theorists shared about laissez-faire economics in the earlier part of the twentieth century. Antonio Gramsci, for instance, argued that state authority produces the economic mechanisms of the market economy:

> It must be made clear that laissez-faire too is a form of State "regulation," introduced and maintained by legislative and coercive means. It is a deliberate policy, conscious of its own ends, and not the spontaneous, automatic expression of economic facts. Consequently, laissez-faire liberalism is a political programme designed to change—in so far as it is victorious—a State's leading personnel, and to change the economic programme of the State itself (1971: 160).

As Thompson (1967) and Polanyi (1957) later articulated, Gramsci shows that the "free market economy" is based on covertly masking the role of the state in the economy's regulation (Jessop 1977: 370; Buci-Glucksmann 1980). Similarly, the neoliberal language of an "unregulated" and "free" market suggests a hands-off approach by the state, thereby obscuring the state's involvement in the process (Sassen 1988; Held and McGrew 2003; Trouillot 2003; Edelman and Haugerud 2005). Indeed, neoliberal policies often extend to the relationship between the state and civil society, and the Western European model of social democracy has historically rested on the notion of a "comprehensive and universal welfare state" (Sandbrook et al. 2007: 14).

Italy's neoliberal reform, undertaken since the 1980s, relates to Europe's "market-radical variant of neoliberalism" (Bohle 2005: 58) and has been structured largely by its role as a member state of the European Union (Kierzkowski 2002; Van Apeldoorn 2002; Bosia 2005). Critical to this process in Europe have been transnational migration, monetary policy and exchange, and transnational political governance (Keough 2006: 433; Borneman and Fowler 1997; Berend 2006). Neoliberal economic policies in the 1980s and 1990s led to broad changes in Italy, including high unemployment rates, threats to long-term job security, and a larger informal economy (Blim 2002; Yanagisako 2002; Fargion 2003; Ginsborg 2003; Stacul 2007), while welfare policies in the 1990s focused, in particular, on pension reform rather than on unemployment and family assistance (Fargion 2003: 313). One fundamental aspect of this process has been called the "casualization of labor," referring to the rise of employment positions with fewer benefits, often with atypical configurations or only for the short term, with fewer safeguards, and with an increasing privatization of labor (Sassen 1998: 146). Public debates in Italy have reflected a great concern about the vicious effects of neoliberal policies, principally the 2003 Biagi Laws that dramatically restructured Italy's labor market (Corriere della Sera 2006). The notion of job "precariousness" for workers (rather than their so-called flexibility) as mobilized by Italy's left-wing political parties, directly critiques the privatization and destabilization of labor and often situates mobbing as a direct outcome of precariousness. The stripping of protections from Italy's labor market has produced a two-tier workforce, which is split economically and socially between long-term and short-term workers—and this split often overlaps with age, gender, and class differences.[4] The space of the workforce has thus become inhabited in new ways, with effects on the consciousness of all workers. These trends have been particularly strong in Veneto, Padua's region: while lifelong contracts were nearly halved, the number of short-term contracts almost doubled between 1991 and 2004 (Veneto Lavoro 2004: 53). Mobbing, I argue, is a form of abjection in that it is produced by labor's rapid devaluation in proximity to lived safeguards and allows actors to name the injustices and human costs of neoliberal orders.

Padua, one of the principal cities of the Veneto region in Italy's Northeast, provides a good site to study neoliberal governance and labor. Italy has a rich labor movement history and strict labor safeguards, yet Veneto has been called "the darling of neoliberal development" (Blim 1990) in part because of its early development of flexible labor strategies (Piore and Sabel 1984). The Veneto region's right-wing politics reflect and further shape anxieties about labor and frame the social and symbolic significance of toil. The right-wing separatist party known as the Northern League (Lega Nord) rose in 1996 to become the fourth largest party in Italy and Veneto's second largest party (Colatrella 2001: 316). The Northern League animates neoliberalism by asserting a specific Veneto identity and Veneto values.[5] Though it includes diverse political and economic allegiances, the league supports two central pillars of neoliberal reform: the decentralization of the state and the reduction of national welfare programs. The party also draws on Catholic notions of diligence and piety to reassert and marshal a particular northern Italian identity, even as it simultaneously affirms the secular order of the state (Ginsborg 2003: 177). Within Veneto's moral economy, work is viewed as a symbol of one's deserving and individualized efforts. Veneto scholar Ulderico Bernardi suggests: "[There is] a certain Veneto way of appreciating *work done as God commands*. Such as the generations of artisans, of farmers, but also of great entrepreneurs, of populists and patricians. [This is] one of the principles shared in the deep identity of Venetos" (2005: 14; emphasis in original). Here, the neoliberal valorization of autonomous labor is reinforced as an act of divine duty. At the same time, middle- and upper-class Veneto worker-citizens see themselves as exploited, because they often feel that their hard labor is stripped from them by the state in the form of taxes for the allegedly unworthy South or to support, via the Italian state, undesirable immigrants.

Italian States

On a macro level, the nation's economic development has been conceptualized as uneven and incomplete, as Michael Hardt and Antonio Negri claim: "The Italian economy did not complete one stage (industrialization) before moving on to another (informatization)" (Hardt and Negri 2000: 289).[6] Similarly, historian Paul Ginsborg identifies neoliberalism as Italy's "ideological warhorse, the freedom of the individual [as] the basic tenet for society" (Ginsborg 2003: 296). On the other hand, Italian citizenship may be distinguished from that of other Western democracies by its weak sense of national belonging, the collective mistrust of the state, and its diverse components of "individualism, collectivism, libertarianism, communitarianism, market capitalism, welfare statism, majoritarianism, consociativism, secularism and clericalism" (Koenig-Archibugi 2003: 87, 98). After a period of ambivalent nation-building, the fascist state built Italian citizenship on an allegiance to the patriarchal state, portraying laborers as central and important figures (ibid.: 93). Mobbing is a symptom, a piece of historical evidence, of a similar sort of incomplete and paradoxical process, since the Italian state combines its support for free market dominance with an enduring commitment, both structural and ideological, to national labor protection and welfare. Neoliberalism need not be envisioned as "a vast tidal wave," as David Harvey puts it (2005: 145), but rather as a highly contested shift that unfolds in the every day (Gledhill 2006; Sharma and Gupta 2006; Muehlebach 2007; Molé 2007a, 2007b).

Mobbing is about everyday exclusion, slow and contentious—and it can be seen as a microcosm of broad transnational and national economic processes. Work is one of the central modalities through which citizens become political subjects of the state, a process resting on a particular configuration of power and the production of difference, regulations, and moral orders (Burawoy 1979; Willis 1977; Aretxaga 1997). Consider, for instance, Article 3 of the 1948 Constitution of Italy: "It is the task of the Republic to remove all economic and social obstacles that . . . hinder the full development of the human person and the actual participation of all workers in the political, economic, and social organization of the country" (Koenig-Archibugi 2003: 96). In Italy, the worker-citizen is central to the state structure and social protections (Horn 1994). Italy has been called an "occupational welfare system" where membership in particular occupational groups is the essential component of garnering welfare protections (Koenig-Archibugi 2003: 102). It was the development of protections to safeguard the worker-citizen, which were established primarily to protect the male worker, that propelled the expansion of social rights in Italy first under fascism and then in the welfare state (Horn 1994). These origins have profound consequences within contemporary Italy and reverberate within the domain of mobbing, including how it is prosecuted under the law and by whom.

The strategizing of workplace inclusion and exclusion, as it is described in mobbing cases, often requires not collective but individual action on the part of worker-citizens. Such a shift is known to be embedded within the processes of neoliberalism, and it has been described as "the decline of social citizenship" (Isin 2004: 217), "individualization" (Beck 1992), construing citizens as "subjects of choices and aspirations to self-actualization" (Rose 1996: 41), and the actions of individuals who "take responsibility to protect themselves from risk" (MacEachen 2000: 323). These terms point to the ways in which under neoliberal conditions citizens are refashioned as more responsible for and capable of providing their own welfare, a concept bolstered by ideologies that view political subjects as rational and calculating (Perramond 2005; Ong 2006b). Stories of mobbing illuminate this process, allowing a view of how this intangible transformation of subjectivity takes place.

Subjects of Mobbing

Within this climate of high economic stakes, mobbing could be seen as a convenient circumvention of lifelong contracts and a transition strategy, however crude, to downsize and tailor the workplace to fit new economic demands. I got a glimpse of this view on one of my first nights in Padua in the late summer of 2004. Diego, a student of mine when I taught English in Padua in 1999, took me out to a pub with some of his friends, a group of thirty- and fortysomething professionals. We approached the long wooden table of men, each with his own pint of some shade of amber. When Diego introduced me with the unusual title of "his American friend here to study mobbing," the crowd hooted with laughter. One man sat up and said plainly, "I'm a mobber" (*Sono un mobber*).[7] Peals of laughter erupted and three other men raised their beers and exuberantly exclaimed, "I'm a mobber too!" (*Anch'io sono mobber!*) in a way oddly reminiscent of the film classic's "I am Spartacus" scene. When the first of the self-proclaimed mobbers, a corporate manager, settled down, he turned to me and in a serious tone explained: "You're an American and in America you don't need mobbing because you can just send someone home. But in Italy, we have Article 18 and the lifelong job contract. You can't get rid of workers unless you mob them."

This notion of coercive downsizing was a common explanatory model for mobbing: it was seen as a specific corporate strategy to dismiss lifelong workers. Lawyer Francesco Gallo, who specializes in mobbing, told me:

In the public and private sectors, employers sought illegitimate means to induce the worker to resign in order to avoid a penalty for firing a worker who could easily have been considered illegitimate or unjustified. Such means were often extremely bad for the worker's health. They were means to attack and deny fundamental human rights for the dignity of mankind.

Even though Francesco views mobbing as a vital issue of human rights, his narrative follows a series of events premised on a logical economic sequence: high labor costs, a capitalist desire to reduce labor and costs, and the need to avoid the legal and financial penalties of worker dismissal. But the idea that mobbing is merely a means of dismissing lifelong contract holders is not a robust hypothesis, as even short-term workers experience mobbing, and it may be carried out by same-level or lower-level co-workers.

Beyond revealing this origin myth, the pub scene gave me insight into mobbing's gender and class dimensions. That men would even jokingly avow being mobbers suggests that they identify with the moral understandings of work as earned, as semi-permanent, and as market-oriented, thus feminizing the Italian tradition of work as a right, as stable, and as grounded in close social and familial networks. Thus, mobbing has double significance: modern yet malign. A mobbing counselor once told me that she'd assumed that mobbing was an American or British invention that had migrated to Italy with "the rest of the Anglo-Saxon economy." Because it is symbolically wedded to an economic regime widely believed to be superior to Italy's, it is not surprising that the position of mobber could also convey a sense of desirable cosmopolitanism, financial savvy, or technological know-how. This position is predominantly, if not exclusively, masculinized in Italy.

While mobbing is often purported to be gender-blind, most mobbing studies indicate that the average mobbee is a woman in her forties who works in the private sector (Associazione contro Mobbing 2006). Gender becomes especially critical in decoding certain absences, such as the absence of sexual harassment charges in favor of mobbing, and workers' identification as freelance (*liberi professionisti*) as opposed to precarious workers (*precari*) even though their employment is short-term and irregular. Mobbing inherits and reshapes gender ideologies in Italy that carry with them a history of sharply drawn dichotomies: between lusty men and alluring women, between masculinity as dominating and bold and femininity as demure and caring.

Living Neoliberalism on the Skin

One of my most surprising findings about mobbing was the extent to which it is imagined, experienced, and treated as a health problem (Molé 2008). Mobbing is considered a threat to workers' health, a dangerous and spreading pathology: in the year 2000, Italy's minister of health, Umberto Veronesi, listed Italy's top two national health problems as cigarette smoking and mobbing (La Repubblica 2000b). In 2003, mobbing was recognized as the primary cause of work-related illnesses (INAIL 2003). A Veneto regional newspaper, *Il Gazzettino*, described the importance of codifying a single definition of mobbing: "No matter what you call it, by now mobbing is considered a sickness. It's actually nearly an epidemic and this is precisely its new frontier" (Bignotti 2005). Mobbing is invoked as an unpredictable violence with dire consequences:

> It's rather widespread and often . . . female and male workers don't have the strength, nor the protection to rebel, maybe even fearing the worst: because in mobbing you

inject a subtle venom into the more or less hidden threat of the worst: a transfer or otherwise, that forces the weak one to be subordinated to everyone, that [produces] damage against one's dignity and one's physical and psychic health. (Filippone 2002)

Why did mobbing in Italy become not merely a labor disorder but a psychological and physical one? How do workers embody, or resist, large-scale social instability? The embodied experiences of mobbing—the heart-racing pulse of anticipation, the weight of everyday dread, the empty gut of alienation—reveal with crystalline focus the micro-level intimacy and embodiment of neoliberal orders. Mobbing is nestled between what might be distinguished as the geopolitical and the biopolitical, at the points of contact between political economy and health, neoliberalism and the body, the welfare state and biological well-being, the organization of labor and gendered subjectivity.

There is a long tradition of theorizing how labor regimes marshal certain kinds of workers, and therefore particular kinds of people, into being. For instance, Gramsci linked the habits and desires of men that were formed in tandem with the rise of the Fordist economy to the nineteenth-century development of a "new sexual ethic suited to the new methods of production" (1971: 204). He elaborated:

> It seems clear that the new industrialism wants monogamy: it wants the man as worker not to squander his nervous energies in the disorderly and stimulating pursuit of occasional sexual satisfaction. The employee who goes to work after a night of "excess" is no good for his work. . . . This complex of direct and indirect repression and coercion exercised on the masses will undoubtedly produce results and a new form of sexual union will emerge whose fundamental characteristic would apparently have to be monogamy and relative stability. (ibid.: 304–305)

For Gramsci, sexual intimacy was made to conform to the demands of a wide-scale economic transformation. Alone, this formulation might compel a more top-down, materialist analysis of sexuality and how sexualized subjects, with multiple kinds of desires, shape capitalism. However, Gramsci's insight also demands that we refrain from assuming that sex, gender relations, and health are cut off from large-scale political and economic processes and structures. Daily practices, identifications, and bodily experiences cohabit in intimate proximity with emergent neoliberal labor structures, modes of governance, and ideological orders.

Other studies also have theorized this link between cultural production, economic change, and bodily transformation: how bodily discipline is a product of industrial time regimentation (Thompson 1967), how capitalist understandings of waste and efficiency shape knowledges about and the experience of menstruation (Martin 1987), how the transnational organ trade steers over the imprinted tracks of global poverty and wealth (Scheper-Hughes 2001), and how illness seems "sent" because it is an effect of global economic structures (Farmer 1990). The management of health, welfare, and bodies under neoliberal conditions reflects the continuing resonance of Foucault's (1978) biopolitics, the management of populations through disciplinary knowledges and practices in which "such entities as economy, population and society [are] irreducible to bodies that constitute . . . them, but [are] shaped by them" (Isin 2004: 221; Horn 1994: 7; Hardt and Negri 2000; Rose 2007; Esposito 2008; Kideckel 2008).[8] The "casualization of labor" (Sassen 1998) is, therefore, not only a change in the relations of production but also a change in the kinds of biological subjects that workers become. Mobbing's legibility is contingent upon changing corporate hierarchies and economic reconfigurations and attests to the ways in which capitalism is fragmented (Yanagisako 2002; Tsing 2004). Mobbing only makes sense by illuminating the existing cultural and historical conditions that make it possible.

Neoliberal configurations of labor and capital produce prohibitions, illnesses, and social values, but none of these can be reduced to the material conditions of neoliberal labor or, in the case of mobbing, exclusion from labor.

The Traffic in Mobbing

This book tracks the social life of mobbing through the northeastern region of Veneto, occasionally bringing to bear information from media, court rulings, and institutions outside the region. I set out with the premise that no single site would give an adequate and deep picture of mobbing—rather, the mapping and plotting of who, where, and what accumulated around this word would be my methodological guide. The circulation of the word *mobbing* is anything but uniform—rather, it sticks to certain kinds of people, places, and institutions. Taking mobbing as my central ethnographic object, I focus on how and when particular actors identify with mobbing as a cultural idiom, and when they do not do so. My research in mobbing clinics, which put me in direct contact with people who believe that they were mobbed, served as my point of entry. To some extent, mobbing has also been commodified, consumed, and codified on an institutional level: it can attract resources and moneys to open a clinic or expand public health services and work injury compensation; it can even transform labor law. I was particularly interested in what kinds of governing projects are promoted—or perhaps decentralized or reassigned—when capital accumulates under the banner of mobbing. I also traced mobbing within the growing community of experts (lawyers and judges, trade union workers, psychologists, medical doctors, public health professionals) and their many projects (codifying work-related illnesses, planning mobbing prevention programs, issuing or interpreting court rulings, organizing labor movements). Finally, I examined how various media (newspapers, television, films, books, websites) helped to spread this discourse to new domains and for new people. I designed and carried out multisited fieldwork for this project from July 2004 to September 2005 in Padua, Italy, building upon my prior residency (1999–2000) and intermittent months of fieldwork (2001–2003).

I conducted research at two corporate sites in Padua, one a multinational company, Contax, and the other a smaller firm, DataGisco, both of which are in the information and communications sector.[9] DataGisco is a midsized firm of 500 employees that had originally been a small family firm. Contax has over 1,000 employees in various office sites in Padua. Both have fairly young workforces, mostly between the ages of twenty-five and fifty-five, and nearly equal percentages of male and female workers. I selected these sites to observe workplace norms, social relations, corporate structures, and employer-employee relations, and perhaps even to witness a case of mobbing. I knew, however, that regardless of whether or not I observed mobbing, I would gain a sense of the social relations in such environments, since mobbing is only one social category within a constellation of relationships, people, and conflicts in workplaces.

One great challenge in studying these institutions was where to place myself along the quite rigid hierarchies and how to occupy myself when most workers were at their computers. I realized that time with executives made me suspect to employees, yet time with lower-level employees made it more difficult to reenter relations with upper-level employees. In order to get around these difficulties, I often "shadowed" different people, reading documents given to me by particular employees at their desks, right beside them, and asking questions about their projects and products. For example, at DataGisco I read a proposal for a public contract to convert archived bank files into interactive, digital software. At Contax, I perused promotional materials and new service packages that the agents were selling to their clients. This strategy worked well because I was able to converse about each company's structure, corporate protocol, projects, products, and history. During meetings, breaks, and mealtimes, I hung out socially with workers, becoming familiar with other aspects of their daily routines.

Beyond the actual workplaces, my research was connected to the broader field of mobbing experts. For example, in 2006, the University of Verona began to offer a master's degree in the prevention of mobbing:

> The master's program, therefore, aims to train professionals who are expert at recognizing stressful situations which may deteriorate into episodes of mobbing. This expert individual will acquire specific methods, techniques and tools for monitoring different situations in which mobbing may occur as well as a thorough understanding of the factors that are directly linked to the phenomenon (stress, overcompetition, management styles, etc.). (Faculty of Education of the University of Verona 2007)

I have drawn on my close day-to-day contact with mobbing counselors, lawyers, trade union workers, public health officials, and medical professionals. This wide array of trained professionals has become critical in producing, disseminating, and codifying knowledge about mobbing—and about the conditions of labor.

Of particular importance within this group are the mobbing clinics (*sportelli*) to which victims of mobbing might turn. These clinics, which are almost always publicly funded, publicize and offer services to assist the victims of mobbing, in addition to promoting education and awareness about mobbing in the Veneto region. I selected three clinics in greater Padua: a European Union–supported institution promoting women's employment; another staffed by local female volunteers, mostly college graduates with degrees in psychology; and a clinic funded by the Veneto regional government which was headed by two women who had been mobbed. Upon noting the increasing medicalization of mobbing, I also got involved with public health institutions beginning in January 2005, participating in the planning stages of a mobbing prevention program involving various Veneto public health institutions, and completing a series of interviews with health officials at various institutions dealing with the problem of mobbing from the medical perspective.[10]

The metaphor of circulation may be a helpful framework for reading this book, given that the chapters deal with a variety of populations and localities, including clinics, offices, and hospitals. Many ethnographies focus on the lives of a particular group, like Wall Street bankers (Ho 2009), Brazilian transsexuals (Kulick 1998a), Malay peasants (Scott 1985), Thai women factory workers (Mills 1999), or Sri Lankan priestesses (Obeyesekere 1986). There is no single group or institutional site behind my story, however; it is unified only by the highly enigmatic concept of mobbing.

Overview of Chapters

Chapters 1 and 2 provide historical background and an ethnographic overview of Italy's labor market, contextualizing mobbing in the Veneto region. Through a critical examination of Italy's expanding neoliberal economy and historically protectionist regimes, I show how mobbing emerged as a cultural discourse about this economic transition. I also contest a strictly materialist analysis of mobbing as simply a strategy of downsizing and cost reduction.

Chapter 2 examines the political origins of mobbing in relation to the notions of protection and precariousness. Mobbing is inextricably tied to the increasingly precarious character of labor and life in a context of neoliberal transition. Asking what propels workers to turn on one another reveals sharply diverse political orientations and multiple understandings of the human present in Italy. I show the political and cultural significance of "precariousness," both as a way to talk about employment and as a way to discuss existential angst and a state of constant apprehension. The notion of precariousness is fundamental to understanding why mobbing exists in Italy. In chapter 3, I delve into the notion of precariousness from a legal perspective by examining the emergence of the mobbing-specific legal category of existential damages (*danni esistenziali*). This category of legal injury reveals a deep tie between mobbing and damage to the soul and a new affective regime.

I then turn to how specific knowlege practices, and gendered regimes inform how workers navigate interpersonal conflicts, exclusion, and difficulties at work. Unspoken regulations shape how actors respond to trouble at work and how they are able to perform and be recognized as flexible and productive workers. Chapter 4 illustrates the gendered dichotomies within the discourse of mobbing, as women are increasingly excluded from the notion of flexible worker. To supplement the case studies of women who have been mobbed, I examine the film *Mi Piace Lavorare: Mobbing* as a critical representation of gendered mobbing.

The last three chapters turn to the ways in which health and bodies—bodies classed, gendered, and habituated by certain labor practices—are redefined in relation to shifting global economic demands and how social and economic devaluations are experienced somatically. Chapter 5 provides a close examination of a newly codified work-related illness, organizational coercion pathology (OCP), that purportedly results from mobbing. I pursue the historical question of how the right to bodily integrity, first established under fascism, gave way to forms of worker compensation and also surveillance under neoliberal conditions. What has been pathologized is not the specific figure of a mobber, but rather the organization of labor itself. Chapter 6 takes up the question of why sexual harassment, unlike mobbing or "organizational coercion," is not considered a health problem or a threat to bodily integrity. There is an implicit distinction between mobbing, glossed as moral harassment, and sexual harassment. That sexual harassment may be viewed as less serious than mobbing shows the sexual and gender inequalities that sustain global capitalism.

In chapter 7 I turn to the twenty-first-century wave of programs aimed at preventing mobbing. I examine how new pathways between worker-citizens and the state are created and then blocked through projects, governed by cohorts of mobbing experts, that promise to eliminate mobbing and improve worker well-being. Such projects reveal a specific Italian imaginary of how workplaces should be, of what may happen in the future, of potentials and estimates—a mapping, in other words, of risk.

1 Toward Neoliberalism

While mobbing is a term recognized throughout the European Union, it has come to have a particular urgency and salience in Italy. Mapping the field of Italy's dynamic political, social, and economic orders uncovers the historical conditions and tensions from which mobbing emerges. The discourse about mobbing reflects cultural apprehensions about the worst of global capitalism, reiterating its risks, effects, and human costs. The rapid replacement of Italy's protectionist labor regime, once one of the world's strongest, with neoliberal economic and social policies has played a significant role in shaping how workers might experience a sense of persecution and harassment at work. The social and economic history of stable work, as well as the speed with which neoliberalism has been implemented, has played a critical role in generating a set of moral orders in which the hasty removal of secure labor breeds fear, anxiety, and dread. Only in the context of Italy's moral economy, in which protected labor has been seen as a right of citizenship, could precarious work be recognized as unethical and even health endangering.

We must first recover Italy's specific cultural and political genealogies in order to understand why high-risk neoliberal labor regimes would seem, to many Italians, to be something economically, politically, and ethically deviant. The devaluation of labor can only be pathologized in a context in which labor is, or once was, valued. Policies that would fashion the Italian labor force into a pliable population of interchangeable human work units are unethical to many Italians, whose ethics animated the creation of state laws and policies in the past. Mobbing has emerged at a historical moment dominated by a sharp decline in labor safeguards, while there coexists a deep cultural value for safeguards in the increasingly market-oriented labor force. The pro-labor and pro-market political movements and ideologies create the moral orders in terms of which Italians may understand what is at stake during neoliberal reform and, in turn, what mobbing disrupts.

Emerging against neoliberal labor reform, the discourse of precariousness in Italy is a publicly debated set of ideas and the centerpiece of a new leftist political platform and social movement. And it has become a site of negotiation about the meaning of work, the rights of workers, and the role of the welfare state in protecting worker-citizens. The idea of precariousness underscores the perspective of the worker and valorizes long-term secure labor: it turns the neoliberal value of flexibility on its head.

Economic Miracles to Stagflation

What makes Italy's economic history unusual has been its rapid industrialization. After the demise of Mussolini's fascist government, Italy's 1948 Constitution shifted from its long-term centralized governance, particularly evident during the fascist regime, to allow for more robust regional governmental control (OECD 2001: 141). In the geopolitical context of post-fascism governance, plans were made to strengthen Italy's economy and to prevent the spread of communism in Europe (Barca et al. 2001: 32). The ruling Christian Democratic Party did not destabilize family-run firms, and it sustained economic growth into the 1950s, particularly in central and northern Italy (ibid.: 35). These factors facilitated the remarkable economic growth between 1950 and 1970 which became known as the "economic miracle," a manufacturing and industrial boom coinciding with the first reductions of the protectionist regime, which swiftly lowered labor costs (Ginsborg 1990: 214). Part of what sustained this extraordinary economic growth was the rapid movement of workers from Italy's South to its industrial North. Some studies suggest that in the early 1960s up to 5 million people (14 percent of Italy's total population) from the South moved to the central and northern regions of Italy (Di Matteo and Yoshikawa 2001: 52). The North, in essence, became an industrial frontier for unemployed and economically disadvantaged southerners.

The southern migration to the North also produced particular kinds of labor relations between employers and employees that led to industrial decentralization and flexibility (Piore and Sabel 1984). The southern workers, largely trained in agricultural sectors and not accustomed to factory labor, contributed to a great deal of strife between laborers and employers as many workers resisted the use of mass-production equipment, and this fact, unifying craftspeople and unskilled workers against employers, resulted in multiple strikes in the early 1960s (ibid.: 155). Thus, workers effectively limited not only their work pace and productivity but also the quality of their contracts and their promotions. In turn, new flexible strategies of management emerged to better control the labor force, and employers began to decentralize production. Workers were spread among smaller firms as a disciplinary measure, and this meant the creation of new jobs, especially for the artisans and craftspeople who left the large industrial sites (ibid.: 156). The existence of large firms encouraged workers to set up collaborations between smaller firms to become more competitive (Pagano and Trento 2003: 199). What is significant and unusual is that these small firms allowed workers to quickly develop the skills to become self-sufficient owners and managers themselves (ibid.). This particular type of rapid development of skilled artisans in small firms, together with the structure of decentralized production, became one of the unique strengths of the Italian economy. This mode of production, dubbed "flexible specialization," thrived in the Veneto region (Piore and Sabel 1984). The concept of flexible specialization stems from Piore and Sabel's description of Italian economic conditions but is also a generalized term for production driven by "networks of technologically sophisticated, highly flexible manufacturing firms; a strategy of permanent innovation: accommodation to ceaseless change" (ibid.: 17). Thus, and ironically, Italy's Veneto region is one of the birthplaces of the neoliberal labor regime— a precursor to what David Harvey would later describe as "flexible accumulation," which "rests on flexibility with respect to labour processes, labour markets, products, and patterns of consumption" (Harvey 1989: 147).

Despite the economic miracle, a significant portion of Italy's population, 19 percent of the workforce, was still employed in the agricultural sector in 1970 (Di Matteo and Yoshikawa 2001: 43). Wages increased in the 1960s and the need for capital remained high, contributing to the relatively stable growth of the Italian economy into the 1980s (Barca et al. 2001: 33). State labor policy in the 1970s stunted the growth of large-scale firms and limited their potential growth by requiring excessive bureaucratic work for the opening of new firms and by very high taxation (Carnazza et al. 2001: 161), leading to what became known as a period of stagflation (Vercelli and Fiordoni 2003: 14). Like many industrialized nations at this time, Italy faced a difficult economic period dominated by "oil shocks" that destabilized the economy, producing high inflation rates and high deficits (Di Matteo and Yoshikawa 2001: 58). The Fordist model of production entered into a period of crisis as the growing strength of small and midscale firms and increased market deregulation overtook the power of large industrial plants and large-scale firms (Vercelli and Fiordoni 2003: 16). Italy's governmental apparatus was also decentralized in this period, allowing greater autonomy to five "special regions" (Sicily, Sardinia, the Aosta Valley, Trentino-Alto-Adige, and Friuli; OECD 2001: 141). Italy's economic deceleration, high inflation, depreciation of its monetary unit (the lira), and high unemployment rates lasted throughout the 1980s (Di Matteo and Yoshikawa 2001: 59; OECD 1997).

Workers Statute and Article 18

A number of new labor protections for workers in the 1970s changed the cultural and social ways in which jobs and work were understood. First, there was a system of "social shock absorbers" (*ammortizzatori sociali*) which improved unemployment protection and insurance and minimized the risk of job loss (Ferrera and Gualmini 2004: 36). The Workers Statute (Statuto dei Lavoratori) of 1970, which followed the intense surge of the trade union movement in 1969, a moment dubbed Italy's Hot Autumn (Autunno Caldo), was instrumental in improving safeguards for workers. A number of the articles of this important legislation specify how workers' health should be protected: one reaffirms workers' right to health and safety (Article 9), another requires employers to verify sick leave only through public institutions of public safety (Article 5). Perhaps the most famous and contentious of these is Article 18.

This article promotes protections for workers in firms with more than fifteen employees who hold "indefinite time" (*tempo indeterminato*) contracts, which give them full-time, lifelong contracts, full social security benefits, health insurance, retirement plans, and accident insurance (Schiattarella and Piacentini 2003: 90).[1] In terms of dismissing workers, Article 18 changed older legislation by requiring the automatic reintegration of dismissed workers when the dismissal was deemed unjustified, rather than allowing the employer to pay a penalty (Ferrera and Gualmini 2004: 38). What this accomplished was to make dismissing workers with indefinite time or lifelong contracts an extremely costly and time-consuming process for employers. In Italian imaginaries, it was Article 18 that created what workers would come to call the "steel barrel" (*botta di ferro*), contracts that were highly protected and stable. Though such contracts can be used for part-time positions, they are distinct from fixed-term (*tempo determinato*) contracts, which are designated for preset periods of time. Employers could be strategic in order to avoid Article 18: the Veneto region, for example, had at one point the most fourteen-person firms in all of Italy (Colatrella 2001: 274).

By the end of the 1970s, Italy had established a labor market organized around great obstacles for worker dismissal, insurance protections for the unemployed, extensive pension and health care benefits, and a strong union role. Notably, labor policies were especially strong in terms of occupational illness and disability, providing for full sick leave benefits (Ferrera and Gualmini 2004: 39). Also by the end of the 1970s, other laws were passed to improve wage indexing, regulate youth employment, expand industrial mobility, and provide for vocational training. This period solidified a view that would remain part of Italy's labor regime and that is crucial in understanding mobbing; it established a system generally aimed at protecting insiders, those already employed, to a greater extent than outsiders, those seeking employment (ibid.: 43). Thus, even before the sharp separation between long-term and short-term employees, which began to rise in the 1990s, labor policies already pitted the employed against the unemployed. For the insiders, however, full-time employment meant a great deal of stability and security.

The Emergent Global Economy (1993–2001)

By the mid-1990s, neoliberal policies began to be seen as the preferred model in Europe in order to achieve high levels of productivity in the global economy and to transform industry, although neoliberalism would require a great deal of policy change in Italy. Many state powers were transferred to regional and local governments, agencies, and the office of the prime minister in order to make Italy more capable of European policy implementation (OECD 2001: 142–146). In addition, the state began to privatize and restructure Italy's banking system to be more conducive to neoliberal economic policies (Bianchi et al. 2001: 164; Pagano and Trento 2003: 200). Adjustments were made according to various features of Italy's demographics, such as the problem of pension spending, given the high ratio of elderly to working people (Vercelli and Fiordoni 2003: 24). Public sectors such as utilities and telecommunications were rapidly privatized, which generated nearly 8 percent of the average GDP between 1993 and 2001 (Pagano and Trento 2003: 200); state ownership in companies went from 30 percent in 1996 to less than 10 percent in 1998 (Bianchi et al. 2001: 183).

During this period, employers had few legal ways to hire cheap or short-term workers and relied on part-time labor, used informal or under-the-table contracts, or simply remained just under the fifteen-employee mark to avoid having to comply with Article 18. However, various measures were taken throughout the 1990s that rendered the labor market less stable and secure: the *scala mobile*, the practice of adjusting wages to the cost of living, was abolished in 1992, and regional and local governments were granted more authority over employment placement services, many of which were privatized (Ferrera and Gualmini 2004: 143, 98).[2] Here, "preventive" strategies meant policies and institutional strategies that staved off long-term unemployment.

The Treu Law, passed in 1997, expanded the use of flexible labor contracts and promoted privatized job placement services, gaining particular success in urban northern Italy (Ferrera and Gualmini 2004: 102). Additional measures included (1) Law 196 (1997), which no longer required that fixed-term contracts (*tempo determinato*) automatically become lifelong contracts but allowed employers to give "wage compensation" instead; (2) the expansion and promotion of part-time contracts; and (3) Legislative Decree 386 (2001), which no longer required employers to justify fixed-term contracts (Ferrera and Gualmini 2004: 102–103). For instance, an employee could be given a three-month contract without justification and could be let go after the contract expired. Various measures were also implemented in the 1990s to reduce welfare benefits, including reducing pension benefits, further decentralizing health care, empowering local administrations, restructuring unemployment benefits, and reforming social assistance (ibid.: 115–116).

Still, in September 1999, the European Union's Labour Commission criticized Italy's employment policy and high unemployment rate and subsequently urged Italy toward further reform (Spiller 2003: 108). Despite Italy's ability to rapidly privatize and implement market-oriented economic policies, it was nonetheless considered an economic liability for Europe as a whole. Promising to correct Italy's economic shortcomings, Silvio Berlusconi, representing the House of Freedom (Casa delle Libertà) political coalition, was elected prime minister in 2001; his coalition would become the first long-standing, postcommunist political government in Italy. Bolstered by his entrepreneurial image, Berlusconi had started a new right-wing and neoconservative political party, Forza Italia, which promised to improve and expand Italy's economy and political position in Europe. With a political coalition consisting of the neofascist National Alliance (Alleanza Nazionale), the deeply conservative Northern League (Lega Nord), and the Christian Democrats (Centro Cristiano Democratico), the Berlusconi-led government would overhaul Italy's labor regime (Ginsborg 2003: 291). In 2003, he passed the White Book (Libro Bianco), also known as the Biagi Laws or Law 30, which was a series of policies to regulate Italy's labor market, encouraging corporatist agreements and increasing flexibility in the labor market through the creation of an array of new atypical and short-term employment contracts from consulting to leasing to internship (Ferrera and Gualmini 2004: 157–160). In the same year, when Prime Minister Berlusconi proposed a revision of Article 18, the trade union CGIL organized a general strike of 3 million workers, and the measure was not approved. Also in 2003, CGIL led a national referendum to extend the benefits of Article 18 to companies with less than fifteen employees, but the attempt was not successful.

From their inception, the Biagi Laws have had a complex, highly politicized, and violent history. In addition to great public outrage at the new laws, the new Red Brigades, a militant communist group, killed Marco Biagi, a professor and consultant for the namesake Biagi Laws, outside his home in March 2002. The Biagi Laws indeed represent a profound clash between three political lineages of the Italian state: the center-right Berlusconi coalition; the center-left two-time prime minister, Romano Prodi, whose 2005 campaign promised to radically modify the Biagi Laws; and the Communist Party (Rifondazione Comunista), which called for an immediate repeal of the Biagi Laws and later demanded the extension of Article 18 to protect all workers, even those in smaller firms (ANSA 2006c).

Berlusconi defended the Biagi Laws in March 2005: "Thanks to the laws and the sacrifice of Professor Biagi, the labor market has been given the most advanced and the most dynamic flexibility in Europe" (Grazie 2005). In May 2006, Prime Minister Prodi announced that the Biagi Laws would be revised, suggesting that indefinite time contracts cost less for employers, while "atypical contracts" cost more (Pogliotti 2006). Prodi initiated a bill to abolish certain forms of labor, including on-call positions and staff leasing, and to establish pension contributions for certain flexible contracts (ibid.). In this publicly staged debate, flexibility became part of a web that drew together Berlusconian neoliberal politics, a transnational imaginary of Italy's role in the European Union, and a labor market understood as progress-oriented and advanced. But like Berlusconi's strong public image as an entrepreneur, flexibility also became inherently mixed up with masculinity and the subject position of the employer. Consider the following story.

At dinner at a restaurant in October 2006 during one of my trips to Padua, the first course seemed later than usual, even for Italy's temporal rhythms. The owner, a woman in her mid-forties, knew my friends as regular clients and came to the table to apologize. "The cook," she sighed, speaking in Veneto dialect, "canceled at the last minute. On a Saturday night! And thanks to the communists, I have to keep this worker!" She shook her head in anger and disbelief: "Just think—it was easier for me to get divorced! But getting separated from this worker, now that will never happen!" Because of the leftist critique of the Biagi Laws, the communists had become a visible actor to blame for undesirable workers. The owner's remarks directly mirror the rhetoric that Berlusconi used in 2005: "Today entrepreneurs can hire young people without needing to marry them. Entrepreneurs are wary of new hires because of the lifelong contract, which obliges them. Nowadays it's easier to separate from your wife than from your co-worker" (Grazie 2005).

Berlusconi's metaphor was an apt synopsis of Italy's historical condition in the 2000s. The new figure of the neoliberal economy was not the monogamous and faithful husband married to his workers, but rather the elite bachelor-entrepreneur able to change partners with ease. Berlusconi, representing the state's authority, had grafted the intimacy of marital relations onto the market-determined workings of capital and labor. And Berlusconi's public persona as a capitalist and billionaire combined with irreverent machismo to become an important cultural trope among the layers of flexibility in this complex discursive landscape—even as producing a more elastic labor market enhanced the desirability of Italy with respect to Europe and the global economy.

Echoing this notion, an occupational medical doctor told me: "The company is not your family. There shouldn't be a love relationship with your worker." Here, he referred to the ideal of familial love and connection as one that Fordist workers would often expect in the workplace; and Italian industry has historically relied upon close, familial relationships between worker and employer, even when they are not tied by kin relationships (Yanagisako 2001). The doctor had been explaining that he thought most workers had inappropriate affective expectations about work, and it was this that made them more likely to feel estranged and mobbed. Like the view of the restaurant owner, the metaphor of a romantic or familial bond, connoting trust and stability, between employers and employees was invoked as a morally wrong and socially inappropriate way to approach the workplace.

Precariousness as Discourse and Social Movement

For many Italians, the 2003 Biagi Laws animated a more urgent public discussion about precariousness (*precarietà*). While precariousness has dominated public discourse in the twenty-first century, Italy bears a deeper historical imprint as a nation long concerned with labor's vulnerability in terms of workers' occupational safety (Cafruny and Ryner 2003; Horn 1994), exploitation, and abuse (Ferrera and Gualmini 2004) in both the industrial and agrarian sectors (Holmes 1999). In the period after the passage of the Biagi Laws, precariousness became a strong Italian and European catchword for economic changes, emphasizing compromised job security and the risks that workers face in a market of declining and limited labor protections. Questioning full employment as a social value, new forms of contracts and the loss of stable employment raised the question in Europe of whether "a core value in Western society is about to fade from the scene" (Procoli 2004: 1). The term *precarious* is a direct revision of *flexibility* in that flexibility was derived from the perspective of the employer: short-term, subcontracted, or atypical workers allow for an elastic labor supply for the firm or corporation, as the workforce can be fluidly adjusted to meet various market demands. But from the perspective of the worker, being at the mercy of an endless series of short-term labor contracts is indeed precarious: uncertain, contingent, dependent upon circumstances beyond one's control.

Italians often use the term to encompass social risks beyond the workplace, evident in this comment by left-wing Partito Democratico della Sinistra (PDS) member Antonio Bassolino: "If flexibility becomes synonymous with precariousness, then flexibility risks becoming an endless thing and provoking a precarious-ization of people's lives and of Italian society" (ANSA 2005d). The discourse of precariousness reveals that what is at stake in losing a stable job is far greater than the job itself and thus is fundamental in understanding labor exclusion and possible job loss: mobbing. Claims about the increasing precariousness of Italian society expose the fictions of economic flexibility; they raise deeply ethical concerns about the relationship between a stable labor market and the collective national body. Neoliberalism deterritorializes both land and populace in the making of an elastic labor market and creates new moral orders under the guise of flexibility, while the idea of precariousness reterritorializes the worker as deserving state intervention.

Anthropologists Jean Comaroff and John Comaroff theorize the makings of "millennial capitalism," or "capitalism in its neoliberal, global manifestation" (2001: 4):

> [Neoliberal capitalism] appears to include and to marginalize in unanticipated ways; to produce desire and expectation on a global scale, yet to decrease the certainty of work or the security of persons; to magnify class differences but to undercut class consciousness, and above all, to offer up vast, almost instantaneous riches to those who master its spectral technologies—and, simultaneously, to threaten the very existence of those who do not. (ibid.: 8)

Precariousness is one culturally and historically specific formulation of millennial capitalism, underscoring the inherent and near-totalizing risk that drives its expansion and mining the "legacy of irregular piecework, of menial 'workfare,' of relatively insecure, transient, gainless occupation" as its starting point (ibid.: 5). But in the Comaroffs' formulation of millennial capitalism, class becomes disarticulated from an explicit narrative about class relations, while the Italian case shows how identifying as a precarious worker (*un precario*) positions one in a political and pro-labor class.

Most visible in sustaining and perpetuating this discourse against flexibility is Italy's Left, which solidifies the semiotic tie between Berlusconi, the center and right-wing political parties, and neoliberalism. Italy's Communist Party

(Rifondazione Comunista) and the ex-communist trade union CGIL (Confederazione Generale Italiana del Lavoro) are fiercely positioned against neoliberal labor market reform.[3] Beginning in 2003, the Rifondazione Comunista (RC) began a campaign called the Struggle of the Precarious Ones (Lotta Precariato) with demonstrations against the Moratti reform, an extension of the Biagi Laws for Italian university employment (ANSA 2004d). CGIL in the same year had begun to use precariousness as a key term for mobilizing demonstrations against the Biagi Laws, staging protests such as A Day against the Precariousness of Work (La Stampa 2003a) and, in 2005, Struggle against Precariousness: Rights and Welfare for Atypical Work (ANSA 2005c). In campaigning prior to the 2006 election, communist leader Fausto Bertinotti accused Berlusconi's government of nourishing "a cancer in our society, a dramatic illness: precariousness. . . . Precariousness is a disease that kills social cohesion" (Cani Sciolti 2006).

Evident in both the RC and CGIL anti-precariousness political campaigns was the important positioning of labor as a citizen's right. In 2003, the secretary of CGIL, Vincenzo Scudiere, explained his position on precariousness: "The laws that the state wants are aimed at destroying the *right* to work" (La Stampa 2003a). In a similar vein, in October 2005, Gloria Buffo, speaking for the Democrats of the Left (DS), said: "Making precarious work stable—this must be our objective; it means giving people who work back their *rights*" (ANSA 2005e). Political actors, then, situate short-term and nonstandard work contracts as an assault on the rights of workers, as both a legal and a moral infringement. The discourse of precariousness animates an ethical imperative to safeguard not only the opportunity to work but also the mandate that work be certain and long-lasting. Within this set of cultural understandings, secure work is not a privilege of the laborer, but rather it is a worker-citizen's right. If, alternatively, as neoliberal ideologies propose, stable work is merely a reward for those who merit it and not a right, then the state may cater to the fluidity of a transnational market.

Speaking before a national meeting of the RC in March 2005, Bertinotti focused on precariousness and, in particular, on its effect on Italy's youth:

> The "nth" firing, the "nth" promise of being hired, dissolved at the last minute. This is the life of the precarious worker. And frankly it is an unsustainable life. We need to make this a memory because it is the story of a generation, of our children, of young people in a time of globalization and neoliberalism, of the capitalism of our time. It is the story of waiting for a future that never comes, of little money, of interruptions, of getting fired, of being called to work, of being left at home, of uncertainty about today and tomorrow, about mobbing and about temporary work. (Carta 2005)

What the Left has recognized and fully marshaled to its advantage is that precariousness now characterizes the lives of an entire generation of Italians between the ages of twenty-five and forty.[4] Some reports claim that 70 percent of new skilled labor positions are precarious, constituting 45 percent of the jobs of workers between the ages of thirty and forty-four (ANSA 2005c). In the Veneto region, this is the generation that remembers their parents and grandparents working in an agriculturally driven economy, poor families with dirt floors in rural homes until the 1970s, and the dramatic period of "modernization" in the 1980s that made the region one of the richest in Italy. Even for the urban elite of Padua, the rise to middle- and upper-class status is a critical collective memory, often viewed triumphantly and as a sign of regional identity, and it deeply shapes their understandings of work and economic opportunity. Unlike their parents' success in small and midsized firms, Veneto's young, skilled, and educated workers are most likely to be precariously employed today. Rather than the poster children of 1980s flexible specialization, they have become the new iconic figures of marginal employment.

The Memory of Protection

While neoliberal economic policies are often considered an extension of certain northern Italian values, such as individualism and bootstrapping, for the most part precariousness is viewed as a foreign intruder. When the notion of firing a worker with ease came up in Italy, someone would almost always refer to this as either the "Anglo-Saxon model" (*modello anglo-sassone*) or simply the American model (*modello americano*). That is, Italians often defined a social and economic system characterized by a weakened labor force with few protections not only as the precarious new economy but also as something explicitly not Italian. Firing, glossed as "sending someone home" (*mandare a casa*), was widely thought to be the dominant managerial strategy in the United States and England. The idea of the Anglo-Saxon model suggests a public awareness that neoliberalism is a result of the economic policies established in the 1980s by British prime minister Margaret Thatcher and United States president Ronald Reagan (Harvey 2005: 88), and it still characterizes the economic policies of both countries. Perhaps, too, the notion of Anglo-Saxon capitalism implies a Weberian sense of capitalism as a particularly Protestant, as opposed to Catholic, endeavor (Weber 2001). Critics, however, point to Europe's use of the term *Anglo-Saxon model* as faulty, as it not only masks the true forefathers of capitalism—including the Scots Adam Smith and the Spanish David Ricardo—but also the great diversity of European capitalisms (La Repubblica 2005). Furthermore, it diminishes and obscures the ways in which Veneto's flexible specialization was itself a strong tradition in the Italian context and hardly a foreign intruder. However, the notion of neoliberal economics as part of an Anglo-Saxon tradition remains strong (Reyneri 2005b: 40). For example, when the European Employment Strategy of 1997 named the four main pillars of economic growth for Europe (employability, adaptability, entrepreneurship, and equal opportunity), the Italian debate centered on the degree to which such reforms were "Anglo-Saxon and northern European policy paradigms" (Ferrera and Gualmini 2004: 105). Italy's labor market as deviant from an Anglo-Saxon economy reinforces the discourse of Italy's economy as "backward" and characterized by bureaucracy and fragmentation (ibid.: 106).[5] The debate about precariousness, in light of the Anglo-Saxon model, shows the Italian capacity to render other modes of production as immoral. That neoliberalism is indexed as Anglo-Saxon persistently reminds Italians that this new form of economic and social policy, generating precariousness, is something unnatural or alien to a certain Italian way of being in the world.

Neoliberal reform was intended to dismantle a labor market defined by its safeguards or protections (*tutelà*), part of a broader ethos of Fordist stability. With the passing of the Biagi Laws in 2003, employers were able to cut costs by using short-term contracts, even though the indefinite time contract, guaranteed by Article 18, was not altered. In effect, the state expanded the possibility for corporations, public and private, to utilize alternative sources of labor, thus shifting the entire labor market as evidenced by a progressive decrease in lifelong contracts granted to workers. For instance, between 1977 and 1983, 51.9 percent of workers had lifelong contracts; between 1991–1997, this number fell to 36.3 percent (Ballarino 2005). In the Veneto region in 2002, only 24.5 percent of workers had such contracts (Veneto Lavoro 2004: 145). At the same time, it was far more difficult for new workers to be given lifelong contracts. The rate of new issues decreased 4 percent between 1993 and 2000 in Italy as a whole and dropped 33.7 percent in the Northeast (Schiattarella and Piacentini 2003: 90).

Holders of lifelong contracts are quite likely, then, to feel particularly threatened since employers are apt to favor flexible contracts. Given these conditions, one might argue that employers have become more likely to mob (push out the old, then hire new workers), but such a top-down explanation cannot, even in a functionalist way, explain same-level mobbing among colleagues with no capacity to fire one another. Moreover, mobbing is not exclusively experienced by workers with lifelong contracts. Because the lifelong contract is a legal possibility and looms large in Italian imaginaries, many workers in short-term or atypical positions are anxious to gain any sort of job security. I believe that this is a key dynamic of precariousness, leading to a rising sense of apprehension and fear for a majority of Italian workers.

Robert Castel (1997) discusses how instability is lived by those who have experienced stability, that is, precariousness gains hold progressively as future generations come to view such a dynamic as natural and self-evident. Precariousness only becomes a social problem because job protections have been a routine social expectation. In Italy, stable work was normalized only for a relatively short period of time, from 1945 to 1975, when the process of industrialization allowed most citizens to garner a lifelong position (*lavoro per la vita*) (Reyneri 2005a: 21). The Italian market has been measured as having an extremely high regime of labor protection (*regimi di protezione dell'impiego*; RPI), a quantitative measure of state labor protections that considers safeguards for regular occupations, temporary occupations, and collective dismissals. Italy had an RPI rate of 3.5 for the late 1990s, compared with 2.9 for France, 2.6 for Japan, and 0.7 for the United States (Boeri and Garibaldi 2005: 46). Italy's shift toward a neoliberal labor regime has taken place in the context of some of the most intense labor protections in the world. The acute suffering of labor exclusion (mobbing) stems from the intensified vulnerability of those who feel they have lost something in the upheaval of the labor market.

Available Work

How does a labor structure in which workers who are marginally employed share the same space with fully employed workers transform and shape workers' psychic interiorities? Within Italy's shifting labor market, the desires, memories, and imaginaries of Fordist stability need not be extinguished because of the proximity, spatial and psychic, between precarious (*precariato*) and protected (*tutelato*) workers. The Biagi Laws legalized over forty different kinds of new contracts, which enabled a rapid reduction in the number of protected contracts such that the vast majority of Italian workers, particularly those employed in the professional or service sectors, soon found themselves in a two-tier workforce.[6] Between 1991 and 2003 in the Veneto region, lifelong contracts were cut from 55 percent to 31 percent of the labor market, while short-term contracts almost doubled, from 22 percent to 43 percent (Veneto Lavoro 2004: 53). The remainder of the 2004 Veneto labor market included training contracts (*contratto di formazione*), used for workers between the ages of sixteen and thirty-two, which decreased from roughly 10 percent to 2 percent; and internship contracts (*contratto di lavoro apprendistato*), used for advanced professional training, which remained relatively stable in this period at approximately 13 percent. The two-tier workforce also represents both the success and the failure of Italy's partial neoliberalization. In part, the state seems to uphold the value of labor as inherently important to citizens, but state policies and legislation supported independent labor, regional autonomy, and the value of flexibility.

Davide Toreglia, a project manager at DataGisco, a midsized service industry firm in Padua, helped me to understand the social dynamics of this two-tier workforce and the salience of precariousness. During my fieldwork, I would often shadow Davide, reading company materials to occupy myself when he was at the computer but being present for the critical moments of meetings, lunchtimes, coffee breaks, desk-to-desk conversations, and visits to sites to manage temporary workers—even, on occasion, to dismiss them. I asked him about his relationships with new workers, and Davide responded:

> It's obvious that the relationships are different. It's not like I treat a precarious one [*un precario*] differently. . . . In a very dynamic job, I don't concentrate much on relationships. I don't have very human relationships [*rapporti tanti umani*]. . . . Sometimes maybe we exaggerate in expecting the new generation to gain work experience for themselves. It's not out of spite: "I've worked and you have to work, too." But I mean, damn, you've never worked before

or you're trying to work now! I say this to guys during the interview: this job is for two or three months now, but you may have a new opportunity, the company is big. And so if you're smart, then you work. Can't change that! . . . You have to plant yourself in there, be available [*disponibile*]. It's not as if I'm asking you to come to work for free, but if I ask you, "Tuesday, I'm starting a job, can you stay an hour?" And you respond to me, "Well, are you paying me?" I'm not saying that's not a worker's right, but it pisses me off [*mi vengono i fumi*].

Davide's narrative relies on the figure of the available (*disponibile*) worker to explain a moral and social reconfiguration of labor. Propelled by an ethic valuing workers' desire for genuine toil, workers' individual smarts could be rewarded by corporations with long-term contracts or more work. This type of logic, only salient in the context of a two-tier labor regime, fortifies the difference between short- and long-term workers, because the latter group, according to these logics, has successfully earned their positions. Inquiring about payment transgresses implicit rules of the labor regime by avowing their identities as workers with rights, a subject position largely shaped by the labor ideologies of the welfare state (Blim 1990; Reyneri 2005b). Davide, despite enjoying a lifelong contract, admits his lack of deep relationships with his colleagues, reflecting a new gendered and classed regime ruled by disaffected and distant work relationships and disavowing Italy's labor history of close ties at work (Yanagisako 2002). For the precarious ones, the promise of work creates a sense of expectation and hopeful possibility that they can acquire lifelong positions as well—if they submit to seeing labor as naturally unstable. And while short-term workers have had to prove the value of their labor and become disciplined, hard-working, and, most of all, risk taking, protected workers holding safeguarded contracts have had to deflect conflict in order to maintain their positions.

As Davide reflects, showing one's availability (*disponibilità*), despite the economic risk it may entail, was something that many workers, particularly among the women I encountered, had already adopted as a work practice. For example, nearly all of the precariously employed middle-class women with college degrees I met reported beginning a job with neither dialogue about nor written agreement of their pay. In Padua, people talked to me about jobs as if it were entirely self-evident that one must portray oneself to employers as patently disinterested in the salary. Francesca, for example, a twenty-five-year-old with a degree in the economics of tourism, had a job working in a hotel on a six-month defined time contract. She had not asked her employer how much she would be paid, but rather discovered her salary based on her first few paychecks. She admitted to me that she thought it would have been "impolite" to ask. Alessandra, a twenty-four-year-old graduate in communications, worked for over two months, forty hours a week, at a firm in Padua without asking whether or not she was being paid at all. Since this was her first job after graduation, she was still eligible for internship contracts, which are without salary. I had met Alessandra through a friend, and whenever I saw her I would inquire, "So, did you ask yet?" She would smile and shake her head. Once, she explained that asking sooner would make a "poor impression" (*brutta figura*). This practice was sustained by the fact that their parents supported them, and many Italians live at home until their early thirties. In 2003, 60 percent of unmarried Italians between the ages of twenty-five and twenty-nine and almost 30 percent of thirty- to thirty-four-year-olds lived with their parents. And this occurred disproportionately for men between thirty and thirty-four years old (37 percent of men versus 21 percent of women; ISTAT 2006: 65).[7]

In the context of socially conservative Padua, with its firm etiquette and self-presentation standards, Alessandra's use of the phrase *brutta figura* is particularly noteworthy as it is usually used to describe practices or events that are damaging or embarrassing to one's public and classed persona: bringing an inexpensive gift, wearing an inappropriate outfit for an occasion, or hosting a party at an inexpensive locale. Its opposite, *bella figura*, is also distinctly classed: wearing brand-name or elegant clothes, having excellent professional credentials, traveling frequently, or, more broadly, acquiring the esteem of others by exhibiting something that solidifies one's class distinction. Avoiding *brutta figura* means abiding by a set of regulations that codify class-based appearance, style, and etiquette. In Italy, this is not merely a public façade or performance but, as Gloria Nardini, author of *Che Bella Figura*, suggests, these regulations are "the very subtle, all-encompassing and public ways in which the expression of Italian identity is imbricated in creating 'bella figura'" (1999: 20). In this sense, one's silence about compensation in order to avoid a *brutta figura* suggests that a closed practice, one suitable to an upwardly mobile cohort, is emerging. But this is not merely to solidify temporary employment. Rather, such financial inquiries would disrupt the tenuous availability (*disponibilità*) that workers, particularly female professionals, must enact in order to secure a long-term work contract. The two-tier workplace results in the separation of *bella figura*, an upper-class consciousness in which one need not ask about money, from *brutta figura* in which economic demands portray one as working class. Fashioning oneself as economically indifferent becomes a subtle technique of self-distinction in the broader context of division and flux.

I encountered precarious workers at mobbing clinics in and close to Padua. In February 2005, Nora Darettin, a middle-aged woman of somber demeanor, arrived at Fiore Montiglio's door with a problem about work. Fiore held a public office, present in every province of Italy, and was responsible for managing a multitude of women's employment issues but, in practice, she largely dealt with mobbing cases. Employed as a check-in clerk at an airport, Nora had come to the clinic after her three-month contract was not renewed: "They told me that I wasn't good. I wasn't fast." The letter Nora received from her boss said explicitly she was not offered another contract because she was "slow." Nora told us angrily: "We're in an airport. We're not on a production line!" Nora aligned herself with neoliberal ideologies by invoking the distinction between material and immaterial products and her role in the service industry. What struck me was not only that Nora was severely depressed and anxious but also that her precarious employment was considered, rather self-evidently, as a serious and profound problem with consequences for Nora's mental health and quality of life.

In March, Fiore was finally able to speak to the supervising manager at the airport and requested Nora's reinstatement. Later that day, Nora returned to the office to discuss what had transpired. Fiore reported: "He said you were unable to adapt to the environment. He said, 'I don't want to hire her precariously. She's very capable for other types of environments, but not the airport.'" According to Fiore, he refused to rehire Nora, acting as if this was for her own good, as if he recognized and sympathized with the harshness of precarious employment—a stance Fiore immediately labeled as manipulative. Nora, visibly annoyed, reminded us that her training had been inadequate and that her employers were corrupt. For example, they had hired the boss's sister with a long-term contract even though she'd been incompetent: "She left a line of people just because she has a lifelong contract. I said, 'Look, if you need a ten-minute break, I'll come in for you.' Basically, this company is pitting the poor against the poor!" Fiore put this into perspective: "Most people with precarious jobs try to hide their errors, but she's beginning to advertise hers. In a precarious environment, everyone hides everything; they deny the evidence. But then again, so do the non-precarious ones." The logic here was that Nora's co-worker failed to be an attentive and vigilant worker precisely because she had job security, revealing yet another increasing perspective: one's contract typology is an interpretive framework for one's interiority. Fiore also revealed a particular sensibility about the new practice of hiding and had her own theory about knowledge production: in such a context, everyone must be doubted, and truths become, by definition, deceptions. Fiore looked at Nora directly and spoke slowly and evenly:

> You have to understand that, in some ways, the world is terrible. In this world, if a job is done well or poorly, not everyone gives a damn. They only care about a favorable economic profit, not how much money is spent on polluting. What is important is getting money. This is objective, not subjective. It is the opposite of slowness. And if justice is important, then we have to busy ourselves with obtaining it. We have to realize that we are not what they want. They need to earn money, but why should we adjust ourselves according to their mentality?

Fiore had picked up on Nora's comment that she was too slow for the job and reframed this slowness as a way in which she was distinguished from the fast, unethical, and polluting capitalists. Her speech seemed to comfort Nora, and she smiled. Articulating multiple available cultural ideologies of work and, in this sense, feeling ontologically divided, Nora identified as a neoliberalized subject with her attention to the superiority of immaterial labor, her refined ability to navigate substate circuits like Fiore's office, and her desire to independently acquire economic and social resources. Yet she also revealed her more Fordist class consciousness, her moral positioning of employers versus workers, and her powerful longing for stable work and an acceptance of her slowness. In the two-tier structure, social practices sometimes have unstable interpretations and meanings: Nora is neither part of the normative protectionist workforce nor fully inhabiting a new neoliberal order.

On another day with Fiore, I met someone struggling with the consequences of a precarious contract that had been discontinued at a particularly inopportune time. Sandra, a woman in her early thirties who worked in a clothing shop, walked into the office with her third-trimester belly rounding her jean overalls. Sandra described how her boss at the store had promised her that she could work "*as if* she had a lifelong contract," meaning with the various benefits and safeguards, so she agreed to remain employed on six-month renewable contracts for a few years. Sandra explained: "After six months, I wasn't changed [to a lifelong contract], and the boss says, 'Don't worry, you're protected,' but then he gave me only short-term contracts." Italian employers are only allowed to renew certain kinds of contracts twice, such as the short-term ones (*contratto a tempo determinato*), before they default to lifelong ones (Cirioli 2006). After informing the shop owner that she was pregnant in December 2004, she was told via letter that her contract would not be renewed when her latest six-month period expired in March 2005. Her boss suggested that Sandra ask for INPS (the Istituto Nazionale Previdenza Sociale, National Institute for Welfare) to finance her maternity leave (a benefit she would have received had she been on a safeguarded contract). She continued: "He mentioned that the contract was expiring. I called him and he says, 'Well, you're pregnant and you can't come back to work. Are you sure you want to come back right away?' I said, 'When I've finished everything. I have two months [of] leave prior to the birth and three months after. But maybe part time. But I can't come back full time.'" Sandra hoped that Fiore would be able to help her secure the maternity leave she would have been granted had she been given a safeguarded contract. During maternity leave, women are paid 80 percent of their wages by INPS, and most national contracts require that the employer pay the 20 percent difference in wages.

Sandra said her boss had promised not to "leave her uncovered" and "did so in good faith." Lina, one of the lawyers who collaborated with Fiore's office, told Sandra that she would not qualify for INPS moneys because she had only three months of INPS contributions in the eighteen consecutive months prior to the birth of the child, which would hardly cover a five-month maternity leave. Unfortunately, there was little legal recourse because her employer's decision was within his legal limits: he was allowed to offer her only two consecutive definite-time contracts. Sandra said she would not be willing to take any legal action against the store owner because she felt that he had acted in her best interest, adding that it was possible her employer had been deceived about INPS resources. Surely, she suggested, he had made a mistake regarding the kind of worker protection she would be entitled to from INPS.

Sandra's case exemplifies the consequences of precarious labor and the split workforce, particularly for women. Women are asked to trust their employers and be constantly willing and flexible in order to secure a favorable employment contract. But despite her faith in her boss, Sandra had become precarious: she had no guaranteed job, financial support, or maternity benefits. Fiore talked to Sandra about the risks that such precarious contracts often entailed for women in particular. Women in Veneto are dismissed, or at a greater risk of being mobbed, once they are pregnant.

Pregnancy represents a key shift for women as over 25 percent of Italian women leave work after childbirth (ANSA 2006b). Nearly all of the twenty- and thirty-year-old women I knew reported lying about their marital status in order to convince employers that they would remain childless for a number of years. To my surprise, women often told me that their employers had openly, illegally, inquired about their marital status and intentions about starting a family. Access to work in the Veneto region for women, in other words, means guaranteeing employers that they will remain underpaid and childless.

The Blank Contract

In addition to the employees who did not ask about their remuneration or accepted unusual and risky contract configurations, there was another way that employers sought to precariously employ workers. In October 2004, a new term seemed to be the buzz of many conversations at mobbing clinics and in the corporate offices I frequented: the blank contract (*il contratto in bianco*). As it turned out, the blank contract was not actually a contract, but a letter of resignation, without a date, that employees would sign when they were hired; employers could, at any time, fill in the date and thereby terminate the contract. Corporations thus bypassed the state by granting lifelong contracts but with the letter as a built-in dismissal policy, which transformed the workers with such contracts into precarious short-term workers without safeguards. Friends joked that such a mechanism was clever (*furbo*), a smart and circuitous means around Italian law; this trope often came up in conversation, even as people didn't lose sight of it as a devious and unjust ploy. Practices that had similar resonance were Neapolitans who rode with blow-up dolls to avoid carpooling rules or Veneto firms officially employing only fourteen workers to avoid having to issue safeguarded contracts (required for firms with fifteen employees).

During this period, in which the desire for guaranteed employment had not lost much of its collective psychic weight, workers were making a compromise:

bearing the risk of immediate dismissal in exchange for the benefits and safe-guards of the lifelong contract. The labor market had expanded its entryways but only via precarious contracts, producing a situation in which Paduan work-ers would independently negotiate their employment (making the requisite sacrifices) in order to secure employment that, at the very least, gave them the benefits and safeguards they desired. But an important shift had been made: employees had to demonstrate their worthiness despite the persistent threat of dismissal. Employers emerged in a more ideal position with respect to the la-borers, who had to battle one another in order to demonstrate their value. Be-cause the blank contract's usage was obscured in rumors and because it was il-legal, it was difficult for me to gauge its prevalence. However, I consider the blank contract to be a highly significant indicator of a rise in corporate exploi-tation that relied on the still-salient Fordist expectation of permanent work.

Sword of Damocles: The Normalization of Fear

The commentary of Elenora Pagnan, one of DataGisco's partners and its director of human resources, condenses a common affective disposition in the Paduan workplace at this historical moment. In describing the labor market, she explained: "During this moment of crisis, this time when you have to cut costs, people who are not productive have to leave the company." Elenora told me that she had been accused of mobbing by one of her assistants, but had de-nied the charges.[8] Later, she said:

> It's not so easy with our Article 18; it's not so easy to fire people. But there should be the opportunity, in the meantime, I think, for more stimulus to the labor market. . . . Because if you know that your job isn't a given, it brings . . . more productivity. . . . So it's not a given that if you lose your job because you've been fired, like "Oh, God, I won't find anything!" . . . Anyway, it could be a good step ahead for the vitality of the company.

Elenora was identifying two underlying logics of neoliberal labor orders: (1) workers are more productive when their positions are not guaranteed, which in turn allows for institutional gain; and (2) greater flux in the labor market al-lows the unemployed to return to work with relative ease. While these were Elenora's proposed ideals, she then contrasted her vision to what she viewed as the reality:

> In Italy right now there's this motionlessness. Like someone keeps his job and meanwhile no one can fire him and no one ever changes. I mean, I think it would be much more dynamic even for the kids to grow more by chang-ing jobs more often basically. Sometimes, someone gets hired at twenty years old, when he's just a boy, and stays in the same job until he . . . he retires! In my opinion, that's absurd. . . . You don't grow, you get old earlier, there's no

stimulation. You don't grow professionally, don't grow as a person, you don't put yourself in competition with anyone. In the end, it gets very monotonous, very sad even.

Building upon the common lament I heard from many managers, the obstacles to easily firing workers, Elenora deployed concepts which reframe stable labor and its accompanying class of laborers as deficient and inferior: geriatric, stagnant, dull, and depressed. She concluded, "And therefore I think, without a doubt, employees always have this . . . sword of Damocles, this constant fear of not having [their] own job." This was not the first time I had heard this metaphor. A reference to Greek mythology, the sword of Damocles is a symbol for an ever-present threat or a sense of impending doom. In the story, the tyrant king Dionysius invited the jealous peasant Damocles to a luxurious and plentiful dinner. While he was enjoying his meal, Damocles realized he was sitting directly underneath a sword, which was dangerously hung from the ceiling by a piece of hair. The king declared he had done this to show Damocles that life as a king was a constant threat, and nobody, not even the poor, should desire and envy the life of the wealthy and powerful. After this, Damocles implored the king to let him return to his life as a poor man.

The recycling of this myth in contemporary Italy serves as a moral instruction about class and wealth in a transitioning welfare state. While Fordist ideologies aim to make economic gain widely accessible and job security guaranteed for all, in Damocles's world, wealth naturally occasions risk, so poverty is the only path to security. Whether the individual opts out or rationally chooses wealth, he bears the responsibility of that choice. But there is also an affective architecture made visible: fear and apprehension have become the emotional hallmarks of economic gain.

Mobbing: A Neoliberal Problem

The discourse of mobbing is fraught with inconsistencies that became more complex as I delved into the real-life cases of mobbees. One starting point is that mobbing and neoliberalism are an entangled pair, with mobbing, at times, becoming a rare site in which the dehumanizing aspects and moral shortcomings of Italy's new labor regime might be corrected, or at least recognized. At times, mobbing cases allow for the reassertion of neoliberal ideals, as for instance, when mobbing is criticized as being a costly and ineffective project for companies: "A worker subjected to psychological violence has an output down 70 percent in terms of productivity. His cost, for a manager, is 180 percent more" (Corriere della Sera 2002b).

Victims, too, are summoned into subject positions congruent with neoliberal values. One news article offered the following advice for potential mobbees: "It's not healthy to be passive and continue to tolerate abuse and unfair harassment. The best solution is to continue to carry out one's job, [not] reacting to the provocations and acquiring evidence for eventual legal action" (Bignotti 2005). This discourse summons into being the neoliberal citizen capable of navigating, on her own, the welfare state and pursuing justice as a product of self-investment. Italy's worker-citizens are hailed as individualized political actors, called upon to assemble proof of their own mobbing. Navigating conflict at work is considered the task of one person, rather than the task of a collective class or group of workers.

But, at times, what might seem to be the mundane characteristics of typical late capitalist employment are cast as urgent and deplorable when framed as mobbing:

> [Victims of mobbing] are accused of low productivity and loaded up with marginal tasks, more so than other colleagues or even inferiors. They are given impossible objectives and useless tasks, drawn up on exaggerated disciplinary actions, stripped of responsibilities, excessively checked up on by fiscal agents, excluded from meetings, threatened with possible office transfer, subjected to obsessive control of their work hours, and sent urgent requests even on holidays and after work. (Corriere della Sera 2003)

Precisely those practices—regimes of deftly managed control, constant demands, and increased surveillance—despite becoming normalized in post-Fordist Italy, were defined as something objectionable and malign. In other words, mobbing encompasses (but is not fully defined as) what is most characteristic of neoliberal capitalism: market slowdowns and detours, changing governing strategies, and relentless compliance with market-directed corporate objectives. Note also that the mobber is absented as the central agent of the action; rather, the persecutory practices and the organization of labor itself become constructed as the agents of mobbing. This point is counterintuitive, but workers don't usually talk about a single social actor doing the mobbing. What often happens is that the effects of ambivalent, confusing, or disjointed work relationships become construed as mobbing, particularly when mobbing is medicalized as organizational coercion pathology.

That globalization creates a deterritorialized and individualized workforce has been well documented (Appadurai 1990; Collins 2003, 2005). I am calling attention to what happens when the workplace is only partially neoliberalized and, in turn, becomes a site in which neoliberalism is simultaneously undermined and advanced.

2   The Politics of Precariousness

Endemic uncertainty is what will mark the lifeworld and the basic existence of most people.

—Ulrich Beck (1999)

We have noted a definite incapacity on the part of companies to evaluate the human and economic damage caused by mobbing.

—Maria Grazia Cassitto, psychologist (in Fiorii 2006)

Employment and Mortality

In the world of Italian blogs about work, one proclaims: "Mobbing is a monster which appears at the tip of your toes, delicately, it intensifies with its little criticisms, then grows into professional and human isolation . . . and ends up with public verbal aggression and culminates in the end of employment" (di Tacco 2008). The blog's author positions mobbing, not the mobber, as monstrous. Mobbing enters and disrupts the individual's body; it is an omen that the worker's social body could collapse. While mobbing discourse like this often vilifies widespread organizational malfunctioning, this large-scale social turmoil is also embodied within single moral anomalies: the mobber as predatory evildoer. This is not surprising as both an agent-less form of social exclusion from the labor market and a hostile work-stripping aggressor are monsters—*capitalist* monsters because what is at stake is workers' economic fate. Italy's mobbing pioneer Harald Ege, who likens mobbing to a "war at work," warns potential victims: "Be courageous and determined! . . . Your job is in play, what earns you a living and lets you live!" (2002: 51). Within Italy's shifting labor regime, workers identify their own employment as vital but also at risk, and their intensifying vulnerability is a signal that new monsters are invading the workforce. If, for Marx, capitalism "implies a symbolic death," then, Annalee Newitz reasons, capitalist monsters represent this "pretense of death" (2006: 6). They "embody the contradictions of a culture where making a living often feels like dying" (2).

On a fall day in 2004, I was at one of the weekly meetings at Dora and Lidia's mobbing clinic. Answering the phone, Dora reacted: "No, no, I don't believe it," and "When did it happen?" When she hung up, her face was lit with exuberance and delight: "Bruno Sgarone is dead." She began laughing uncontrollably. "Dead?" squealed Lidia. "A heart attack," Dora grinned. Turning to me, she exclaimed in Veneto dialect, "He was one of the worst mobbers we have ever seen. He took away a disabled woman's chair! He came on to his employee! Mina, she came here and told us everything, Mina was suicidal because of him. One of the women had to take 120 drops [of medication] just to sleep, and it's been three years since she's had a Sunday at home." Dora's eyes turned distant and serious as she remembered: "You should have seen their faces. They were like zombies." Lidia, who often finished Dora's sentences, whispered, "Zombies—filled up with pills." Then, recalling their unusual display of laughter in the face of death, she said defensively, "It's not like we did this or anything. But it was not a good person that died today."

What I had witnessed was mobbing as a moral litmus test to measure the metaphysical and the sacred: one way to determine a worthy life and its zombie alterities. The subject position of "mobber," in this case, had recast the meaning of Bruno's death and the meaning of the precarious lives of those who had survived his mobbing. Despite mobbing's shifting or vague definition, or its newness, it had clearly become a profound way to make sense of the world. But also evident in the reactions to Bruno's death were mobbing's material traces: the missing chairs, the therapy interventions, the sleeping aids, psychopharmaceuticals. The image of the zombie positions mobbing as a medium that produces the living dead, which charges the workplace as a site of haunting and foreboding force. It is compelling that the *victims* are also made monstrous. At the moment in which workers become subject to this harassment and yet remain in the precarious labor regime, they lose their humanity.

What also struck me about this moment was Lidia's defensive assertion that they had not "done this." Lidia was asserting her innocence and seeking absolution. But from what? Her statement indexed a sense of guilt in delighting in the death of another and reflected two kinds of belief in unseen forces: a Catholic belief in a higher power that had enacted justice, and a superstitious or magical belief that their wishes for his demise had actually caused Bruno harm. In an earlier discussion about how mobbing makes victims depressed and suicidal, Lidia had confided: "When you are mobbed, the only thing that you are left with is: 'I'll kill you one day.' It's something that you know you shouldn't do. But it's like postpartum depression—you don't have your head in the right place." Finding solace in silence, Lidia never wanted to fully recount her story. What I knew was that she had worked for a cleaning service, and the harassment she endured had provoked severe depression. In her telling, Lidia situated a combative angst within a medicalized discourse of postpartum depression, characterizing mobbing as a life-and-death crisis and homicidal rage as an uncontrollable, natural outgrowth of suffering.

The polarized outcomes of mobbing seemed to be either rampaging murderer or lifeless zombie: "If you are sick, stay home! Neglected depression . . . can have very serious consequences: a chronic depressive is often more similar to a zombie than a person" (Ege 2002: 172). Mobbing creates zombies not only by their exclusion from work but also by further subjecting them to the medical regime. The zombie is also liminal, situated between the dead and the undead, what Avery Gordon (2008) calls a "ghostly matter." She argues that this kind of circumstance is how subjects come to indirectly and "obliquely" know a form of power whose "oppressive nature is denied," and thus, hauntings often beckon and demand action (ibid.: xvi). In the case of neoliberal reforms—alienating but imagined as liberating—workers are called upon to not betray their class cohort *and* to become hypervigilant and suspicious about others. Everyday workplace events and people are rendered volatile and unpredictable.

If employment is entangled with mortality, then it is no surprise that mobbing is saturated with the language of war. An Italian sociology of work handbook for mobbing prevention defines mobbing in these terms: "The victim of mobbing is also a mobber in terms of his colleagues, in a sort of fratricidal conflict (almost like that among gladiators) that ends up eliding every solidarity and every bit of belonging: a war in which the weakest is destined to succumb like a soldier that kills the mobber and immediately after kills himself" (Nistico 2003). Undermining brotherly love, mobbing is figured as the ultimate fruitless battle, and a mortal one. Not only does this passage foretell that workers will increasingly succumb to self-interest and greed, but it also seamlessly uses the metaphor of killing for the termination of employment.

Mobbing, as these texts document, is bound up with an awareness of life's fragility, a recognition that one's delicate existence can be, at any moment, endangered. The idea of precariousness, the knowledge that one is subject to unknown perilous conditions, which includes the idea of neoliberalism as intensifying workers' capacity for rage or Zombiedom, sustains the existential urgency of mobbing. The broader context of economic flux ignited this widespread paranoia and sustained a sense of precariousness that was not merely economic but affective, immaterial, existential. But while taking seriously these public stagings, which weave together employment and vitality, and work dismissal and death, this distinction also becomes a means to understand why only certain actors, those for whom this discourse waxes most salient, become likely to identify with or against precariousness and mobbing. By situating the precarious worker (*precario*) and the victim of mobbing (*mobbizzato*) in dialogue with a third figure, the freelance worker (*libera professionista*), I will expose how such positionings are classed, gendered, and, on a deeper level, built upon different understandings of work's life-giving or life-taking capacity.

One objective is to make sense of situations in which subjects failed to identify with or to name mobbing. At the moment of the massive overhaul of Italy's labor market, how individuals identified their employment contracts, their labor practices, and their positions became at once a political act, a gendered identification, and an ethical claim positioned in relation to neoliberal ideologies. Precariousness, in a broader sense of vulnerable and sometimes volatile interdependency, whether explicitly acknowledged by subjects or not, runs deeply through the experiences of diversely positioned worker-citizens. On one hand, precariousness is economic, referring to a particular configuration of unprotected and short-term employment in Italy's labor market; on the other hand, it is existential, understood as a pervasive instability that haunts multiple aspects of contemporary life. Because of the latter dimension, especially workers' sense of deepening alienation and exclusion from social life, precariousness incites certain affective disorderings that enable mobbing: fear, apprehension, paranoia. Thus, during this period in Italy, the workplace became resignified as a site in which one's core value hung in the balance; precariousness thus critiqued neoliberalism, and it ultimately produced an understanding of the neoliberal workplace as preternaturally dangerous and foreboding.

Expirations

In 2004, the Communist Party launched a new campaign, with posters in urban centers and placards carried in anti-precariousness protests: When Do You Expire? (Quando Scadi?). The When Do You Expire? campaign deployed images of young Italians, gazing deeply and solemnly outward, holding up signs that said "I expire on . . ." (*Scado il*) with a particular date which, at least on one level, referred to a contract's ending date. But what was also at play here is "expiring" as diminished value, as deterioration, as death, which is particularly salient as the subject is the individual: *I* expire, not *the contract* expires. The public campaign asserted that work's end coincides with death, drawing on public imaginaries that apprehend the end of work as a metonym for the end of one's life. As viewers identified with the featured workers, they also related to a more profound message: neoliberalism occasions dehumanization. Solidifying a newly recognizable class of subjects, the precarious, the Quando Scadi? campaign summoned these workers to rally against oppressive labor policies. The campaign identified them as vulnerable, threatened, and unpredictable— and as a collective.

Utilizing similar imagery, Andrea Bajani, the author of *I Break Down but I Can't Get Hired: A Travel Guide for Flexible Workers* (2006), writes about a generation of Italians living with discontinuous work. The result, Bajani argues, is the sensation of living "with an expiration, without a way out from a state of permanent precariousness" (Il Sole 24 Ore 2006). Similarly, CGIL mobilized an anti-precariousness political campaign called Don't Forget Me (Non Ti Scordardime), which had five guiding mandates for the "rights of the precarious workers," including cancellation of the Biagi Laws; equal compensation; maternity and sick leave; inclusion in national unemployment; and local welfare and other benefits (professional training, nursery schools, cafeterias, transportation programs) (CGIL Foggia 2006). While the trope of forgetting may be softer than that of expiration, it nonetheless reasserts the capacity, necessarily part of Italy's new labor regime, of casual employment positions to marginalize and alienate. The work of the CGIL provides evidence that the Left is refiguring and aiming to strengthen the class consciousness of workers with specific rights and specific demands.

Both of these examples articulate unemployment as expiration in the context of leftist discourse, an agenda to restore rights to short-term laborers, and emphasize their shared classed devaluation. Articulating marginalization from the labor market as an existential circumstance is political, tied to the broader leftist project of critiquing neoliberal policies and, implicitly, a new affective regime.

Freelance Precariousness?

Before I turn to mobbing, in which the connection between lived instability, apprehension, and persecution is easily deciphered, it's important to recognize why the term *precarious*, though widely present in the city of Padua, sometimes didn't materialize as a way for subjects to define their positions. A good example is the story of a contract renegotiation at Contax, in which nearly all of the employed had semi-permanent contracts, yet identified as neither precarious nor mobbed, but as freelance.

Contax is a multinational company in the communications and information technology industry, an employer of over 1,200 in its headquarters and satellite offices in Padua. It is organized into three divisions: corporate, including product development, marketing, and human resources; sales, handling both private and corporate accounts; and customer service, which is limited almost entirely to call centers. I was situated within one of the sales divisions, which was housed in a separate space from the massive tower of headquarters, under the head manager, Gianni Mastinini. The look of the office was sleek, technological, and clean. Contax's signature color is yellow, and its logo, its font, and that color were everywhere in the office—in posters framed on the wall and on pens, cups, notepads, folders, mouse pads, and calendars. Only Gianni and the accountant had separate offices; the agents shared seven tables and five computers, where they spent most of their time setting up appointments either to sell more Contax services and products or to maintain their client base.

The mood and tone of the office were indubitably set by Gianni. Having worked with Contax when it was an Italian-owned company in the late 1990s, he had generated a small empire of satellite sales divisions, specialized call centers focusing exclusively on his clients, in addition to managing around fifty sales agents. Gianni's elite class position was evident in his dress, his speech, and the material things that surrounded him, from his finely crafted, hand-tailored suits to his Porsche. The disjuncture between the Contax agents' and Gianni's wealth was a source of strain among the agents: picking up a car magazine from the office table, one employee remarked to me dryly, "This is the real problem in this office."

Gianni's presence was formal, authoritative, and somewhat cold. When I visited the office, he would always ask one of his three administrative assistants, an attractive, dark-haired, petite woman, to bring me espresso. He loved to discuss his firm, the growth of Italy's economy, his travels, and his wine and food consumption; and I recorded many of his spirited monologues. He also had a particular way of speaking: barely apparent was his southern accent, as he'd been in the Veneto region since university. He had an exaggeratedly precise enunciation and a penchant for using the first name of his interlocutor. Often, one of my opening questions would elicit a response from Gianni that might last an hour, such as one fall day in 2004 when he pontificated on the growth of capital:

> In our world, two plus two doesn't equal four. Two plus two can equal three, it can equal zero, it can equal ten. So, what does that mean, Noelle? You can invest a lot, but that doesn't mean your result will be immediate. You may have an immediate result. You may not have a result. You may have a big result. I don't count results; your result comes with time. . . . Every day. Selling is like shaving, every day. . . . Today you do business, tomorrow no, the day after tomorrow no, the day after next, yes again. So, you have to be constant.

Capital, within Gianni's neoliberal logic, can be slippery and elusive and defy rationality; there are no set or guaranteed economic returns for any given labor or investments; the single constant is individual effort. Even if capital wavers, its unpredictability can be conquered by self-determination and dedication— epitomized here by the masculinized daily ritual of shaving. Gianni thus fashioned himself as able to control transient and risky capital by his own tenacity and endurance. He also spoke proudly about Contax's transnational economic success which, he explained, derived largely from its speed: "[Contax] is much faster than other companies because they can react in a second. A small and svelte company is always fast." "So, if the market is going like this," he said, curving his hands and running them across the shiny glass table, "then we adapt like this." Smiling, he slid his fingers in the opposite direction. "If the market goes that way, then we adapt that way. It's velocity. The faster you are, the faster you get a profit." Comprehending Gianni's worldview required careful attention to the ways in which he identified with Contax. The notion of precariousness is entirely omitted from this worldview: adaptation and velocity have replaced upheaval and apprehension.

At times, I felt his urgency, as if he were selling Contax and its merits to me:

> We're a certain kind of company. As I say, "We were, we are, and we will be" [Ci siamo, c'eravamo, ci saremo]. . . . Contax is a company that says, "Go! How can we do this? Let's do business [fare business] together!" . . . We exploit this feeling and it transmits security. . . . Contax has always given their clients freedom: "You are free to choose; if you want to stay with me, I'm happy, but you can leave in the morning." . . . In the end, you'll come back. The client who feels they can leave comes back more easily.

A global producer, like a talented lover, is confident enough in the services he provides that partners are offered freedom of choice: the promise of consumer or sexual freedom ensures long-term allegiance. Freedom and feeling intertwine to cement the producer-consumer relationship; they shape the kinds of ideologies with which Gianni identifies. In terms of affect, the mode here is sexualized detachment and pleasure, in striking contrast to the fear of expiration for the precarious. Of course, it is only within the structure of providing goods and services that one can rally behind the aloof pleasures of capitalist relations.

On another occasion, linking capitalism with a heterosexual erotic charge, he joked proudly about some investment offers: "I'm tired sometimes. I feel like a woman whom everyone desires." Desires, economic and sexual, often merged in Gianni's worldview. To conceptualize Contax's clients, Gianni returned again to an explicitly sexualized understanding of capital: "We rape our clients [*i nostri clienti li violentiamo*] by constantly changing their contract agreements from under them." He shrugged, "The world will be like this." The violent, sexualized metaphor describes the movement of capital between production and consumption. Embedded here is a dark imaginary of capital: the producer activates a client-consumer relationship with a deceptive illusion of ultimate freedom yet relies on violent submission. Richard Sennett pointed out such paradoxes within neoliberal regimes: "flexibility begets disorder, but not freedom from restraint" (1998: 59). Gianni's remarks about his clients echo the issue of contract manipulation for his employees: they were subjected to a sudden and important contract change and yet reminded that they were "free" to stay or go.

A Risky Offer

One morning in February 2005, I entered the office as the agents were preparing for an important meeting with Gianni regarding a contract change; he had already called and postponed the meeting from 10:00 to 11:00. At 11:30 he arrived, and the meeting began soon after. I sat with the agents around the meeting table, while Gianni set up the digital projector and his PowerPoint presentation. "Today," he announced, "we're going to talk about money."

How sales were credited and how the earnings of the agents would be calculated were both suddenly, and quite radically, changed at this meeting. Prior to this meeting, the salespeople had been paid a small fixed monthly salary (€200, equivalent to about US$240) and paid per scheduled meeting with a client, earning additional commissions for sales and when clients upgraded their services. They had, on average, a thousand clients per agent. Now, they would earn a predetermined amount based upon their client retention rate, with clients closing their accounts, making delayed payments, or reducing their spending deducted from the total. What Gianni had done was to translate how Contax calculated his earnings, as a function of all his sales agents' earnings, into a more stringent rule for the agents.[1]

Gianni tried to explain a bit more, emphasizing that instead of being paid per visit, they would be paid based on the total percentage of their clients who stayed with Contax: "Is that clear?" Clara, a woman in her early forties, responded sourly: "Only for a twisted mind like yours." Gianni smiled and responded evenly: "This company wants numbers." Cris, an agent in his late thirties, immaculately manicured, ironed, and stylish, retorted angrily: "I find it wrong that Contax is making me pay for their client loss. Frankly, it's outside of the parameters of my job and unprofessional of Contax. They really have big heads! . . . You've earned well up until now and you weigh us down! Now I'm paying for it." Gianni's composure remained steady as he responded coldly: "I agree with you. But if the job is unpleasing, then there are other jobs. You must be active, strongly attentive. What choice do you have? One, you get pissed off and you leave. Two, the better thing to do is realize that it's this or this [*é così o così*]." Playing with the phrase "this or that," Gianni's "this or this" implied, in Italian, that change is inevitable. Clara scoffed: "Then our work is invisible!" Gianni was unmoved: "Enter into the logic of the company! What are you going to do? Leave or adapt." Abruptly, and with the differences anything but resolved, Gianni tried to end the meeting on a positive note: "I'm convinced this will all go well." As everyone dispersed for lunch, the frustration and outrage were evident.

In this meeting, Gianni enlisted moral ideologies based on market competition and buttressed by a view of economic forces as unstoppable, summoning workers to "enter the logics of the company" and properly manage their own risk-filled employment. I initially wondered if his "adapt or leave" policy might be construed as mobbing or imposing precariousness, yet no one at Contax, either that day or afterward, named Gianni's actions or their positions as such. Part of this was shaped by the fact that workers at Contax identified with, and perhaps desired, a class and political subject position that was more closely aligned with a neoliberal ethos of individualized labor and market rule. Such a regime is able to produce worker-subjects increasingly disarticulated from employers, other workers, and the state.

The day after the contentious meeting, Gianni was not in the office, and I spent the morning chatting with Cris. It had taken me a while to earn Cris's trust, but in the six months I had spent at Contax, we had established a closeness I didn't share with other workers. Cris told me emphatically:

When you lose human contact, you become a number. They're all lovely, all darling. But in the end, that doesn't guarantee numbers for the big company. I'm talking about how Gianni is with us. And how Contax is with Gianni. It's not just Contax; the world is just like this. It's good to do this job, earn some good money, earn by making the branch manager earn a lot. That's what Gianni does. He exploits people. Any company will eventually cut corners, it's always been like this. . . . But what if I get injured tomorrow? Or if I'm sixty or seventy years old and [I've] been earning $20–$30,000 a year, what's left in [my] pockets? . . . The agent should be motivated. In reality, we aren't agents, we're sub-agents. The agent is Gianni.

Picking up his business card and holding it toward me, he pointed at the logo, "I have this on my card, but really I don't work for them. I represent them, but I have no connection to them." The powerful and ever-present company logo represents to Cris not a group of directors, but rather a distant, reified, and detached entity. Cris's contacts with that entity are truncated, a kind of capitalism in which "capital and its workforce become more and more remote from one another" (Comaroff and Comaroff 2001: 13). In addition to representing a global company, the Contax logo has become a reified manifestation of Cris's alienation from the corporate structure, whose workings have already become natural and self-evident. For Cris, then, precariousness is dehumanizing, but it is not something to be battled against: it is merely an intrinsic dimension of global capital. I asked Cris if he thought Gianni would mob new agents, if the current agents left under the circumstances. Cris sighed and said: "He won't need to because they'll never stay in the company. They'll all leave shortly after being hired." In this sense, undesirable work conditions replace individual mobbers; Gianni's new articulation of labor's remuneration would preemptively regulate workers.

Another aspect of precariousness is not knowing, unpredictability; for example, at Contax knowledge about clients was tightly controlled. Despite Gianni's promises to keep the agents updated on client information, he kept the pathways of information highly guarded. A few weeks after the meeting, Cris and another agent, Franco, were discussing how some companies allowed their sales agents to check orders and track the arrival of goods with real-time precision. Cris said: "They'll never let us do this." I asked why. "Because," he explained, "we would know too much. They leave you hanging [*Ti lasciano in ballo*]. They change everything all the time on you. Once you know something, they change it on you again." From Cris's perspective, "they," a collection of various actors at Contax, seem to work in a coordinated and intentional fashion to make things purposefully difficult for workers. On another day, Cris reported that Gianni had remained on his phone during a meeting and paid little attention to the conversation: "Gianni looks at numbers, not at ethics and morality. I think he's supported from up above, pampered by the CEO." The recent contract change, which forced Cris to choose between precarious remuneration or unemployment in a precarious labor force, had heightened his suspicions and feelings of persecution regarding Contax. In a labor market where lack of information, silence, underhanded deals, and misinformation had social and economic consequences, day-to-day events were transformed into practices that could be essential to one's social and economic viability. Bits of information seemed saturated with willful purpose, causality, and intention; coursing across the diverse ways in which Paduan workers identified themselves were waves of acute apprehension and suspicion.

Italian Masculinity and the Freelance Worker

In mid-March, the problems at Contax remained unresolved and palpable; Cris described it as a generalized atmosphere of "bad feeling" (*malu-*

more). I asked what would he do if he left, and he said, "The only thing to do is leave and sell other things. I want to be taken seriously, not look for a job as an employee [*dipendente*] but rather as a freelance professional [*libera professionista*]." Cris did not see himself as part of a class of workers devalued by Gianni's adapt-or-leave policy nor as socially marginalized by his semi-permanent and high-risk contract. Fashioning himself as a freelancer in relation to the antithetical other, the antiquated Fordist *dipendente*, he embraced the status of late modern worker, "a new type of 'high tech' nomadic worker" (Beck 2000: 75). Cris was not alone in this kind of identification. In early May, I was on a trip to clients with Luca, an agent in his late twenties who was considered handsome and was well liked by most employees. He played a special role in that he was sent immediately after clients had terminated their contract agreements with Contax. Marshaling his charm, he would rush out with corporate gifts, discounts, and problem-solving capabilities to try to retain the client.

Sitting on the passenger side of his BMW, I noticed his perfectly shiny waved hair, long eyelashes, and meticulously ironed white shirt. I asked him about Contax's management, and he replied, "Contax is huge. I have to deal with things on my own and that's it. When you work for a corporation, you're a number and that's it. It would be nice to say that you're part of a Contax group. But this way, I can say when I think Contax is wrong." Looking straight ahead, he announced proudly, "I'm not a company man. . . . I'm lower than Gianni is, fine, but I'm motivated to work. I'll always do something on my own, not be hired by someone else [*alla dipendenza di qualcuno*]. I'll do something that's mine." Luca saw employee status as the antithesis of independence; he rejected the conformity and uncritical collectivism bound up with being a company man. While he was driving, Luca received a phone call. "That was my mom," he grinned. "She calls me so I know everything will be ready when I get home. This way, I waste less time and then I go out again." That Luca lived at home was not surprising; this was quite normal for his colleagues at Contax. Through a triumvirate of labor dynamics, demographics, and gendered norms, the largely invisible labor of Italian middle-aged women supported the emerging neoliberal regime and the lifestyles of Italy's youth. Living at home enabled a more luxurious mode of consumption: Luca's freelance professionalism was accompanied by his adornment with high-fashion brands, weekly trips to tanning and hair salons, and café and club sojourns in Padua's chic center. Luca's colleague and friend Marco summarized it perfectly: "You don't have vacation, sick days, and they can still fire you [*lasciarti a casa*].[2] We pay the contribution for retirement, and you have to do it, not your boss. For now it's okay, but when you have a family it's not okay. But for now it's a good way to learn how to sell. And you can get yourself stuff. I got a car, a boat, your nice little vices."

I was reminded of a similar occasion when Gianni, frustrated with the upper echelon at Contax, spoke to me as if he were addressing them directly: "I'm an entrepreneur, and so I don't work for you. I'm not your employee [*il tuo dipendente*]," emphasizing the final words as if they were terribly distasteful. The term itself, *dipendente*, obviously derives from the notion of dependence—workers are dependent on employers for their salaries and benefits—and it is refigured within these logics as undesirable and low status. Men were disproportionately likely to be freelance workers: only 5 percent of freelance professionals were women in Italy in 2005 (ANSA 2005a). This is another case in which masculinity is structurally and symbolically appended to willful and individually managed employment (Schein 2000: 134; Ho 2005, 2009).[3]

Within the vast category of precarious contracts—which includes apprenticeship, internship, temporary, and subcontracted—freelance contracts increased 60 percent from 1995 to 2002 (Carboni 2005: 50), and they proliferated in Italy after the Biagi Laws. They offer no long-term safeguards and no sick days, vacations, or pension. In addition to applying to a group that was almost exclusively male, what distinguished them was the requirement of a special individual tax code, which could be acquired only with the help of an accountant, thus requiring additional capital—another class distinction. While Cris drew a sharp line between freelancer and employee, the former was actually strategically used as a low-cost substitute for regular full-time employment. In 2005, Italian employers reported savings of 40 percent compared to other kinds of short-term contracts, and 89 percent of workers with such contracts were employed at only one company at a time (ANSA 2005c). The difference was that freelance status aligned these men with neoliberal values of rationality and individualism, even as their own positions were undermined by the state's reduction of labor protections.

Corporate Skin

By July 2005, no changes had been made to the contract, and most of the agents remained. I stopped in to talk to Gianni in his office, which was adorned with models of Porsches, and he shared his plans for the next few months:

> I'm going to open a new window in September. I have to change the air. I won't eliminate anyone. I'll just put someone by their side who is better. Either you start running or you leave. Noelle, it's a shitty life, but that's what it is. If you stop, you lose [*Chi si ferma é perduto*]. . . . We have to change our skin. There are lots of people that don't change their skin. But you can never say, "I've made it." Every day you start from zero. . . . No one gives you anything. You have to do it yourself. . . . The market is a market that works this way. You can't do anything else.

Gianni's strategy would be to intensify the pressure on workers in order to compel them to conform to new shifting standards or quit. In the world of mobbing clinics I also frequented, Gianni's plan would be readily understood as mobbing. But Gianni, in this context, was not considered a mobber. His oft-repeated slogan "If you stop, you lose" employed a southern Italian idiom valorizing the benefits of velocity and clarifying the consequences of immobility, coupled with a neoliberal ethic: there was no unpunishable stillness. With the premise of guaranteed labor both vilified and outmoded, these logics position citizens who are not able to independently secure work as deficient in speed and capability, and subsequently less worthy as individuals; this resembles what Douglas Holmes has called "fast capitalism" in which "the abstract principles of market exchange are rendered as ethical imperatives" (2000: 92). Victims of mobbing, by contrast, demand compensation and recognition precisely because they view secure labor not as archaic but as essential.

I left Padua in late August 2005 and learned via email that by December a number of agents had left Contax; in March 2006, Gianni fired both Cris and Clara. The skin, it seems, had been changed. Following his termination, Cris sought legal support to obtain the salary and severance pay that were due to him according to his contract. Cris and Gianni are examples of neoliberal political subjects who define themselves by how they view their economic and social self-management even as the precarious labor market fuels and shapes the ways in which they relate to one another. The events at Contax also reveal how coerced resignation, even if not explicitly defined as mobbing, is part of the context of labor precariousness.

Apprehension and Fear in the Mobbing Industry

The case of Fiore Montiglio shows how practices of labor exclusion are woven through with suspicion, doubt, and distrust and implanted within an explicit framework of mobbing. Beginning in September 2004, Fiore handled cases of gender discrimination and managed cases of mobbing against women. Fiore was in her early fifties. Her hair, a layering of bright whites, silvers, and grays, rested lightly on her shoulders and her thick bangs fell to the top of the clear plastic frames of her glasses. She was originally from Lombardy and had moved to Veneto later in life to do archival work; she often commented that she had taken years to master the Veneto dialect—and to understand the Veneto people, whom she described as "right wing" and "racist." Fiore had a gentle and thoughtful manner but was entirely assertive and frank. Once, over lunch, she jokingly asked our waiter if he minded the company of feminists. He laughed and said he'd always believed women were "the better sex." That, replied Fiore without a moment's pause, is precisely what is said by men who are most convinced of women's inferior status. Defiant, intellectual, and politically radical, she had a strong group of women friends of all ages who often remarked that she was "mythical" (*mitico*)—Italian slang for outstanding or extraordinary people or things.

Fiore, like many professionals working in the mobbing field, was employed with a short-term contract. Problems began in early October 2004 when Fiore received an anonymous letter from a worker within the provincial government headquarters. The writer complained of poor working relationships among the employees, rigid schedules, constant employee surveillance, and financial mismanagement and corruption. Fiore's office generally catered to workers out-side of her own public office, but she was eager to help this anonymous col-league. She scheduled a meeting with human-resources personnel, demanding less scrutiny of employees' entry times. She then composed an update for her website and asked the technical manager to post it. When this task was de-layed, Fiore concluded that it was done maliciously; she suspected it was de-layed under explicit instruction from her administrators. From there, things in-tensified and Fiore regularly scrutinized daily events for malice. Fiore explained that "they"—the province-level officials—were keeping "a close eye" on her and admitted to me, "I think I'm being mobbed." To my surprise, the very woman whose responsibility it was to resolve mobbing problems felt that she was a target.

At a nearby café that had become our habitual lunch place, Fiore reflected on recent occurrences that might have contributed to her being mobbed: she had taken up the in-house complaint, had made inquiries about office finances, and was "hard working and honest." In addition, she had supported one candidate for the national equal opportunity minister while other officials in the Ministry of Labor had backed someone who had no prior work experience in women's affairs: "They should be ashamed of themselves! [*Ma si vergona!*]." Finally, she had preferred not to employ the administration's lawyer, instead selecting her own, preferring a woman lawyer for her case work, someone independent of government relations. "You see," Fiore explained, "this is why they are working against me." Between sips of jasmine tea, Fiore claimed that photocopies were probably already being secretly made of all her correspondence and cases.

In the next weeks, I witnessed how and which everyday events became evi-dence of mobbing. When a file was lost, Fiore believed that someone was steal-ing materials from her office closet. A few weeks later, an estimate on the pub-lishing cost of a manual disappeared and then "miraculously reappeared" a week later. "But, there was nothing out of the ordinary in the estimate, right?" I had asked, trying to understand why this might have been stolen. "They're just watch-ing us," said Fiore. That afternoon, Fiore went to see one of the office managers, a man whom I had always noticed because he whistled while patrolling the of-fice and had an atypical fashion signature of bright orange or purple jeans; that day, he was adorned in radiant grape. In his office, he stood with one hand hold-ing an unlit cigar, the other fingering his wispy beard. Fiore demanded that the locks on her office cabinet be replaced immediately; her materials, she stated firmly, related to sensitive matters, and the private cases of the mobbing victims needed greater security. The manager walked to the cabinet and peered curi-ously at the lock. Make only one copy of the new key, ordered Fiore. But in the months that followed, many things were still reported missing, and Fiore often wondered just how many copies had been made.

In late November, I arrived to find Fiore and her two assistants scrutinizing some documents from the accounting department with the details of the ex-pense account for the office. Fiore had not yet been paid, a delay that she insisted was orchestrated to push her toward an early departure. "I can't just tell him that the numbers are wrong because he [the accounting department manager] will just say he made a mistake. He's a clever one."[4] Fiore explained that there were nearly €2,000 of expenditures that could not be accounted for. And, she exclaimed angrily, "I'm not making a cent! [*Non prendo una lira!*]."

In Fiore's view, the administration was conducting extensive and elaborate practices to alienate her and keep her on guard. Seemingly chance events in the office were reenvisioned as highly skilled intentional actions—from moving her office to the third floor to problems with the heating and air conditioning. On one early summer day, the air conditioner in her office was turned up high, making the office very cold, and Fiore interpreted this not only as mobbing but also as a deliberate attempt to impair her health. Even actions in my life were interpreted as circuitous techniques of attack and sabotage. One day, I passed the mail clerk, and she did not greet me with her usual morning hello. Fiore was convinced that the clerk was "instructed" to demean everyone around Fiore and her friends. On another occasion, I mentioned to Fiore that I had received such vague directions from counselors at another mobbing clinic, one co-funded by Fiore's office, that I missed the appointment entirely. Fiore believed that one of her superiors had convinced them to isolate me as a way to oust her: "Noelle, they are mobbing you to mob me." I was bewildered and found my own sense of trust in others begin to unravel. Fiore had served in tandem with another official, who had been on leave during this time. In September 2005, after my departure, the other woman returned to work full time and no longer wanted Fiore to handle cases—though Fiore, by law, could continue to fulfill her duties. By December 2005, Fiore had cut back on her work time, and she left entirely within six months but continued to send letters requesting pay that was due. When I saw Fiore in July 2008, she was still owed back salary and travel expenses.

Fiore's experience shows how mobbing, as a cultural category and practice, emerges as part of the broader context of not just economic but also affective and psychological precariousness within a semi-neoliberal regime. While Fiore's case bears some of the classic characteristics of mobbing cases, it is nonetheless rather exceptional given her professional role. Fiore believed that her managers and colleagues were capable of purposefully infiltrating the mundane practices and events of her life. Because her experience rested, in part, on her beliefs rather than documented actions, her case raises further questions. Medical anthropologist Byron Good (1994) famously pointed out what he calls the "problem of belief." He recognized a tendency to describe practices falling outside of medical knowledge as "beliefs," ghettoizing certain knowledges and remedies in ways that problematically reproduce dichotomies like real versus fake, rational versus irrational, and objective versus subjective. In investigating mobbing in Italy, I sought to avoid attributing what blurs these categories as merely an individual's belief and, instead, recognized that mobbing lives in the vexed threshold between these very dichotomies. Indeed, to say mobbing is not real would be empirically false. In Fiore's case, her sensory experiences, her interpretations of everyday life, and her sense of personhood were articulated with mobbing and the broader context of a precarious workforce in real ways. A site of liminality, mobbing is connected with various forms of precariousness: economic, psychological, medical, affective, existential. Both the hostile practices of persecution and the heightened sense of being persecuted are produced in this historical moment of uncertainty, apprehension, and flux.

The case also raises the following question: How does a uniquely Italian experience of mobbing emerge from not only the two-tier labor force and neoliberal discourse but also a sensibility rooted in Italian notions of suspicion? For Comaroff and Comaroff, neoliberalism coincides with "the rise of new forms of enchantment" (2001: 293) and, specifically, the rise of "occult economies." In Europe, these include rumors of cults, organ theft, and kidnapping (ibid.: 312), which derive from a more pervasive trend: suspicion surrounding forms of capital accumulation and circulation. In Italy, co-workers might arouse suspicion insofar as they embody an intangible fear: the snatching away of workers' stability and economic resources. Still, notions of the occult have far more historical significance in Italy than the rise of neoliberal discourse. Work on magic and witchcraft (de Martino 1959; Galt 1991; Hauschild 2002; Pandolfi 1990) and the evil eye (Ankarloo and Clarke 1999; Migliore 1997) in Italy or in the context of Mediterranean anthropology (Dundes 1992; Pitt-Rivers 1954) support a deeper genealogy for notions of the supernatural, immaterial realms, and malign intentionality. Also unique to Italy is what Alessandro Cavalli characterizes as "a markedly higher level of distrust in institutions" (2001: 122). Cavalli suggests that vigilance is often oriented toward underhanded practices and fraught with "the presumption that anyone holding a position of power has achieved this in a shady way" (ibid.: 132). A historically grounded cynicism about national leaders, the state, employers, and institutions, moreover, may exacerbate the contemporary forms of hypervigilance that have resulted from neoliberal labor policies. I am not suggesting that such modes of awareness are homogeneous across Italian workers. Rather, I'm calling attention to how suspicion and sometimes paranoia—particularly within institutional frameworks— are and have been available affective techniques. There is also evidence, as Michael Herzfeld suggests, that uncertainty underlies hierarchical relationships in a Mediterranean context: "Trust turns on a questionable but necessary capacity for predicting and anticipating the actions of others and thus represents attempts to control present time. The continual suspicion that marks everyday experience is corrosive. . . . In such situations actors . . . strive for a temporary suspension of temporality" (Herzfeld 2006: 174–175).

Mobbing, as both a cultural narrative and an embodied practice, allows for navigation of a labor regime that fundamentally undermines fixed temporality. In this sense, Fiore, like Cris, was precarious, as Nancy Ettlinger suggests, in that she lived "a condition of vulnerability relative to contingency and the inability to predict" (2007: 320). Here, the notion of precariousness extends well beyond the employment regime and includes basic notions of human life—such that it becomes an existential condition.

Your Death, My Life

How precariousness discourse frames mobbing was illuminated in a conversation about the origins of mobbing. Many political actors have developed theories on mobbing that expose an ongoing reformulation of a disturbed worker-citizenship and an emergent theory of human baseness. In September 2004, I interviewed trade-union activist, Communist Party leader, and regional-government labor official Carlo Grattini. When I entered his office, Carlo moved from his desk to sit with me at a round meeting table that was covered with political posters and flyers from various anti-precariousness demonstrations. Balancing a heavy midsection over his outstretched legs and leaning forward on the chair, Carlo had thick black ringlets framing his bearded face and falling in coils around his dark eyes. He spoke reflectively:

> The fact is that they are no longer citizens; people are goods, they are objects. We live in a working society [*società lavorativa*]; if you lose work, or when work becomes precarious, then we enter into a precarious society of uncertainty and insecurity. There is no longer global citizenship. You are alone, you are autonomous. . . . Depriving me of work means depriving me of citizenship.

Reiterating widely circulating left-wing discourse within the anti-precariousness movement, Carlo imagined that the welfare and well-being of the national collective rely on the position of labor. Later, Carlo emphasized the point again: "Above all for a working society, [work] is not an accessory [to citizenship]; it is a facet of citizenship. Depriving me of work means depriving me of citizenship." While workers seem increasingly to be encouraged to find alternative means to create their identities outside of the work environment (Sennett 1998), Carlo maintained that work is the essential foreground for subject-making, the site of producing Italian citizenship. Therefore, and in direct opposition to the freelancers' disdain for employment, he figured labor relations as central within the process of late modern subject-making. At the same time, he recognized how precariousness furthers processes of individualization and isolation:

> Mobbing's a phenomenon in expansion. . . . The precariousness of labor, above all "bossing" [*bossing*], or mobbing by your boss, has always existed. What is particularly evident now is mobbing between colleagues, horizontal mobbing. This aspect is the culmination of precariousness. I can think about saving myself if I isolate you: *mors tua, vita mea* [your death, my life]. If the pack isolates you, then we've found the first subject that will have to go.

Here, Carlo was making the distinction between vertical mobbing, also known as bossing, the situation when one worker holds a superior position to the other, and horizontal mobbing, the situation with two same-level workers. His formulation points to how this interworker hostility comes from the loss of class consciousness: in-class hostility is one brutal outgrowth of the labor market's uncertainty.

Carlo's formulation of *mors tua, vita mea* has precedents in the discourse of mobbing. In their legal history of mobbing, Giorgio Ghezzi and Daniele Ranieri make a similar point: "Behind the mobbee's back the pack advances and, like vultures, this 'mob' of pseudo colleagues lives on the other's disgraces . . . driven by the old saying 'mors tua vita mea'" (2006: 54). Within this rhetoric, mobbing is an act of self-defense, which rests on the idea of a person's uncontained egotistical core. It arises not as some sort of circumvention of labor safeguards but as a preemptive and self-saving strike on the part of the worker. The violence has succeeded at the moment when the individual, in competition with a group, becomes the quintessential neoliberal subject: individualized, risk managing, and fearful (Beck 1992; Ong 2006b). But the *mors tua, vita mea* narrative closes the action with a corrective finale: the same subject, seemingly enviable, executes fear-induced aggression yet fails to achieve the desired stability. It is within this failure, I contend, that we recognize these subjects as the result of neoliberal transition. The potent hope for long-term job security reflects the legacy of protectionist labor regimes, while the preemptive attack is indicative of late modern anxiety, a form of affect potently stirred within mobbing and precariousness discourses. Indeed, it is between the desire for safeguards and the fear of precariousness that almost-neoliberal subjects emerge—to some extent individualized and risk bearing yet still seeking safeguards as something psychically and politically within their grasp. The mobbees are more individualized than the precarious ones, they hold a Hobbesian vision of the world, and amid their acute disorientation, neoliberalism becomes the catalyst of their suffering. Meanwhile, the precarious ones identify with a collective and seek simultaneously a hopeful collaboration with others and the defeat of neoliberal policies.

The two figures, the precarious worker and the victim of mobbing, are thus fully separate; indeed, they must be distinct in Italian political imaginaries, as was made clear to me in a chance meeting in May 2005. I saw a flyer for a new mobbing clinic that had recently opened; it was operated by a local trade union in another city. When I met the local organizer, Toni, I sensed some suspicion on his part when I introduced my project as studying both mobbing and precarious labor. Toni's eyes narrowed. "But they are two completely separate things!" I offered an oversimplified explanation, claiming that they were intertwined in that mobbing eliminated a pool of long-term workers, while precarious contracts prevented workers from ever becoming permanent workers. "Well," he shrugged, "that's one way to look at it." Toni went on to explain that his clinic would focus primarily on union-mediated resolutions, juridical interventions, and psychological support. "Work culture," Toni reminisced, "was once more solidaristic, aimed at the group; now it's more individualistic." Mobbing, he explained, was an outgrowth of this "excessive individualism" and was the "culmination of precariousness." Echoing Carlo, Toni asserted that precariousness had ignited the psychic and social conditions to grow mobbing, which was, in effect, the aftermath of labor's demise.

According to alternative logics, one might understand mobbing as coercive downsizing, a circumvention of labor laws, as caused by labor protectionism, not precariousness. But by holding mobbing to be separate, precariousness becomes a primary and unifying ill for workers and a solvable problem, not a totalized new labor regime, while mobbing is evidence of the moral failure of neoliberal labor policies. Thus, the precarious one and the mobbee retain their ontological distance: the precarious one engenders classed resistance while the mobbee is figured as the de facto victim of neoliberalism's ever-tightening grasp.

Precarious Subjectivities

How do people respond to their own and others' precariousness? In the Veneto region, workers' subjectivities were precariously dependent on transient and economically volatile conditions, for example, Cris as a freelancer and Fiore as a victim of mobbing. They both shared the memory of pre–Biagi Laws Fordist security, labor protections, political movements to install long-term contracts, and anti-precariousness demonstrations. The experiences of Fiore and Cris, despite the divergent ways in which they identified themselves and their labor, reflected the conditions of highly capricious employment. Cris and Fiore both believed that their superiors had maliciously tinkered with the mundane practices and events of the workplace, and they both were ultimately eliminated from their job positions. Yet, despite their different political views on neoliberalism, they both viewed it as an inevitable and highly coordinated process; here, they both diverged from the precarious ones, those who identify precariousness as an object of anticipation, not yet arrived in full.

Economically and existentially vexing, precariousness persists like a repeating fractal: it multiplies along a trajectory of interconnected workers, yet, as the cases of Cris and Fiore lay bare, these workers are deeply alienated from one another. Working in a recursive loop, mobbing and precariousness are formidable twins; precariousness is constitutive of the material and symbolic thingness of mobbing: it is both a cause and an effect of mobbing. An ethically charged workplace imagined as "your death, my life," a stark imaginary in which standalone actors fight to the death for social inclusion, materializes in relation to individualization and risk but also, and necessarily, in relation to the sensory and psychic proximity of welfare protections and stability (Molé 2007b). Italy's late modern worker-subjects refocus our gaze on neoliberalism's most neurotic internal paradoxes: individualization yet dehumanization, and uncertainty despite desires for safeguards.

3   Existential Damages

There is nothing better for a man, than that he should eat and drink, and that
he should make his soul enjoy good in his labor.

—Ecclesiastes 2:24

Putting the soul to work: this is the new form of alienation.

—Franco "Bifo" Berardi

The soul that we are constantly constructing we construct according to an
explanatory model of how we came to be the way we are.

—Ian Hacking (1998)

Mr. G worked as an engineer for Telecom in Pisa, where he was responsible for
the Tuscan maritime area (Tribunal of Pisa, April 10, 2002, in Meucci 2006:
490). He had been instructed to minimize the overtime of his staff and had
taken measures to follow those orders. However, his actions provoked a union
reaction and, in response, Mr. G filed suit to protect his job position. Following
disciplinary action by Telecom, Mr. G was transferred to Florence in June 1999
and was told, informally, that this was done to appease the National Union Co-
ordinating Group. He was moved once again to Pisa by the next month. At that
time, Mr. G was denied the monthly raise in salary that his colleagues had received, and he filed suit in the Florence Tribunal (which he later won, in January
2001). In January 2000, Telecom hired a new engineer for the Tuscan maritime branch and Mr. G was stripped of his professional role. Although he presented his case to the attorney general's office (*procura della repubblica*), he was
still fired later that month. He was rehired in February and transferred, once
again, to Florence, and Telecom took legal action to justify the legitimacy of the
transfer. At this point, Mr. G sued for mobbing, professional damages, and loss
of dignity, and he contested the transfer. As part of his ruling on the case, Judge
Nistico, citing Article 2087 of Italy's Civil Code, reflected on the case:

> This obligation belongs to the Civil Code insofar as it is inspired by shared criteria
> for humanism at work [*umanesimo del lavoro*]. Which means, despite the current
> examples that indicate the contrary, the view that has always been maintained that
> our legislature is not [operating] from a market perspective, in which the worker as-
> sumes the role of "human capital" or "human resource," [which are] the expressions
> in the dominant corporate subculture. Rather, he is an endowed subject, even in his

work contract, with his own character and his dignity. . . . The law, in fact, protects not only the worker's psychological integrity, but his moral personhood [*personalità morale*]. The lack of respect for this obligation to protect, therefore, allows for compensation for existential damages upon verification of the case. (Tribunal of Pisa, April 10, 2002, in Meucci 2006: 287)

The total damages, including injury to the plaintiff's professionalism (*il danno alla professionalità*) and existential damages, were valued at €80,000.

Mr. G's case raises a number of questions about work harassment, workers rights, the value and transformation of labor, and the Italian state. Does the Italian legal system, as Judge Nistico suggested, employ logics outside of or even antithetical to the rapidly growing neoliberal values and ideologies within the country's labor regime? In order to unravel how existential damages came to be a legitimate form of legal compensation, we must interrogate the moral and cultural underpinnings of labor, citizenship, ethics, bodies, and materiality. What guidelines about just labor and just human conditions undergird this category? Upon what implicit understandings of human potential and the body do existential damages draw? We must grapple with two intersecting forms of immateriality: immaterial labor and immaterial damages. What I will trace is how understandings of the body, divided between and tied to both material and immaterial realms, help to make sense of existential damages. If biological damages recognize physical and mental bodily harm, then how do existential damages compensate injury to the soul, understood as a subject's moral and affective core, and what does that suggest about governance and Catholicism in Italy?

Because work is likened to vitality, mobbing's capacity to threaten an end to the employment relationship allows it to be positioned as potentially deadly. In addition to being imagined as gravely endangering the well-being and health of the victim, as one concerned teacher put it, mobbing "is capable of stealing your soul" (Servedio 2010). A career pediatrician working in a hospital, after having won a case of mobbing, which had included his abrupt exclusion from weekly meetings and isolation at a desk in the corridor, reported: "I gave my body and soul to the hospital" (Craighero 2008).

It is paradoxical that what seem to be increasingly regular dimensions of neoliberal labor, such as isolation and uneven exertion, are simultaneously normalized and injurious. Because existential damages reference the soul (*A.N. Fideli V. Comuned Loiri Porto San Paolo*, no. 194/00, 2003) examining the body is central to the task of reconceptualizing Italian worker-citizenship, which has become reduced to a psychosomatic body for which labor is medicalized while also being fashioned upon spiritual grounds as a physically irreducible being for whom damage and protection can only ever be approximated. The infrastructure of the state intervenes in positing a citizen as part biological matter and part intangible, even temporally fragmented essence.

The notion of existential damages does not merely mirror a dualism between mind and body but becomes part of a recognition of human capacity and spirit and the extramaterial investment required of modern labor regimes. At their best, existential damages recognize the demands of immaterial labor, that is, the psychic, cognitive, affective, and conceptual labor of workers. While post-Fordist labor has been theorized as emotionally, affectively, and psychically taxing, in order to understand existential damages in Italy, we must also think through what toil means in the Italian context and take seriously that certain forms of labor can be figured as spirit breaking. This form of alienation, as well as the potential for its legal recognition, has roots in three historical Italian sites: Catholic understandings of human subjects as split between the body, the organic perishable matter, and the soul, the immaterial human essence; Marxist and leftist pro-labor movements' denunciation of the alienation of labor as a social death; and the new affective demands of immaterial labor regimes. While existential damages might seem a leftist utopian project, only certain forms of alienation count, and recourse is available only for individualizing subjects capable of managing the state's uneven juridical apparatus.

Existential damages in Italy, as in other European countries using the common law of torts, are a form of immaterial damages (Von Barr 2000: 366). First used in 2000 (sent. no. 7713, June 7, 2000, in Meucci 2006: 286), the term "safeguards the socio-relational profile of the individual that is protected in all of his activity and express manifestations of personhood" (Tribunal of Agrigento, February 1, 2005, in Meucci 2006: 509). Unlike the biological damages awarded for the mobbing-related illness organizational coercion pathology, existential damages represent what often remains disembodied: the loss of the worker's future potential and deprivation of her full human actualization and the employer's duty to guarantee moral personhood and dignity (Article 41, par. 2, Constitution; see Meucci 2006: 286). The Italian courts have come to understand mobbing as both a material and an immaterial wound. This is uniquely derived from the nation's cultural and religious understandings that tie the good life and vitality to stable, long-term work and that see workers' moral and affective personhood as worthy of safeguarding.

Governing Materiality, Governing Immateriality

How do we begin to unravel what it might mean to be damaged existentially? Within the literature of psychological and medical anthropology, the question of the existential is bound to the body and embodiment (Csordas 1994), and also to human suffering and death in the often tragic attempts to manage, mediate, organize, and value human mortality. But this is a question that is impossible to quantify. The states of wellness and illness both become measures of possibilities: "[Health] is the feeling of a capacity to go beyond initial capacities, a capacity to make the body do what it did not initially seem to promise" (Canguilhem 2008: 474). This understanding of the body's capacities implies that injury might be measured in lost human potential, something which can only be approximated. In addition, this understanding of health as fundamentally existential parallels a particular understanding of suffering that Arthur Kleinman has theorized: "Suffering is converted into technical problems that transmogrify its existential roots" (1995: 35). We have numerous examples of this problem of conversion in the ethnographic record. Lochlann Jain, for instance, writes that late-stage cancer trials must necessarily present the risks and dangers to patients, but the trials also represent a "ghosting of the[ir] lives. . . . deaths maintain an everywhere and nowhere quality" (2010: 90). The recruitment of patients for trials hinges directly upon how life is quantified into future chances, which mask and elide the "life-or-death binary" (ibid.).

At times, state law, like medical policy, becomes the indirect arbiter of life or death. Interested in the "growing emphasis on the role of compassion, sympathy, and benevolence in political life," Miriam Ticktin examines the social and political complexities of a clause in French law that grants extended stays to illegal immigrants in the event of serious illness (2006: 34). Since illness has become a means to stay, the choice to treat or cure has become, ironically, a choice about deportation. Thus, in France, the biological is "a flexible social resource" (ibid.: 35) even though "biology is not the domain of the incontestable" (40) and thus is grounded in the outer limits of materiality.

Governing projects, we find, become existential in that they manage human potential and seek to rectify or alleviate human suffering, or they produce, take, or disallow life. Jean Comaroff and John Comaroff, for instance, have written that the people subjected to European capitalist culture in South Africa had "impose[d] on them a particular way of seeing and being, to colonize their consciousness with the signs and practices, the axioms and aesthetics, of an alien culture" (Comaroff and Comaroff 1989: 267). Here, the notion of governing someone's way of being reveals a unique starting point for the Comaroffs: a view of personhood that values the essence of a human being more than a strictly material configuration of a subject, one that examines the state as "an institutional order of political regulation and a condition of being" (ibid.: 268).[1] Political and regulatory operations emerge from and in turn shape the existential conditions of subjects.

Twenty-first-century work has also suggested modes of governance that dwell in intimate and immaterial spheres. In the context of post-partition India, Veena Das traces how the "magical aspect of the state" might be "mimicked,-literalized, and embodied," drawing attention to the involvement of the state in everyday life (2006: 183). In teasing out the transcendental and extrasensory qualities of governed subjects, the shift in scholarly inquiry has been toward recognition of how surveillance and control might be forms of affective governance (Hardt 1999; Muehlebach n.d.). Other studies call attention to the ways in which the governing of citizens' bodies may produce violence, even if compassion, both somatic and spiritual, is involved. Though damage to the soul may leave some material traces, such as hostile letters or uncomfortable office conditions, a review of when existential damages have been awarded in Italian courts shows that this process does not fully depend on the material traces of human suffering and thus enables a different reading of the limits of the biological.

Italian Archives of the Existential

Italian political theorist Roberto Esposito offers a compelling alternative to Cartesian divides: by mobilizing a distinction between *body* and *flesh* in his examination of biopolitics, the soul remains a constitutive element of the subject (Esposito 2008: 159). Rather than the more common differentiation between body and soul, he examines both phenomenology and the Christian roots of the opposition between body and flesh, in which the soul is housed within the body and distanced from flesh (ibid.: 163). The body, then, in this compelling blend of Christian and Foucauldian theories, is simultaneously material and immaterial because of the relegation of the somatic, earthy, and carnal aspects of the body to "flesh." Within Christian understandings, it is "only the spiritualization of the body . . . that is capable of redeeming man from the misery of his corruptible flesh" (164). According to Esposito, who is characterizing modernity not the classical period, biopolitics does not retain the soul, as in Christian ideology, but nonetheless keeps hold of "the presence of a transcendent principle" (165). Esposito marshals Nazi biopolitics as one example of acting on the body: containing this transcendental element in the form of "racial heredity," it resulted in a "bio-spiritual incorporation" (ibid.). Esposito's framework enables a productive rethinking of the body-soul apparatus, which will be useful as we examine the historical grounding of modern biological bodies with souls. Similarly, in his reflections on multiple personality disorder, Ian Hacking adapts Foucault's biopolitics to the "memoro-politics of the human soul," where the soul "invokes character, reflective choice, and self-understanding" (1998: 215) and "stands for the strange mix of aspects of a person that may be, at some time, imaged as inner" (6).

In *The Politics of Life Itself*, Nikolas Rose, seeming to diverge from soul-oriented modes of governmentality, calls for the examination of somatic ethics as a way to recognize the increasing role of biology in forming and transforming late modern citizenship (Rose 2007: 255). For Rose, the rise of this type of ethics relates to a redefinition of biological existence as the core of personhood: "If our ethics has become, in key respects, somatic, this is part[ly] because it is our 'soma'—or corporeal existence—that is given salience and problematized—to some extent at least, our genome, our neurotransmitters—our 'biology'" (ibid.: 257). Underlying these insights is a sense that corporeality can be invested, unearthed, and scrutinized by scientific means, and, therefore, that it is knowable. Within Rose's logic, the rise of biocapitalism and the management of life in advanced liberal democracies rest almost exclusively upon and regulate a biomedically defined body (ibid.: 26). My concern centers on the ways in which biopolitical theories account less fully for the immaterial aspects, or sacred formulations, of personhood. What this points toward is a cultural specificity of existing religious and moral orders that have preceded or altered the ways in which biopolitical governance takes hold, or even fails. Given the Italian Catholic ideology of a terrestrial body containing a sacred soul, the modes of governance may not act upon biology in such an exclusive and totalizing way. In other words, the Catholic notions of toil and the soul see existential damages not as relating to the soma, nor as affecting only secular biological material, but as both sacred and secular.

Rose's earlier work positioned the soul as a central object of governing projects: "The government of the soul depends upon our recognition of ourselves as ideally and potentially certain sorts of person, the unease generated by a normative judgment of what we are and could become, and the incitement offered to overcome this discrepancy by following the advice of experts in the management of the self" (1994: 11). This mode of governance acted on the soul insofar as it was aimed at the subject's intimate realms: motivation, morality, desire, experience, identification.[2] While related, this work did not fully anticipate nor explain the acute interest in the soul among contemporary Italian thinkers of late capitalism. Among theorists of the Italian autonomist movement, a neo-Marxist grandchild of Italy's workerism movement (Smith 2009), the demands of labor call upon the soul and enter the existential domain, a position also shared by other neo-Marxist or New Left theorists, such as Maurizio Lazzarato. Rose's notion of the soul as the complete subject is similar to the way in which Lazzarato suggests that immaterial labor has produced "a kind of 'intellectual worker' who is him- or herself an entrepreneur" (Lazzarato 1996: 145). Similarly, Italian theorist Christian Marazzi positions immaterial labor in this way:

We are witnessing the birth of "cognitive laborers," a class of producers "commanded" . . . by technologies that are increasingly mental, symbolic, and communicative. The new machine that commands live labor and makes the worker produce is no longer [a] physically identifiable and specifically situated tool, but tends to be located within the worker herself, in her brain and in her soul. (Marazzi 2007: 29–30)

In other words, both body and soul are called upon to generate post-Fordist labor. If work itself shifts toward requiring more of the full person in order to execute it, then it follows that when this particular kind of work is at stake, so too is the full autonomy of the worker, her status as a person, the very core of her existence. The soul's incorporation into the mode of production has, within this formulation, bleak effects: Marazzi suggests that late capitalism has induced the collapse of "symbolic order," which has resulted in a devastating fragmentation of human life (ibid.: 14).

Autonomist leader Franco "Bifo" Berardi traces the rise of "cognitive labor"—labor that relies upon workers' investment of affect and language, which he calls *semiocapitalism*—to the 1970s, in tandem with the proliferation of digital technologies. For Berardi, the division between the body and the soul also parallels Fordist and post-Fordist modes of production: "Industrial factories used the body, forcing it to leave the soul outside the assembly line, so that the worker looked like a soulless body. The immaterial factory asks [us] instead to place our very souls at its disposal: intelligence, sensibility, creativity and language" (2009: 116). Within these logics, immaterial labor has far greater potential to harm the worker, who now requires more stringent legal and political protection. Berardi also aligns the height of Fordist production with existentialist philosophy; both focus on alienation, the belief that manual labor objectified and commodified what was "essentially human" (ibid.: 92). He positions existentialism within capitalism's history as lending cultural recognition to workers' estrangement, and he criticizes existentialism's desire for a kind of labor that enables self-realization. One can make a similar theoretical and historical parallel between post-Fordism and Italian leftist theorists, in that the focus on workers' investment of their soul at work acts as a structure of feeling which names the stakes of immaterial labor. In other words, if we take seriously the contemporary historical and epistemological trajectory of the soul in Italy, then leftist theories become a way of knowing that both anticipates and re-creates a cultural understanding of late capitalist labor as taxing the soul, which we also find in Italy's neoliberal juridical apparatus.

Understanding how Italian leftist views might become part of the neoliberal state is an issue which has been carefully investigated by Andrea Muehlebach (2009). She shows us that the two are only apparently divergent by examining how volunteer labor, articulated as a moral and pious form of toil by the Left, has been summoned in service of the increasingly elusive welfare state. Drawing from Carl Schmitt's notion of *complexio oppositorum* (complex of opposites), Muehlebach illustrates how Italian neoliberalism contains within itself its own opposite: "The market neoliberal, in other words, is accompanied by what one might call a moral neoliberal. . . . The result is the somewhat unexpected reinvigoration of politics at the very moment that politics often seems irredeemably lost" (Muehlebach 2009: 499). Muehlebach's theoretical insights further elucidate why, in the case of mobbing, the Italian state appears to extend the conditions that result in workers' precariousness and devaluation and yet recognizes and compensates for the human and moral effects of precariousness.

Legal Origins

Italy's legal history of existential damages shows a recognition of existential personhood, and there are also traces of the soul in other categories of damages awarded due to mobbing. Damage to workers comes from a particular right protected under Article 2087 of Italy's Civil Code, which insists on the employer's duty to protect the "psycho-physical integrity" of the worker. From this, the employer must adopt measures in order to protect both the "physical integrity and the moral personhood" of workers. In the 1980s, a critical ruling preceded a series of changes in the understanding of "biological damage" in terms of legal settlements, "not only in the strict sense of patrimonial damage, but for all of the damages that hinder the self-actualizing activities of human beings"

(Constitutional Court, no. 184, July 14, 1986, cited in Buffone 2005), thereby allowing consideration of "moral" damage. The notion of moral damage in the realm of workers compensation expanded to include intangible loss and paralleled similar codifications of *prejudice physiologique* in France and "pain and suffering" in the United States (Buffone 2005). Moral damage amounts to "spiritual suffering" and thus it is not necessary that a subject suffer physically or psychologically in order to demonstrate moral damage (Amato et al. 2002: 20, 112). In addition, biological damage is not always configured as a perfect parallel to physical damage of the material body but "refer[s] to the integrity of [a worker's] discriminatory reflections on his activity, the situations and relationships articulated in his life . . . [and] also refer[s] to the spiritual, cultural, affective, social, athletic, and every other environmental sphere and the way in which the subject realizes [*svolge*] his personality" (Constitutional Court, no. 356, July 18, 1991, in Meucci 2006: 288–289). It will be important to keep this in mind so as to avoid imagining the state as perfectly and evenly associating biological damages with the material body and existential damages with the soul-carrying body. For Mario Meucci, the treatment of biological damage "doesn't indicate a well-defined and univocal reality" within the courts (ibid.: 296).

Finally, under Article 2087, existential damages have also been awarded in mobbing cases in which the measurable biological damages were not sufficient to capture the kinds of damage suffered by the mobbee. Existential damage to workers is the immeasurable loss of actualizing themselves as persons in the workplace: "altering their life habits and the relational assets belonging to them, upsetting the quotidian and depriving them of the occasion to express and actualize their personalities to the external world" (Serrao 2005: 14). Existential damage, then, names a kind of future-oriented loss of potentiality in one's career and personal life (Amato et al. 2002: 128). Psychological damages "negatively affect [the] psychic health of the victim, while, vice versa, existential damages . . . do not compromise [the] mental equilibrium of the victim so gravely as to determine a true and actual pathology" (Meucci 2006: 290–291). Cases related to mobbing, tried under this article, have awarded significant amounts for these specific damages: the Pisa Tribunal awarded 10 million lira (US$5,000) for biological damage in 2001 and, in another case, approximately US$30,000 for existential damage (Amato et al. 2002: 160). Following the progression of modern labor from physical to increasingly psychological toil, Article 2087 has shifted from biological damage to existential damage for work harassment. Torts law has thus responded to a series of rights of workers: "to not be unjustly fired, to not be demoted or degraded professionally, to not be forced to work in conditions without security, to not be mortified or harassed unjustifiably as might come in various hypotheses of mobbing" (Meucci 2006: 287).

The first recognition of existential damage for a case not about mobbing, for which it is awarded almost exclusively, was in a Supreme Court case in 2000 about child neglect (sent. no. 7713, June 7, 2000). The case was filed against Francesco Capptelletto for negligence in the economic support of his biological son, Daniele Hu Cheng, by the biological mother, Donatella Hu Cheng. The Supreme Court ruled that the father's absence constituted a unique kind of damage with respect to the son—representing a fundamental assumption of what was necessary for the child's well-being and growth—and thus existential damages were awarded (Meucci 2006: 294).

Since this case, existential damages have been awarded for mobbing and for professional demotion. In 2003, two of Italy's high courts (Court of Cassation, sent. nos. 8827–8828; Constitutional Court, sent. no. 203) issued what has become known as the "twin" (*gemelle*) sentences, dividing non-pecuniary damages into three categories: biological, moral, and constitutional (*di valori costituzionali*) (Musi 2008: 22). Existential damages remained differentiated from moral damages and biological damages, the latter based upon medical evidence, as had already been established. The problem, according to Italian legal theorist Emanuela Musi, was that this ruling rendered existential damages a catchall category for any kind of non-pecuniary personal damages, creating the opportunity for claims of injury as trivial as the "over-stuffed inbox, delayed phone connection, bad haircut, lost baggage, and stress" (ibid.). Attorney Luigi Modaffari (2008) likened the twin sentences to extending existential damages to correspond with the constitutionally nonexistent "right to happiness."

After the twin sentences, juridical clarification was widely demanded. In 2006, the court further distinguished between moral and existential damages: the latter was "not merely emotional and interior but objectively certifiable" (sent. no. 6572). Furthermore, existential damages compensated for interference with a "worker's right to liberally express one's personality at work," and the ability to collect the damages would be demonstrable through "dequalification, isolation, and forced inactivity [*inoperosità*]" (Court of Cassation, sent. no. 4712, February 25, 2008).

Most broadly, existential damages are a legal mode of compensation when there has been a failure to acknowledge "the right to develop human personhood [*svolgimento della personalita umana*]" that affects "the daily existence of the individual beyond medically certifiable physical damage" (ibid.). Thus, existential damages do not require a concrete lesion, a financial loss, or the presence of punishable action but rather indicate damage to the "healthy fruition of pleasure and [the] gratification of relational life and social relationships" (ibid.: 295). Though existential damage is defined in numerous ways, what runs across these definitions is that it is considered a form of immaterial loss: loss of selfhood, loss of future possibilities, or relational loss. It is an injury not only of work's harshest extremes, but of work's absence.

Governing Immaterial Labor

Immaterial labor refers to a post-Fordist economic shift in which both the product investment of labor are no longer tangible items, but intangibles: ideas, services, networks, new applications, information. Mr. A, originally from the southern Italian city of Catania, began working for the Ministry of Labor and Social Security in Siena, a hilltop Tuscan city, in 1973 as an administrative assistant. He had over twenty years of work in this position when things began to go awry. In 1996, he was asked to substitute for his colleague in the city of Poggibonsi, a twenty-five-mile commute, and he did so for three years. He returned to Siena in January 2000 and found great turmoil. Stripped of a personal computer, he was thrust into what he called "the most complete inactivity" save for what he dubbed "sham responsibilities" and the "mortifying" task of filing correspondence. Mr. A described his office as "a small room, nearly a closet, . . . with stacked boxes; there was even a water heater." For Mr. A, the situation became unbearable, and he said: "We [were] dealing with work responsibilities that didn't exist. . . . I could only speak with the walls and the piles of paper, but with nobody from outside. . . . Doctor Aquino, the supervisor, she didn't propose anything for me, sometimes she would ask me if I could file a little letter or find the *gazzetta* [newspaper]" (*U. A. v. Ministero del Lavoro e delle Politiche Sociali*, Tribunal of Siena, 2003). It got worse: "I wasn't even greeted," said Mr. A. "I would greet people without it being exchanged so I stopped greeting others and even speaking." One of his colleagues testified:

> When I was in Siena, there were other people beyond Mr. A who complained about the situation of the absence of service orders and the lack of precise work responsibilities; there were other complaints. People who previously had had a role that was well defined in the suburban office and transferred to Siena had lost them and they found themselves without a well-defined role (though these complaints were lessened in time). (Ibid.)

Here, we see not only immaterial products at the center of the narrative and ruling, but also the emergent flexible labor regime with its ill-defined work responsibilities, unpredictable workloads, and intensifying isolation.

Mr. A decided to take action and sued the ministry for mobbing. In the first court ruling prior to the ministry's appeal, he was awarded damages for professional disqualification and biological damages to compensate for the mental and physical strain of his working conditions. According to the 2003 ruling, the lack of a computer was key evidence of Mr. A's marginalization as he lacked "a work instrument and an office worker's status symbol." The ruling likened Mr. A's case to that of Bob Cratchit in Charles Dickens's *A Christmas Carol*, summoning the image of Scrooge's warm office and Cratchit's cold and inferior room. Though the court found no evidence of malicious and intentional action against the plaintiff, it did find that the employer had violated Article 2087 of Italy's Civil Code, that is, the employer's protection of the worker's "physical integrity and moral personhood," which made Mr. A eligible for existential damages. In his case (Tribunal of Siena, April 19, 2003), the existential damage was defined as the "daily" degradations of "his way of being, of mentally relating, of behaving and relating, damages accrued from the lived frustrations, from deluded hopes and expectations, from the loss of self-esteem because of marginalization, mortification, and humiliation . . . damage to the worker's image in his professional environment" (Meucci 2006: 444). The court recognized a loss of future potential for Mr. A: "The work damaged his esteem. . . . the chance[s] to have influence and work responsibilities were cut, his work had changed. . . . these were the conditions which created an atmosphere, a climate that was, for him, hostile." The economic award for the existential damages was €3,500.

In Mr. A's case, the juridical regime enabled the reinstantiation of tangible evidence or, at least, visual and witnessed forms of experience, even as it recognized precisely those alienating practices that constitute a neoliberal labor regime. Measuring something that is as ephemeral and intangible as human personhood, within a juridical system, often takes the form of determining which things can and do take physical form, as well as what matters. In the case of Mr. A's mobbing, these things were the tangible loss of the computer, the silence of lost greetings, the degraded office space, the juridical court case, the quantifiable award, and social recognition. He had been forced to navigate the conditions, both material and immaterial, of late post-Fordist labor: intangible products, isolation, mental exertion, the desire for productivity, imagined prosperity and mobility, and, significantly, the disappearance of the work-life binary. Stefano Harney writes, "[Immaterial labor] separates in its appeal to spirit, affect, and creativity, and collapses in its mourning of the commodification of these capacities" (Harney 2006: 78). The loss of Fordist stability, itself a wound to human possibility, is coupled with economic and investment demands upon the spirit and affective resources of workers.

Yet, despite the rise of post-Fordism, the Italian work regime also retains the value of protected and socially engaged work, an imaginary which holds on to material symbols (the computer) and which produces high moral stakes when this kind of labor is put at risk.[3] In other words, the recognition of existential damages is due not only to the emergence of immaterial labor but to a recognition of this imaginary, which is, as Michael Hardt suggests, both "corporeal and affective, in the sense that its products are intangible: a feeling of ease, well-being, satisfaction, excitement, passion, even a sense of connectedness or community. . . . what is essential to it, in its in-person aspect, is really the creation and manipulation of affects" (Hardt 1999: 96). It is only in this type of labor context, in which labor represents an affectively charged form of production, that mobbing becomes a more vital displacement, an example of a new moral order in which the stripping of information and of modern work tools can mean social death and thus an existential wound. The existential marks this ineffable loss and the ethical limits of the employment relationship even as it, paradoxically, becomes what defines normal labor.

Immaterial and Precarious Labor

The labor regime in Italy is not only immaterial but also precarious. It is necessary to be mindful that the cases of Mr. G and Mr. A occurred within a re-

gime of semi-permanent and atypical employment, which intensifies the possible losses to and stresses upon worker-subjects by rendering them constantly
unstable and at risk. Valerie Walkerdine has examined such new psychic demands in the context of Great Britain: "The process obliterates the relatively
safe space of the long term contract or expectation of a lifetime's work with one
employer and transfers onto the worker the responsibility to embody safety
within themselves" (2006: 28). For Walkerdine, the labor regime demands a
self-responsible subject who is capable of internally navigating safety and security, rather than depending upon public or state resources to do so. Precarious
labor, in tandem with immaterial labor, specifies the kind of psychic exertion
required: one must patrol anxiety and marshal an internal sense of safeguards.
While immaterial labor might enable and demand creativity, abstraction, and
analysis, precarious labor raises the stakes: one must do all of that while self-
managing one's anxiety.

Christian Ethics, the Soul, and the Juridical

Though immaterial and casualized labor has required an important shift,
a necessary and fundamental reconfiguration of work, in the development of
existential damages, so too has the recognition of workers as beings with bodies and souls. How has an underlying Christian ethics informed Italian juridical discourse and practice? The early 1990s collapse of the political party of the
Christian Democrats was symbolic of an overall "secularisation and shrinking
of Catholic sub-culture" (Pollard 2008: 160). At first glance, one might link the
secularization of politics in Italy in the 1990s to the strong casualization of the
work regime and the influx of neoliberalism as heralding a modern, and increasingly secular, subject. However, Catholic values and beliefs underwrite modern
subjectivity. Michael Herzfeld's (2009) examination of eviction in Rome ties the
practices of usury and corruption to an underlying Catholic belief in original
sin and to the role of the church, the former insofar as human subjects are necessarily flawed and the latter concerning the underhanded exchange of indulgences, whether for sins or private rule binding, which allow for governing
through individualized deal brokering. Similarly, Andrea Muehlebach (2007)
has argued that volunteer labor in Italy depends on a Catholic notion of unre-
munerated toil as sacred and selfless, such that the state can shift caretaking labor to underutilized and often underemployed groups: youth and the retired.

What may be taking root within Italian society today cannot fully erase the
strong influence of Catholicism: "97 percent [of the population were] . . . bap-
tized Catholics" in 2002 (Garelli 2007: 10). Franco Garelli declares the dominance of the church to be still deeply salient, beyond moral orders and religious
practices: "The church in Italy is much more than a historical memory, a heri-
tage of the past. Priests, bell towers, churches and religious institutions are not
merely components of the panorama of Italian folklore; they are also integral
and structural elements of the prevailing social relationships" (ibid.: 9). Also

of considerable influence has been the influx of immigrants in the late twentieth century and early twenty-first; Catholicism is rarely their religion, and that, for some scholars, has produced a new and enduring push for the promotion of Catholicism as a hallmark of Italian citizenship and identity (Pace 2007: 88–89).

Disturbance of the Transient Soul

The 2003 case of Angela Fideli from Tempio Pausania, a small town on the island of Sardinia, illustrates the connections between the soul and existential damages most explicitly (*A. N. Fideli v. Comune di Loiri Porto San Paolo*, no. 194/00, 2003).[4] Judge Ponassi referenced both moral and existential damages, naming two Supreme Court decisions (8827/2003 and 8828/2003) as assuring "protection of the subjective moral damage, contingent suffering, from the disturbance of the transient soul [*al turbamento dell'animo transuente*]," which counts as damage to the "inherent values of the person and not merely as subjective moral damage."

Angela worked as a police officer (*vigile urbano*) for the town of Loiri Porto San Paolo beginning in 1996. She professed that the relationship with her superiors, including the town mayor, had deteriorated and she faced "illegitimate disciplinary sanctions, refusals of her requests for mobility"; eventually, she was stripped of her responsibilities and "ghettoized below her professional and human profile." Following additional and intensive disciplinary actions, which led to economic penalties including a reduction in her salary, Angela was diagnosed with depression. She sued the town for mobbing in December 1999 but lost. She appealed, and in the 2003 ruling, the judge found evidence of mobbing: she was the victim of a "persecutory strategy in an environment in which the plaintiff was subjected to a series of behaviors and practices of unjust objectives which damaged, marginalized, and discriminated [against] her, until it provoked damage to her health" and to her "moral personhood [*personalità morale*]." For example, her "sober and correct" request for a transfer was not only denied but also met with "a profound annoyance regarding her personal relationships" and thus was motivated by "personal" rather than "technical-juridical" reasons. Moreover, the township told Angela that she should no longer carry a weapon as her "anxious personality [*personalità non serena*]" would put either her or the public at risk, which the judge ruled was an "explicit and unmotivated request" and constitutive of "persecutory intentions" toward the plaintiff.

Other evidence for the town's malign intent included her exclusion from public safety tasks and confinement to administrative police activity; punishment for two incorrect behaviors with citizens, one of which was issuing a fine to a man for leaving his car to obtain a newspaper, which her employers deemed "foolish" on her part and listed as motivation for her subsequent demotion; and, more generally, "physical and psychological isolation." The judge determined that Angela was "systematically" isolated and confined to "a small room underneath a stairwell which no other employee had ever been assigned" as an office and which also served as a passageway for other employees. Her request to work overtime hours for the November 1999 elections was denied, representing a patently "discriminatory" act, which deprived her of wages. Finally, she was scolded, and a further punishment recommended, for failing to greet the mayor, and she also received a severe letter in which she was told that her behavior did not "conform to correct principles" and was indicative "of little regard and trust toward everyone." In addition to the "excessive" nature of these punishments, the judge found a particular inequality in that the mayor referred to Angela with the informal "you" pronoun while, to him, Angela used the formal address, thus illustrating what was "a character conflict in which the objectively weaker subject is subjected to the authority of the other." In his final ruling, the judge declared: "There is no doubt that this persecutory conduct enters into the definition of mobbing. The worker has proven a causation between the said conduct and a series of prejudicial consequences . . . which merits compensation . . . for harm to the inherent value of the person," which he analogized to moral and existential damages.

Angela's professional identity was harmed by her isolation and demotion, which were achieved in part through highly symbolic material losses: the forced removal of her weapon and her shabby office. But language, both via disciplinary letters and in epithets, was also marshaled to effect a state of isolation and humiliation. Her professional judgment and character were called into question in her request for a transfer and in the degree of criminal activity she sought to punish. The underlying epistemological assumption was that her day-to-day existence on the job, her identity as a police officer, was undermined such that her "inherent value" and "moral personhood" were damaged.

At first glance, Angela's case seems absent of severe harassment and maliciousness. Recognizing a threat to her inherent value cannot emerge unless the mundane practices and fulfillment of work come to be recognized as crucial to human existence. But why then posit damage to the transient soul? The notion draws from a Christian epistemology of personhood as divided between an earthly existence, a perishable material or "flesh" in Esposito's logic, and a saveable essence that endures past death. Thus the notion of *transient*, though used subtly within the legal discourse, encodes this Catholic sense of a spirit entity of the human body, transcending material realms. This sense of transience also reflects the way in which Foucault characterizes Christianity as a "salvation" religion, which is "supposed to lead the individual from one reality to another, from death to life, from time to eternity" (1988: 40). The political subject becomes figured as a site of spiritual and moral repositioning, even as she becomes malleable and shaped by marketization. What is remarkable about Angela's case is the recognition of the strained relationships and day-to-day hardships, even the symbolic power struggle in linguistic address, as injurious, because these are the hallmarks of immaterial production. The state promotes a regime in which workers like Angela must become self-responsible and risk managing, yet it also deems the very conditions they must navigate to be harmful.

Affective Demands: The Case of Alberto

My day-to-day presence at DataGisco helped me to understand the immaterial investment of workers firsthand and how the post-Fordist regime puts demands on workers' souls. Formed over a decade through a series of mergers between eight smaller companies and employing nearly 500 people, DataGisco specializes in information technology and digital communications, environmental sciences and geography. I worked most closely with two divisions, the Map, Information Technology, and Environmental Division (MITE) and the Digital Archives (DA); there are also divisions focusing on banking and finance, public administration, research and development, and internet resources. The MITE division competes for mostly public works projects, such as the building of bridges and roads, and collaborates with engineers, architects, and designers. The DA department also competes for various public and private projects to make digital archives, via scanning or database entry, of large paper-based archives and document systems. At the time of my fieldwork, DataGisco had two executive officers, Ettore Del Vecchio and Franco Santonini, who formed the apex of an organizational structure that included six division directors.

Roberta Tullini was the technical director of the corporate branch that encompasses both the MITE and DA divisions. In Italy, there are not many examples of women in positions of corporate leadership, which made Roberta part of a very small minority. In 2003 in the city of Padua, there was a quite low employment rate for women (34.7 percent), and in the country as a whole, women held only 6 percent of the positions as corporate directors or managers (Veneto Lavoro 2004: 83). While many workers shared with me that they viewed Roberta as a competent manager, just as many were critical about her management style. Her floor of DataGisco, where I was situated, was undoubtedly dominated by her presence; her high-pitched peals of laughter were one of the few distinctive sounds on the floor and could be heard above the noises of keyboard clicking, computer whirring, phone ringing, and paper shuffling. Employees would share a knowing smile or roll their eyes on the many occasions when she laughed. Roberta was also one of the few people to physically move around the large, cubicle-divided floor. She spent little time in her enclosed, glass-paneled office—the only semi-private space in this entire division.

After a year of fieldwork at DataGisco, I conducted formal interviews with various employees. Married and in his early forties, Alberto Albetti was a project manager in the MITE division and handled environmental consulting in particular; he had worked with Roberta, who was one of his supervisors, for over ten years. Alberto had been hired in 1990 by one of the smaller companies that later merged to form DataGisco, and he had close connections with the men who became the CEOs of DataGisco, including Ettore Del Vecchio. I had witnessed conflict between Alberto and Roberta and wondered whether he viewed their interactions as a form of mobbing, but I did not want to put words in his mouth. I framed the question carefully, "Well, let's be frank, are there people who are a bit pushed toward the door, either by Roberta or other people?" He met my gaze and raised his hand in the air with a wistful smile. I said, "You? Seriously?" In a single, slow gesture, he shrugged and jutted his chin forward and upward, a typical Italian way of conveying a kind of reluctant admission, a sense of hopelessness. He described how his job position had been disrupted and constrained by various economic processes, including poor company profits, a stalled economy, and delays on particular projects. One of Alberto's most anguished moments, which for him most crystallized the reality of his persecution, was when he had been blamed for a company-wide computer virus, because he had not updated his software. While Alberto identified as being "pushed toward the door," he did not explicitly use the term mobbing. We also discussed his case informally after the initial interview:[5]

> I'll tell you very honestly that I've had problems with Roberta for a long time. And lots of other colleagues have problems with Roberta. But up until three or four years ago, we got along okay.... She has a personality that's very particular, really impulsive, not inclined to listen. Well, she *appears* to be listening, but then she doesn't care at all and makes up her own mind....
>
> I believe that Roberta is very smart about organization and managing personnel.... She's much much less good at managing those that can bring in work, those that basically have more years of experience, have different opinions. [If you] sit her down at a table and say to her, "I don't think the same as you, and I believe there are other and different things to be done"— in these cases, she hardens, puts up a wall.

Much of Alberto's critique of Roberta draws from and contrasts her with notions of the appropriate affect for Italian women: emotional availability, cooperativeness, receptivity. He also distinguishes between her positive ability to manage low-level employees and her difficulty in interfacing with higher-level workers, the group with which he strongly identifies. He later added that he believed she hired employees without college degrees in order to increase her own authority, paraphrasing this strategy as "You've gotten here from nothing, so now you'll do what I say or else I'll fire you." He positioned her as a person who cruelly threatened new workers, showing little regard for others, little care. In this narrative, Roberta was positioned as a menacing and threatening figure in the workplace because she embodied the lack of care and concern about workers that was being simultaneously experienced on a massive scale as part of the demands of neoliberal labor.

The legibility of Alberto's persecution was bound up directly with Roberta's lack of appropriately feminine affect:

In about a month, we earned back €100,000. And she didn't even say, "Nice! Great! Good result!" It was as if she were saying, "Oh, guess who I ran into the other day on the street?" Cold water, nothing, zero. So it's clear that it's not about the sector's profits. It's a scripted game. It's as if I started being something they didn't want to handle any more.

When Alberto mimicked Roberta, his voice became flat and devoid of warmth, which he illustrated with the metaphor of "cold water" to mean "deadpan" or without emotion. The affective distance and isolation that Alberto read from Roberta's speech were identified by him as a key indicator of his marginalization. The absence of positive evaluations, in the broader context of vigilance and suspicion in the workplace, were signs of her "game," which implies a predetermined and intentional coordination between actors.

I asked whether his concern about being ousted had impacted his life, and Alberto further described the emotional effects of his workplace marginalization:

You lose sleep at night. You also lose smiling, the desire to joke around and laugh, tease people, mess around with folks a bit, yeah, and also with myself.... I've lost the ability to smile about things.... Now, I'm slowly, slowly trying to get back to laughing like before. Because, in the end, it's just meanness that doesn't deserve more than two seconds. But, when it happens to you, you try to defend yourself.

Alberto's sadness and despondency were similar to the complaints of workers who do identify as victims of mobbing. However, it was clear that these affective disruptions were in direct relation to the kind of investment—hopeful, engaged, cognitive, affective—that his position demanded.

Unlike some of the other narratives of mobbing in this book, I actually witnessed Alberto and Roberta interact around the office many times as well as in meetings with Ettore. Their dislike of one another and their strained relationship were evident and were frequent topics of work gossip. In April 2005, I attended a meeting of all the division heads and Ettore. In a newly renovated meeting room, with bright yellow walls and framed images of golf courses, we sat around a shiny wooden table. Before the meeting began, Alberto counted the people in the room, silently mouthing numbers and pointing to each person present, and then moved a chair from a nearby office to accommodate another person. He then placed in a prominent position a high-backed chair, in which Ettore later sat. Roberta eyed him suspiciously and told him there were already enough chairs (which there were not). She told me afterward that she thought it was "absurd" that Alberto was attempting to "impress" Ettore with the "larger chair." I was surprised by her reading of his actions as necessarily for Ettore as there had clearly been insufficient chairs in the room.

Alberto explained to me that the most important and critical issue fueling the conflict between him and Roberta was that she came between him and Ettore, the CEO. He then shared the following about Ettore:

I found out from a colleague . . . that Ettore has a certain way of doing things. You say, he's the boss. But he doesn't really want to be the boss. He doesn't want to pull you by the ears and tell you, "Great." He'll give you a note that says, "This might need to be done. Let's talk about it." In a way, you know, a bit vague. If you tell me that I have to go climb a tree, I will go climb a tree. [Imitating Ettore, cocking head] "Well, I don't know, let's see, seems like we should go climbing, but I don't know." [As a result,] I don't know if I have to go climb it or not. If you want it, I'll do it, and if you don't want it, I won't, right?

There was once this problem when there were just four of us. We had two computers, and there were four of us. A sales promotion for computers came out, and I left him the page from the newspaper with the ad and a note that read: "If you want, let's talk about it." My colleague told me that he got pissed off, "How dare he! What is he thinking?" It was simply a joke. . . . He got really distant that time. . . . Ettore will be bloody pissed off at you, but he still greets you, he smiles at you, he shakes your hand—but deep inside himself he's thinking about killing you.

To Alberto, Ettore displays an unclear communicative and impenetrable affective style, but it's not as much of a problem as Roberta's style is. Alberto critiqued Ettore for lacking a desire to manage while Roberta, he argued, exploited her desire to govern others. Alberto's fear that he was being slowly eliminated made him more apprehensive about what these gestures and utterances meant; this effort at deciphering, in and of itself, shows a kind of unrecognized cognitive and affective labor on the part of contemporary workers. Alberto also expressed frustration about Ettore's inability to give him clear commands. His metaphor of climbing the tree suggested his desire to perform as a good worker: he wanted to properly complete a task, if only he could identify which task he must complete. But the vague boss who cannot effectively make demands on the worker does not give him the chance to effectively show his merit. This puts him at a disadvantage because he cannot show himself to be "worthy" of his employment position, obscuring the pathway to valorized and stable work. This is particularly disorienting in the context of the neoliberal Italian workplace where information, sociorelational or otherwise, is a vital commodity and the stakes for long-term employment have radically changed. The effect of Ettore's approach, as an administrator and as someone who deceives others about his interior state, was a pervading sense of ambivalence and doubt for Alberto. More importantly, Alberto recognized that the affective order in his workplace had been disrupted; it had become uneven, unpredictable, strange. What might seem mundane, even including signs of compassion and care, could be secretly charged with hostility and anger.

Poor and secretive communication practices were pressing signs of corporate abnormalcy for Alberto: "That's the whole thing, it's a matter of understanding and of the scarce transparency of things. It's better to say shithead, but to your face, rather than keeping it inside and thinking it or maybe even saying it to someone else. Better than creating misunderstandings; maybe it would be easier to be healthy." "Transparency" as a social value cuts across discourses of free-market capitalism and Western ideas about emotional maturity. Since around the turn of the twenty-first century, it has become a buzzword in the discourse of ethical corporate practice and often creeps into discussions of neoliberal corporate governance (Strathern 2000a; Best 2005). Alberto also linked expressing affect explicitly—transparently—in language as a sign of health and a desirable quality.

The importance of masked sentiments may be because they represented Alberto's exclusion from critical knowledge about others' underlying affective dispositions. The unspoken is as highly significant as the spoken (Kulick 2005), and Alberto felt that the uncommunicated anger was what most endangered his position within the company. Later, I asked if his communication with Roberta was more direct, and he replied:

> She's not good at hiding her feelings like Ettore. If she's pissed, you can tell because of the way she moves, she won't look at you, she's agitated, she'll say something gruff. Meanwhile, with Ettore, you can never tell. . . . That's the biggest problem. The problem is that I don't work for Roberta, I work for Ettore. . . . I tried to explain things to her but she won't listen, really won't listen. I'm quite willing to listen to someone else's reasons, but the other has to be willing to listen to my reasons in order to find common ground. Either we won't try and just not get along, but [if things are going to change] we have to listen to each other to understand the problems because one of us gets angry because the other is angry.

Unlike Ettore, Roberta was described as someone whose expressions of anger were unpredictable and volatile: her affect was far more transparent, visibly embodied, and audibly apparent to Alberto. His assertion that "I don't work for Roberta, I work for Ettore" uncovered his more abiding allegiance to Ettore as the CEO, even though his day-to-day projects were most directly supervised by Roberta. Alberto had begun his career working closely with Ettore, but now he had little contact with the CEO except through Roberta. Such a reconfiguration of corporate relations is not uncommon in the Veneto region, where small companies merged throughout the 1990s. Yet negotiating the new terrain of hierarchies, which has generated new protocols for workplace communications, was not a simple process. Alberto viewed Roberta's initiative and desire to handle problems on her own as unjust, yet he seemed to desire a more authoritative stance from Ettore. Underpinning this is a language ideology with moral views about the way in which anger should be expressed and by what kind of gendered subject (Ochs 1992; Kulick 1998b; Irvine and Gal 2000). When I asked if he had ever tried to resolve things with Roberta, Alberto described a moment in which his *own* response was not transparent:

She won't accept. [Shaking head] . . . She won't listen, there's no way. She just starts crying and runs away. If you tell her, "You're tall, beautiful, blonde, fantastic," that's fine. Once, I told her just to tease her, "Oh yeah, you're so great, no joke, there's no one else like you!" She doesn't get sarcasm. She's like: "And so, well anyway, what's the problem? Tell me." No, she takes it as a compliment and goes away, get it? It's tough. It's tough to understand this stuff, you know?

In Alberto's narrative, his sarcasm might be likened to a sort of "hidden transcript" (Scott 1985). In responding to me, he embedded an exchange between the two of them where he used humor to criticize her managerial and relational style. He reenacted his joke, evoking the figure of the "beautiful blonde," a term which in Italy is almost always used in reference to a woman. Part of the joke was that he did not believe that she was a beautiful blonde woman, and it seemed to Alberto to be self-evident mockery when he complimented her both on her outstanding managerial style and on her feminine beauty. As affective masking trumps transparency, Alberto practiced sarcasm as a way to make his anger less evident precisely because of how carefully he monitored the escalations of conflict with Roberta.

One week after my interview with Alberto, I was at DataGisco for the day and had lunch with Roberta and her two closest friends and project directors: Davide Toreglia and Caterina D'Antonio. We passed Alberto as he was coming back from one of the cafés and the two of us exchanged greetings. As he walked by, he told Roberta that he was coming by her office later. She waved a hand at him, as if to respond to what he had said, then swiftly turned around and walked close to Caterina and Davide as we continued to the café. At lunch, Roberta told us that Alberto had been annoyed that morning and had been "angrily" shoving things around the office; "Tun tun tun," she said, imitating the sound of objects hitting the desk and giggling.

Davide Toreglia was the thirty-seven-year-old head of the Digital Archives division and a distant cousin of Alberto. Davide had begun working in the smaller company with Alberto and Ettore before it merged with DataGisco. Unlike Alberto, Davide had a close relationship with Roberta, whom he called "Berta," and shared lunch and coffee breaks with her on a daily basis. Throughout the year I spent in Padua, I was often invited to grab a quick panino with them at their favorite café—one not frequented by many other DataGisco employees. In addition, I closely followed some of Davide's projects, spending time in meetings and at work sites and discussing projects with him. All of his closest staff members confirmed that he had a rather abrupt style of management; he was often unaware of and, to a degree, insensitive to how certain orders would impact workers. He viewed himself as someone who was in command. Once, when I heard him muttering about all the "bullshit [*cazzate*]" he had to handle, I asked him to talk about it with me. He sighed and responded: "I'd *like* to work, but I have to always say, 'Do this! Do that!'" On another occasion, when Davide wanted to fire a temporary worker for not completing her tasks efficiently, he was met with some resistance by the worker's immediate supervisor. Davide, however, remained aloof, announcing sternly, "No. Today, she's going home [*va a casa*]."

In May 2005, I met Davide at his favorite café after work. He described how he and Roberta got along:

> She has a personality [*carattere*], but she's also got a lot of responsibilities. She has to kind of impose herself [*imporrsi*] on others, but when she does this, she shouldn't lack respect. . . . She starts yelling. Sometimes, when she makes this mistake, I've said something to Berta [about this], knowing that we're friends, so it affects her more.

Davide then repeated the notion of Roberta "having a personality [*ha un carattere*]." Her flaws, then, make sense as a result of her "personality" and her responsibility in the company. The way in which this concept is often deployed in Italian is quite different than the English expression of having "personality." Whereas in English, it suggests a kind of quirkiness or uniqueness, in Italian it implies a person who is rigid, obstinate, harsh—affectively obtuse. Davide softened his criticism by ascribing Roberta's flaws to what he posited as an ongoing, durable condition: "having a personality." A difficult personality, in this sense, was something an individual "has," not something she "does," and thus had the effect of morally absolving her for acting harshly with employees.

I had heard Roberta complain about Alberto many times during lunch breaks, so I felt comfortable asking Davide why, in his opinion, they didn't get along. Right at the moment when I began to ask him, Davide broke into a hearty laugh and gestured for me to turn around. There was Roberta, about ten feet away, stopped on her moped. Davide had told her earlier that day that he and I would speak that evening. Grinning, she asked us how the interview was going, then wished us a good weekend and zoomed away. "See what I mean?" Davide said to me, shaking his head in disbelief. "She's incredible." Her unexpected visit to his interview was another reminder of her ability to constantly monitor employees (and visiting anthropologists). Once she left, he finished describing his thoughts on Alberto:

> He's always calm, does his work. . . . He doesn't work with me, [but] I know about this whole thing. I have fights, I have problems, but . . . I just swallow it. But she has her way of pushing it. I have to do white and you have to do it black, so I just shut up because the director has decided black.

I asked, "But what about Ettore?"

He trusts Berta a lot. Contacts [with him] are infrequent. Once, they were more frequent, [but] clearly with a company of 500 people, if everyone decided to go to him, [it would be too much]. So Berta brings everything to him. She takes the load of problems and brings them to Ettore. It's the hierarchy. . . .

She would feel bad if I bypassed her and went to speak to him. If I [want to] go to Ettore, I warn her right away, but I think it's the woman [in her]. . . . I mean, because she's a woman, not because of who she is as a person [*come donna, non come lei*]. It's true!

Davide distinguished himself from Alberto, not in the level of difficulty in managing a relationship with Roberta, but in his affective and communicative response to her. Using the term "swallowing [*mandare giù*]" suggests that anger is imagined as a substance that can be blocked; the same bodily metaphor of swallowing has been linked to anger suppression in Brazil (Rebhun 1994). New practices which guard and monitor the appropriate expression of anger and sorrow make this "swallowing" an important affective and economic strategy, the erasure of that which disturbs corporate hierarchies. Davide was able to maintain his powerful alliance with the supervisor of his division, Roberta, and avoid direct verbal conflict with her. Swallowing his anger was certainly a form of "emotion work" (Hochschild 1983). However, in this case, there was an extra layer of affective labor involved in addition to the labor of managing good relations. Here, the labor was defensive: social actors had to properly manage and suppress their affect in order to displace and stave off workplace conflict.

Davide viewed Roberta's actions, such as her dislike for employees speaking directly with Ettore, as fundamentally gendered. Davide suggested that this was not specific to Roberta's particular character, but rather was a characteristic of all women. Yet the issue was also a structural one in that Davide was more likely to be concerned about Roberta keeping her privileged relationship with Ettore, the top executive—a rich resource of capital and knowledge—because of the widespread work conditions in Italy that make employment more precarious.

Fundamental to Alberto's case is a new kind of immaterial laborer with a particular and highly complex set of cognitive, affective, and communicative demands. Though there were some salient gendered differences, by and large what distinguished alienated or inappropriate employees, within which I group Alberto, Ettore, and Roberta, was their intensity and the high calibration of their affect. Davide most embodied the normative new post-Fordist laborer in his swallowing of his anger and his cool detachment. The others, whether they were deceptively cool or explicitly incensed, betrayed the broader shifts that demand workers become intensely invested and engaged yet be dispassionate and evenhanded. Despite the imagined ideal of detachment, many workers are extremely vigilant, cautious, and fearful.

Psychic Discomfort

There is also evidence, though not necessarily using the discourse of a soul, of this demand for complex emotional labor and affective self-management in other cases in which existential damages have been awarded. In the case of Maria Stella, Judge Atanasio of the Milan Tribunal explained existential damages as covering injury to personhood, not limited to psychological or physical illness: "The distinction between illness and simple psychic discomfort may be distinguished by diverse consequences that are produced by this phenomenon, consequences which might constitute both a true and real psychic illness producing permanent effects for the victim, and . . . discomforts of less gravity that might be qualified as existential damages" (quoted in Meucci 2006: 506). But what kind of subject is imagined as injured by "discomforts" less grave than illness, but serious enough for juridical, and necessarily social, recognition?

Maria Stella was employed as a teacher for ENFAP (Ente Nazionale Formazione e Addestramento Professionale), an organization for ongoing professional education, in the region of Lombardy (*B. Maria Stella v. ENFAP Lombardia*, June 29, 2004, no. 1142/01 RG).[6] According to the ruling, Maria Stella was mobbed by two of her superiors (one female, Ms. C, and one male, Mr. F) over the course of six years. For instance, Maria Stella dealt with a fight between two of her students for which, several of her colleagues testified, Ms. C had blamed her, provoking anxiety attacks. Ms. C was accused of excluding Maria Stella during meetings and using offensive and gendered epithets to describe her and her colleagues ("hens in a henhouse, cackling happy geese, sheep, big sheep, brainless, fishmongers at the market"). Though Ms. C justified such terms as part of a friendly relationship with the teachers, Judge Atanasio disagreed: "she should have recognized the gravity of her behavior given her responsibility in her official role; thus she created a climate of psychological intimidation characteristic of mobbing."

There were other episodes. Maria Stella, following a disagreement with a colleague about two students' class performance, was criticized for having an eighth-grade education level; she was asked to work at a Sunday promotional convention shortly after her father passed away; and she was asked by Ms. C to inform the supervisor of her colleagues' complaints at workers' health and safety meetings. Ms. C was vexed when Maria Stella asked for, and was granted, a year-long sick leave and when she began using formal address (*lei* rather than *tu*) in their conversations; she claimed that Maria Stella stopped greeting her upon her return from sick leave. Maria Stella's case hinged upon a turbulent and contentious relationship with her supervisor, and, like in Angela's case, linguistic choices signified imbalanced power relations between employer and employee.

Much of the trouble between Maria Stella and Ms. C focused on how Maria Stella managed her time and worked with students. The gendered dynamics of mobbing often put women in the position of reprimanding or disciplining other women or, more broadly, they focus on women's lack of flexibility, their inability or unwillingness to become a pliable worker. Ms. C had asked Maria Stella to take additional coffee breaks that Maria Stella did not desire to take, and had marked up her time card to ensure enforcement, which was, according to the ruling, "an expression of Ms. C's desire to abuse power." Maria Stella was admonished by her supervisor when she didn't allow a student to use the lavatory, justifying her decision by saying that she hadn't seen a medical certificate to indicate why the high frequency was required; on another occasion, she was blamed for her student's allergic reaction. The way in which Ms. C had handled it, according to the judge, "discredited Maria Stella in front of her students." On another occasion, Maria Stella wished to take a regional professional course and Ms. C assigned her to another one not matching her professional level and experience. Maria Stella was asked to complete a risk evaluation though the task did not match her professional qualifications or profile, and Ms. C defended herself by stating that an imposed two-day deadline for the evaluation required her to ask Maria Stella. Ms. C was also responsible for changing Maria Stella's schedule so she would have to work seven consecutive hours; Judge Atanasio noted that she was given a heavier schedule than all of her colleagues, which he saw as evidence of mobbing. In these incidents, Maria Stella was criticized for what was coded as hypercompliance with school regulations (breaks, lavatory use), and she failed to comply with the last-minute practices typical of flexible labor regimes (last-minute evaluations, schedule changes). Maria Stella's interpersonal conflict, and the recognized form of both material and immaterial damages, emerged at the moment when she failed to embody the demands of production in full.

For Judge Atanasio, the appropriate form of labor production was what was at stake in Maria Stella's disagreements with her other supervisor, Mr. F. In 1999–2000, it was reported, Mr. F hoped to manage the school in a new way, saying, "the structure . . . ought to be managed like a company," and he accused Maria Stella of "rob[bing] money from the institution." (The judge didn't find consensus in the testimony to determine whether this was an actual or a figurative theft.) Mr. F criticized her ability to educate her students, some of whom were rude and offensive to Maria Stella in response to her public disciplining. In May and June 2000, Maria Stella complained of high temperatures in the rooms and was told it would be unlikely she would encounter the same difficulty the following year, insinuating the end of her contract. Maria Stella was threatened by Mr. F for not attending the screening of a film used for professional training. One colleague had witnessed Mr. F threaten: "If you don't come to [the] screening, I'll fire you. I'm telling you [this] as if I were the father of the family." In October 2000, he held a meeting with Maria Stella and a colleague and demanded: "What do you teach? Professional theory? What a big word! You understand what I'm saying? Let's take a step back: shall I explain it in Neapolitan or Milanese?" Here, Mr. F used Maria Stella's Neapolitan identity, a more precarious and abject subject position in northern Italy, to attack her (e.g., Schneider

1998). Compared to her female superior, Mr. F's harassment was more explicit, directive, and public. Maria Stella was compared with a better, more efficient imaginary worker, one who would be made compliant by threatening her employment contract, one readily tamed by his assertions of paternal authority.

Judge Atanasio reflected on the complexities of work relationships: "The peculiarity and the importance of this phenomenon [mobbing] emerge from the fact that the management of social relationships replaces volunteerism and spontaneity with that of necessity. As a result, one cannot voluntarily remove from oneself the ineluctable responsibility of sustaining oneself and one's family." What was deemed violating was the loss of spontaneous affective bonds surrounding work, the harm incurred to social relations when they become dirtied by material obligation. The notion of "spontaneity" should not go unnoticed as it indexes a kind of affective labor newly lavished with nostalgia under neoliberal conditions. The notion of Italian volunteer labor, as Muehlebach (2009) has outlined, is charged with a Catholic and leftist understanding of moral labor as the fruit of unmediated compassion for the other and as unsoiled by material gain.

The judge made clear that the damage was imposed externally rather than being an internal flaw or a psychic failure on the part of the victim: "The systematic and repetitive nature of illicit behavior reveals another end: that of giving a certain objectivity to the distinction between illicit behavior and illness or psychic discomfort. . . . the psychological discomfort [*disagio psicologico*] derives from illicit and damaging comportment and not the personal hypersensitivity of the offended person." The judgment was quite significant: €30,000 for the biological damages of permanent disability; €4,200 for temporary disability; €7,300 for partial temporary disability; and €28,000 for existential damages.

Maria Stella's conflicts with her superiors often emerged at the moment she failed to embody the role of a dispassionate yet passionately invested worker-subject. Much of the troubles focused on how Maria Stella seemingly failed to contain her students (performance, discipline, order, bodily functions) and to perform authentic work (resisting demands, opting out of additional obligations). Maria Stella was also subject to vicious ad hominem attacks and derided in a way designed to delegitimize her professional authority. But seeing this case as an example of either the failed flexible worker or the victim of malicious superiors would miss how Maria Stella was the victim of a new labor regime understood as callous, affectively bereft, and uniquely capable of undermining the core of human connectivity. That she was asked to represent her colleagues at the health and safety meeting was more of an affective and social violation in that the position might have strained her already vexed relations with her colleagues were she made responsible for their wellness. Mandated breaks can only be read as threatening and injurious when what is at risk is one's self-realization or soul, a historically specific understanding of human potential under late capitalism. Equally striking were the more subtle signs of injury: the form of linguistic address, once again, signified an imbalanced power relation between employer and employee and a harsh exclusionary practice. Being scheduled to work so soon following her father's death, Maria Stella was the victim of an economic order deprived of compassion and without sympathy for her family's mourning.

What was remarkable about Maria Stella's case was the recognition of the affective toll, the strained relationships and day-to-day hardships, as injurious to the person, even though these very affects and behaviors constitute the neoliberal work regime. Mobbing becomes a proxy for late capitalism, and, in certain moments, we can see that the state, even as it promotes a regime in which individuals must become self-responsible emotionally regulating subjects, also deems these practices to be injurious.

Governing Bodies with Souls

The Italian state has been fragmented among various political ideologies, including socialism, liberalism, and welfare, such that religious identity in Italy holds a particularly significant and unifying place. For sociologists such as Enzo Pace, Catholicism has become a mark of distinction among an increasing diversity of ethnic, racial, and religious groups. Yet, a renewed site for safeguarding and avowing human existence has emerged which, however explicitly secular it may remain, reveals that Italian political subjectivity has retained the sacred notion of a worker-citizen worthy of salvation. While existential damages, on one level, compensates for the wounds of late capitalism, it is necessarily an exclusionary process: only particular worker-citizens and only certain kinds of distress are recognized; neither every claim nor every claimant count equally. The law provides one site in which the state prescribes and remakes not only citizenship but also subjectivity and difference. On this point, Bill Maurer suggests, "The paradox here is that liberal legal orders rest on the differences among selves, as well as excluded others, as the law's raw material" (2003: 777). Jain reveals precisely this issue in her examination of the "culture of injury" in product design in the United States, where tort law "does the political and social work of determining what will count as an injury" (2006: 2).

In 1990, Jean Baudrillard expressed "pessimism" about new capitalist systems: "You are no longer brutally snatched away from your daily life to be surrendered to machines, you are integrated in the systems, along with your childhood, your habits, your human relations, your unconscious drives, even your rejection of work" (quoted in Toscano 2007: 104–5). The notion of existential damages recognizes, if imperfectly, this shift: labor is consuming and requires not just a part of your personhood, but all of it, body and soul.

4 Feminizing the Inflexible

The company that bought us has a very precise philosophy: total flexibility.
— From *I Like to Work: Mobbing* (*Mi Piace Lavorare: Mobbing*, 2004)

I want more autonomy, more flexibility.
— Giulia, self-identified mobbee

You can't have the keg full and the wife drunk.
— Veneto saying

Neoliberal work regimes reduce labor costs not only by outsourcing, but also by building and sustaining a growing body of peripheral or semi-permanent labor, often dubbed *flexible labor* (Harvey 1989; Sennett 1998; Collins 2006). Within the semantic architecture of flexibility is the figure of a pliable, adaptable, docile worker. However, for working-class and middle-class workers in Italy, the idea of flexibility has been reframed, rapidly and publicly, as precariousness: as high risk, estranged, uncertain. From a moral standpoint, the discourse of precariousness casts flexibility as an immoral and intruding social value incompatible with Italian notions of just welfare citizenship and with Fordist orders. Mobbing, if understood as a strategic and covert means to reduce the number of permanent and even semi-permanent employees, would thus be a process able to generate a regime of labor of precariously employed workers. But a close investigation of mobbing shows it to be far more circuitous and less linear, yet consistently gendered. National reports about mobbing and gender vary widely; however, some statistics indicate that as many as one in three Italian women have been mobbed, and 39 percent were mobbed by other women (ANSA 2005b). Researcher Elena Ferrara, a contributor to the European Commission's Daphne Report, dedicated to "raising awareness of women and mobbing," reports that 62 percent of mobbing victims are women (Ferrara 2004: 21). Like other mobbing literatures, the report emphasizes women's tendency to mob other women due to jealousy, hypercompetitiveness, and deviance from gender norms.

Mobbed women may be denounced as inflexible, unable to follow orders, and incapable of swiftly adapting to corporate regulations such that they become the bulk of Italy's precarious workforce. That is, the ideal of flexibility is salient in discourses about inappropriate or weak workers even though, at the same time, many Italians refuse to recognize and adopt the normative value of flexible labor by deeming labor markets precarious. Not only are Italian women disproportionately excluded from being recognized as flexible, despite the practices they adopt and the work they perform, but, in certain cases, women's proclaimed desire for work and their willingness to work become grounds to name them as unsuitable and ill adapted to work environments. As the inflexible becomes feminized, mobbed women are then routed into Italy's so-called flexible workforce where post-mobbing employment is far more likely to be in the form of short-term precarious contracts. Thus, flexible (precarious) workers are produced through discursive constructions and exclusionary mechanisms that proclaim certain workers to be inflexible.

Many studies, by contrast, have detailed how women in industrializing nations are considered to be the central figures of flexibility par excellence (Kondo 1990; Mills 1999; Collins 2005). In her study of the sexualization of *maquiladora* factory workers in Mexico, Leslie Salzinger (2000) reveals how women come to be coveted as workers because of cultural beliefs and discourses that link high productivity and pliability to women workers. Within the global labor force, women's persistent refashioning as desirable workers is animated by assumptions that their gender "naturally" makes them fit for certain kinds of labor, and "natural" characteristics such as "nimble fingers" are exploited as highly economically valuable (Safa 1981; Fernandez-Kelly 1983; Martin 1992: 113). Carla Freeman, for example, delves into the complexities of how women in Barbados came to be considered ideal and docile data entry workers (2000, 2002). Yet proclamations of and performances of flexibility do not always allow women to achieve social recognition as flexible. Even when Italian women both desire and perform flexibility, they are nonetheless labeled as inflexible and excluded, via mobbing, from the workplace.

There is an additional doubling within flexibility. According to Emilio Reyneri, who examined the contours of Italy's labor market, the desirable worker must adapt to changing work schedules, entrances and exits from a specific corporation or location, and mobility within the enterprise (2005a: 22). But he suggests that such employment actually erodes workers' identification and limits their affiliation with corporate production; thus, the very process of being employed in this fashion makes it more difficult to cultivate the "elevated polyvalent professionalism" and changeability that are desired (ibid.: 24). Italy's neoliberal restructuring has also been characterized by an increased number of quality checks and a heightened degree of surveillance throughout the process of production, whereby the responsibility of control is shifted increasingly to workers. Inflexibility, wielded as a rationale against targets of mobbing, is thereby already conditioned within a regime which heightens workers' poor performance. Mobbing, in other words, has become a means to restructure the workplace according to gendered divisions, with inflexibility its attendant rationale.

Anthropologists Emily Martin (1992, 1994) and Aihwa Ong (1999) have studied the concept of flexibility as a defining cultural paradigm of global capitalism; it crisscrosses the ways in which people understand economies, ideas, citizenship, states, and, importantly, their own bodies. I'm particularly interested in how seemingly far-reaching notions of the flexible become intimate: embodied and experiential. Martin has explored how the notion of flexibility, particularly within models of the body's immune system and defenses, resonates from the Western medical field to various social understandings. She raises the important question of how the discourse of flexibility produces certain kinds of desires and shapes subjectivities: the "intense desirability—even the seductiveness—of the ability to be flexible and adaptable" changes the ways in which actors think about the world and about their own bodies (Martin 1994: 149). This insight may help us understand how and why the harsh criticism of being inflexible manifests as psychological and physical trauma.

Mobbing expands Italy's precarious workforce, if circuitously. But this is only one of many gendered threads that tie together how and when Italians deploy mobbing. Many women, for example, report mobbing by same-level and lower-level colleagues, further illustrating how mobbing, in practice and as a discourse, is not simply a top-down corporate strategy. Moreover, Italian mobbing experts, often in the field of occupational psychology, have conceptualized mobbing and its origins based upon an underlying assumption of gender and sexual difference, not just economic scarcity. Thus, gender has become intertwined in various ways in the process of employee creation—and elimination.[1] Homing in on the paradoxes of worker elimination shows the existing labor regime in Italy to be not a rational system that seeks cost reduction and maximized production, but rather a profoundly fragmented and deeply gendered process.

Refiguring Patriarchy

Italy's feminist movement in the 1970s and 1980s contributed to changing patriarchal regimes which had been deeply extended under the hypermasculinized figures and pro-natalist family structures of Italian fascism (Horn 1994) by expanding women's social roles from the realms of domestic caretaking and motherhood to the workforce (Spackman 1996; Krause 2006). The feminist movement also played a significant role in hard-won legal battles for the legalization of divorce and the legalization of abortion in 1974 and 1978 (Ginsborg 1990: 394, 351). Despite important gains, however, employment in Italy has been historically marked by gendered hierarchies and sharp differences between women's and men's employment rates (Baranski and Vinall 1991; Caldwell 1991; Bassi 1993; Gregory 2000). In 1961, the employment rate for women was 22 percent, and it was still quite low, 36 percent, in 1993 (Ginsborg 2003: 35). In the 2000s, Italian women's participation in the labor force remained low with respect to other European Union member states (Bernardi 2000; Ginsborg 1990, 2003). For example, the Paduan workforce was characterized by a sharp gender division: employment rates were 60.1 percent for men and 33.5 percent for women in 2002 (ISTAT 2003). Regional disparities were also the rule: women's involvement in the workforce in 2000 was as much as three times higher in northern Italy than in southern Italy (Bernardi 2000: 137). And the majority of the women in Italy's workforce, 63.5 percent, were between twenty-five and twenty-nine; studies show that women's participation in the workforce tends to follow their reproductive cycle (Martineli et al. 1990: 151).

Italy's relatively low occupation rate for women could suggest that women take on roles as mothers and caretakers. However, Elizabeth Krause (2001) has pointed out that the national discourse on reproduction portrays women as "irresponsible" caretakers who are neglecting the nation, as the low birth rate is compared to the incoming immigrant populations. Working women without children, in this environment, risk being indexed as deviating from their more appropriate social role in the domestic realm (Krause 2001; Ginsborg 2003). Yet Italian women tend to continue to take on all caretaking and household responsibilities, even after they enter the workforce—a double task more conducive to having only one child (Ginsborg 2003: 71). Other important demographic factors may play a role, such as Italians marrying later, limited work opportunities, and enduring taboos against having children out of wedlock (ibid.). In 2001, women, on average, married at age 27.8 and had their first child at 28.5 (Toma 2003: 314). For Italian men, careers have tended to replace fatherhood as the dominant symbol of masculinity, and the great majority of Italian men in their twenties and thirties live with their parents, delaying having families of their own. As historian Paul Ginsborg suggests, the family is a paradox since "the very strength of the Italian family contributed to its numerical diminution" (Ginsborg 2003: 72). Italian women seem to be neither fully at home nor at work. With Italy's low birth rate and low full-time occupation rate, Italian notions of femininity have shifted away from the realms of marriage and motherhood but have not significantly shifted toward full participation in the labor market or public sphere.

In order to gain a better understanding of the gendered dynamics of mobbing in Veneto, we must first analyze the employment rates and contract types that produce the basic parameters of the labor market. At the time of my fieldwork in 2003, the Veneto region enjoyed a low unemployment rate, 3.4 percent; however, the unemployment rate varied significantly by gender with a rate of 1.9 percent for men and 4.8 percent for women in Padua and neighboring provinces (Veneto Lavoro 2004: 20, 83). The gap between men's and women's employment was also high for the Veneto region: 65 percent for men and 39 percent for women, and only one in four women in Veneto had the most safeguarded, lifelong contract (*contratto a tempo indeterminato*) as opposed to one in three men (ibid.: 83, 102). And while part-time labor constituted only 15 percent of the total labor force, it made up one-third of women's employment (102). Overall, women in this northern region were less likely to gain long-term stable employment, were more likely to be given short-term or part-time contracts, and were more likely to remain unemployed, rendering their labor more precarious than men's, economically, socially, and politically.

Psychiatric Perspectives on Mobbing

Psychiatric discourse deploys gender as a central means of parsing mobbing's origins and psychic dynamics. In March 2005, in a plush red-and-brown high-ceilinged conference room that was adorned with hundreds of coats of arms, I waited with a group of about sixty others for a greatly anticipated talk on mobbing by Renato Gilioli, one of the leading mobbing experts in Italy and co-author of *Mean Bosses, Mean Colleagues* (*Cattivi capi, cattivi colleghi*; Gilioli and Gilioli 2001). By training, Gilioli is a psychiatrist, and in 1996 he founded his clinic, the Center for the Prevention, Diagnosis, Cure, and Rehabilitation of Work Maladjustment Pathology (Centro per la Prevenzione, Diagnosi, Cura e Riabilitazione della Patologia da Disadattamento Lavoro), whose patients were the subject of his talk that day. Summarizing findings from his clinical records, Gilioli shared the basic demographics of this group, describing them as between the ages of thirty-five and forty-four, with an eighth-grade education, at a regular employee level (as opposed to lower-level workers, 18 percent, and executives, 12 percent), and predominantly from the private sector (64 percent).

Turning to the gender dimensions of this phenomenon, Gilioli said that he had found a nearly even distribution of men and women mobbees (52 percent male and 48 percent female). Though he positioned this as proof of an equal distribution of mobbing, it actually suggested that women were almost twice as likely to be mobbed because of their significantly lower overall employment levels. He suggested that men and women could also be distinguished in the objectives for and styles of mobbing used against them. For men, Gilioli asserted, mobbing often involved being transferred to a new office location, demotion from a higher position within the workplace, a change in superiors, irregular work flows, or the assignment of meaningless tasks to complete. Gilioli used the term "strategic mobbing [*mobbing strategico*]" for this type of mobbing, and claimed that 72 percent of men's cases in his study followed this model. Strategic mobbing was most likely to occur when men returned to work after an accident or extended sick leave, or during a corporate merger or reorganization. In contrast, he continued, 68 percent of women's cases in Milan were more likely to include what he called "emotional mobbing [*mobbing emozionale*]," involving "exclusion, marginalization, isolation, humiliation, affronts, taunting, and sexual harassment." He elaborated on the idea of emotional mobbing as an effect of women's purportedly natural sensitivity and as a result of women's relational practices of pettiness, jealousy, gossip, and unimportant but constant strife. He reported that the onset of mobbing for women was usually related to reporting sexual harassment, returning from maternity leave, or returning to work after plastic surgery. "Times," he noted somberly, "are particularly delicate after breast enhancement surgery." I asked Gilioli if he had any information regarding the gender of mobbers, as opposed to mobbees. While he did not have exact statistics, he said that men tended to be mobbed by other men, while women were mobbed by both men and women. His comment "Women are attacked on all fronts" was met with laughter and some "it figures [*figurati*]" comments from the predominantly female audience.

Within the psychiatric discourse of mobbing, strategic mobbing most likely results from economic shifts and, at least implicitly, the market-driven need to maintain low costs of labor. Thus, the verbal and practical weapons for mobbing men, according to the psychiatrist, are used to hinder their professional mobility: constant demotion, lack of new tasks, lack of advancement, disorganization of hierarchies. The proper advancement of men's labor is interrupted by an incoming force of corporate merger or accident, both construed as beyond the scope of the worker. Mobbing, pathologized and intrusive, signals the moment when men become passive victims, deprived of their labor and their presumed economic advancement, rather than the successful agents of global capitalism. The male mobbee was figured as a man who was dispossessed of labor, information, and productivity as a result of tighter economic markets, not any preexisting gendered aspects of the worker himself.

Women's labor, according to Gilioli's logic, is not necessarily altered by the movement of transnational labor and capital, but rather, women's purportedly innate affective and relational ways of being become risk factors for mobbing. The effect of this discourse is that women, unlike men, are constructed as more likely to be ill adapted to new workplace regimes. Stereotypically feminine characteristics such as sensitivity, fear of isolation, and expressiveness become precisely those characteristics that render women more vulnerable in the workplace, reinstating a gendered Cartesian dualism between mind and body: mobbing targets men's minds and women's hearts. That which is already socially construed as typically feminine, then, rather than neoliberal market shifts, make women more vulnerable to mobbing. Sexual harassment, which is inextricably linked to women's sexuality, becomes both a precursor and an effect of mobbing. In other words, women who deny sexual advances may be punished by mobbing, and women may be sexually harassed as a means to intensify mobbing. It is necessary to underscore here that sexual harassment becomes a "natural" workplace feature for women, bolstering another related idea: women's sexual subjectivity at work is necessarily generative of conflict and strife. Plastic surgery, and particularly breast enhancement, may over-eroticize women in the workplace in ways that transgress notions of appropriately sexualized or asexualized workers. Mobbing therefore is a punitive effort to discipline and exclude eroticized women workers, whose sexuality and desire find visible manifestation in large breasts. Thus, harassment and exclusion punish not simply the bodies of women, but their desire to be desired in a forbidden place: the office. Psychiatric knowledge about mobbing, then, is highly instructive and regulatory for women about what kinds of behaviors in the office are risky and what kinds of practices disrupt gendered and moral orders.

Visualizing Working Figures

Working-class imaginaries have populated Italian films from industrialization to neoliberalization (Bedani 1995: 2). Even though women have not emerged as classic working-class figures in popular imaginaries, women have emerged as symbols of neoliberal labor regimes and as victims of mobbing onscreen. In order to better understand this transition, I will briefly trace two iconic working-class figures before examining the mobbee's screen arrival.

Part of Italy's neorealist tradition, Vittorio De Sica's *Bicycle Thieves* (*Ladri di biciclette*, 1948) tells the story of an unemployed man, Antonio Ricci, who is finally hired to post bills around the city and requires a bicycle to fulfill the new position. He obtains a bicycle, which is then stolen. The film focuses on Antonio and his son's search for the missing bicycle and on Antonio's attempt to steal another bicycle to continue working. The plight of the unemployed, as symbolized in Antonio's bicycle, represents "the breakdown in civic values," and Italy's postwar labor regime is here portrayed as eroding the connections between those most exposed and vulnerable (Ben-Ghiat 2001: 42). Antonio's alienation from both employment agency workers and similarly impoverished citizens reveals "an implicit denunciation of a particular socioeconomic system," while his "solitude and loneliness" become the psychic stamp of Italy's Fordist worker (Bondanella 2001: 59).

The 1960s and 1970s economic modernization produced a figure who epitomized the most absurd aspects of post-industrial labor: Fantozzi, the protagonist of *Fantozzi* (*White Collar Blues* in English; Salce 1975), the first movie in the 1971–1999 series of books and films. Several moments of the film display Fantozzi's desperate and hilarious debacles: his unnoticed entrapment in the office bathroom for eighteen days, his infelicitous attempts to clock in punctually, his daughter's humiliation in the company's poetry contest, and his role as the target for countless food and drink spills at the company party. In the twenty-five years of Fantozzi films, he becomes the white-collar clown, while the pointless endeavors of post-industrial labor regimes inform his juggling act. Fantozzi's everyday yet tragic abjection has given him the notorious title of "the father of mobbing," both colloquially and in court rulings on mobbing (Antonietta 2007).

Unlike the still-playful Fantozzi, Anna is the haunted face of casualized labor regimes and mobbing as the working single-mother protagonist of *I Like to Work: Mobbing*, which director Francesca Comencini made in collaboration with Roman mobbing clinics (Comencini 2004). Anna, an accountant, is played with grace and vulnerability by Nicoletta Braschi, an acclaimed Italian actress and the adored star of *Life Is Beautiful* (1997). We quickly see Anna's good-natured relationships with colleagues in a pizzeria scene in which two women co-workers remind her that she is "protected" (*tutelata*), referring to her life-long contract. That Anna is the targeted mobbee and has this kind of contract is important because the viewer sees how a worker, despite being reminded that she is "protected," can experience circumstances that completely evacuate any idea of protection. The calm safety ruptures and soon we witness Anna being subjected to a series of humiliating acts at the hands of her manager and colleagues: her ledger is stolen to undermine her credibility; a colleague appropriates her desk, leaving her to wander the halls; and her manager has Anna meticulously monitor every transaction at the photocopier. Anna begins to doubt all of her colleagues, many of whom begin avoiding and isolating her. The film suggests that workers should beware of trusted colleagues' betrayal and shows the persecution that often accompanies neoliberalism's arrival and its capacity for destruction. The company for which Anna works—its scope, product, and organization—remains generalized and anonymous throughout the film. As the opening credits roll, we hear the male voice of a new post-merger manager:

> All of us must work to conquer the new effects of the market. We should confront this new market by being number one, knowing that we are second to no one. It shall be only by our shared enthusiasm that we can obtain those results, and it is the only way for you to defend our jobs. Nowadays you defend your job by conquering more work.[2] You don't defend it any more as if it were an act that someone bestows upon us *ab divinis*.[3]

Laying bare the emergent neoliberal discourse, with its attendant military metaphors of "conquer" and "defend," the new executive's speech crystallizes Italy's historical shift in how work is conceptualized: as a sacred right of citizenship or as victory booty. The executive hails the employees, regardless of their contract typology, as soldiers who must defend their labor and conquer others', thus redefining already-won work as inferior and base. That he consigns the notion of secure employment to the supernatural realm, to divine intervention, casts these ideal workers as naturally modern, secular, competitive, rational, self-striving actors who can depend on only themselves.

In another scene, workers meet with union representatives regarding a posted announcement that some of them will be transferred to a new and distant office. The union leader, a bespectacled middle-aged woman, leads an assembly of the company's outraged men and women. From the start, gendered roles are defined: the mostly male managers stand in for the new economic regime in contrast to the feminized representation of collective labor activism. She warns:

> The company has brought us a very precise philosophy: total flexibility, the complete availability of all employees. They're not interested in your personal problems, family loads, everyday fatigue: they count for nothing. Total flexibility. It means availability twenty-four hours of twenty-four hours. . . . People are fragile things, they break easily, the harassment they will carry out against you might be

extremely violent. Remember that violence doesn't mean they physically assault you. It's enough that they leave you with nothing to do. They can take away the dignity of any one of you. Any one of you.

The company is a microcosm of the Italian economy and the new management is neoliberalism's embodiment: new labor policies have been "brought" and are henceforth trackable by employees. The psychic destruction unleashed is understood as dehumanizing, indiscriminate, and debilitating and is capable of striking the human core and destroying one's inherent self-worth. Combating the arrival, then, requires acute social surveillance. In this context, the union representative hails women in particular:

> The transferred department is made up of nearly all women. So what does this mean? Their objective is to bring you in front of a choice between family affections, established relationships, and work. You shouldn't choose. This is the true error! It is not right to put women up to this choice. It is not right. Women should continue to work and to maintain their relationships. But it is also normal for you to seek out your own individual decision[s].

This speech chronicles the problem of corporate reorganization in gender-specific terms, hailing women as most victimized because of their role within the family. The women are asked not to "choose" between work and family, and they are simultaneously comforted about the "individual decisions" that must be made. Thus, rather than issuing a unifying call to all workers as an alienated or exploited class, the critique unfolds according to gendered and individual parameters. Given the trade union CGIL's cooperation in the making of this film, this may be indicative of an actual shift in union strategy within Italy—calling upon individual choice as opposed to collective action—and at the same time, her invitation effectively recasts them as self-fashioning and free-choosing subjects.

Early on, Anna says to a colleague: "It seems as if everyone's against me, everyone, seriously everyone." The film beckons worker-citizens into preemptive vigilance by illustrating Anna's apprehension and her resulting mental breakdown: it is here that paranoia is fastened to the mobbee. Unlike Antonio's bleak loneliness or Fantozzi's futility, Anna's dejected and isolated disorientation is a sign of late capitalist transition. She is the embodied figure of apprehension and dread who confirms the existence of many everyday fears: fear that one's labor is unappreciated, fear of secretly plotting supervisors, fear of unpredictable and hostile colleagues, and fear that no contract or productivity could serve as effective safeguards.

Mobbing Protagonist Extraordinaire: Anna

The narrative of mobbing in *Mi Piace Lavorare* masculinizes the logics of a flexible economy, while feminizing those workers unable to conform to the new standards, that is, inflexible workers.[4] In the beginning, Anna is depicted as ideal along three vectors. She is an appropriately feminine woman: she dresses professionally in neutral-toned suits, lightly applied makeup, pinned-back hair, and brainy brown glasses. She is a productive employee: her colleagues marvel at her great "meticulousness" and financial discipline, and Anna shyly admits: "I allow myself nothing, nothing [*Non mi permetto niente*]." And she is a good mother: she politely declines an invitation from a male colleague, citing her responsibility to her preteen daughter, Morgana. Anna's gracious refusal situates her perfectly within a particular Italian feminine ideal: sexually desired, yet exhibiting control, especially with respect to her motherly duties. In scenes full of affectionate touches and a familial sensuousness, we go inside her modest home and see the loving moments between mother and daughter, and we view Anna visiting her ailing father.

The first hint of trouble comes when she can't find an important notebook during a meeting with a client. Panicked, she scurries around the office, searching anxiously, only to be told afterward that it was purposely taken away, because she will no longer be keeping those books. Anna continues, however, to show herself as a productive employee: she enters her office to her colleague's dry questioning: "Didn't you have a day off? Well, you really do like working, don't you?" On another morning, Anna finds that a colleague has taken over her desk. After silently gathering her belongings, Anna walks dejectedly to a communal office with eight other workers and tries to continue to labor. The viewer begins to see how "liking work," an earnest desire to labor and toil, can have severely negative consequences. Moreover, her will to labor emerges as the protagonist's tragic flaw: she does not recognize its futility.

While initially the viewer might consider the new administrator, who remains nameless in the film, to be Anna's primary antagonist, the escalation soon becomes difficult to pin on a single individual or event. Anna is seen eating alone in the cafeteria, not being greeted by co-workers, and looking increasingly anxious and frightened. Days later, when she finds her computer mysteriously malfunctioning, Anna is asked by the new administrator to find some invoices in the company's basement warehouse. That night, she sneaks into the administrator's office and reveals his malicious ploy by finding the requested items in his desk. When he asks for them the next day, Anna responds that the files may simply be misplaced or in someone's desk. Scowling, he offers Anna another "chance," which amounts to training a new hire, a woman in her early twenties who is, for Italian audiences, indexing the hiring of younger, temporary workers.

In addition to generational competition, the film highlights how women seek to dutifully cooperate with the new emotional and economic regime of the firm. Anna's friend, for example, a woman who recently gave birth, announces at a five o'clock meeting: "I must show them I'm working." In the horribly fluorescent-lit bathroom, she tries furiously to pump breast milk and, unable to finish, she pours the drops down the drain and rushes out of the bathroom in tears. Evoking sympathy and horror, this scene shows the violence of neoliberal capitalism disrupting familial and patriarchal orders, iconically represented as the nursing mother unable to provide nourishment. Similarly, in another scene, Anna proudly wears a white leather jacket, a gift from her daughter, and the new administrator chides her: "Did you forget to change out of your pajamas today?" Mobbing, envisioned as the brutal culmination of neoliberal capitalism, threatens traditional familial orders.

Anna's next task is to dutifully record every transaction at the hallway photocopier, where much of the time she sits without anything to do. Anna goes to the administrator and pleads: "It's just that I don't have anything to do. I don't do anything. And not working tires me greatly, much more than working. I like to work [*Mi piace lavorare*]." Anna's plea to work is heartfelt and emotional, as if she is pleading for a return to normalcy within the corporation; it animates a more resonant and broader view that the loss of labor means something very big is at stake for Italian society. Dissolved are the social democratic logics that high productivity would enhance the value of a worker.

Anna is then transferred to an all-male-employee storage warehouse, complete with porn-adorned walls, and given the assignment of enhancing the workers' efficiency with a timer and clipboard. As tensions rise, she confronts her boss directly: "I can't stay down there. There's a very, very aggressive atmosphere. I'm the only woman and I'm having a bit of trouble. I'm a bit afraid to be there." Forced to remain in that assignment, Anna soon finds that the men have received notification of imminent job cuts and they blame her, calling her the corporate "spy." Here, the factory workers locate a single actor to blame for the precarious labor regime, and we see the emergent narrative that worker precariousness incites mobbing. The camera shifts between Anna's perspective and a third-person shot in which five large men crowd around her, closing in on her physically, shouting and pointing their fingers at her. There is a palpable physical tension in this scene, and the viewer senses a heightened risk of Anna's physical or sexual assault by these men. Screaming "Don't touch me! [*Non mi toccare!*]," Anna runs out of the office, locks herself in the bathroom, and collapses. The manager's refusal to reassign her, together with the announcement of job cuts, seems to have been maliciously and intentionally orchestrated to induce her breakdown. The culmination of mobbing surfaces through the anomalous presence of sexual tension and conflict in a traditionally all-male workplace: the site of manual labor and Fordist orders.

Home on sick leave, Anna is tenderly taken care of by her daughter, although she remains pale, bedridden, and exhausted. She is visited by an "occupational doctor [*medico del lavoro*]," a form of "medical police" that originated in the nineteenth century in Italy, who under Italian law may check on workers out on sick leave. After her return, the head executive calls Anna into his office and shows her a letter of resignation:

> We've left you with the same activity as before. . . . You were supposed to work as a team; instead, you created a void all around you. You had a series of problems

with colleagues and finally, the episode with the factory workers who—because of you—were about to strike on me. You have a bunch of personal problems, for pity's sake. . . . But you also have a responsibility to the company. I think that you are not suited to this company. You have great abilities, but with respect to the company's rhythms, you are not right. Perhaps you need a calmer company with a smaller scope.

The executive describes Anna as unfit for the fast-paced company and negligent of her corporate duties, blaming her for several social disruptions for which she was not responsible.

The letter of resignation is a clue that the boss is utilizing this tactic as a means to avoid having to directly fire Anna. The resolution follows rapidly as the film cuts sharply to her meeting with a union representative, who counsels her on pressing charges for mobbing, and then cuts quickly to Anna, collecting a check for the mobbing case she has successfully pursued. In the final scene, she and her daughter exit their house with suitcases in hand. Anna fumbles for her phone and wonders out loud if she should call her new job. Morgana stops her, smiling sweetly, "Stop being scared of everything! I'm here with you!" They then joyously run down the street, an ending that reestablishes multiple moral orders: secure labor and restored familial love. But Morgana's plea to her mother to resist her all-encompassing fear reveals the film's unresolved tension: familiar labor protections and dutiful productivity have been rendered faulty and fragile, and, as a woman, Anna remains disproportionately likely to be hailed as inflexible, despite her efforts.

Mobbed by Her Staff: The Case of Michela

Various aspects of the film, though not the seamless narrative, resonate with the lived realities of mobbing I witnessed in Padua. In April 2005, I met Michela Lorenzetti at a mobbing clinic that was staffed mostly with women working in the public sector and local volunteers. It was a weekday afternoon, and we met in a small room, lovingly furnished with two soft sofas and low lighting that made it a warm and comfortable space. We were joined by Daniele, a graduate student in clinical psychology in his late twenties, and Helena, who was in her mid-fifties and had established some seniority among her colleagues given her long-time involvement in labor rights in Italy.

Michela was in her late forties, with blonde hair and turquoise eyes framed by glasses with black plastic rims; she was employed with a lifelong contract at a university-affiliated teaching hospital in Padua as a staff coordinator for approximately fifty therapists in the physical and rehabilitative therapy ward. She had come to talk about how the group of physical therapists that she supervised, together with hospital administrators, were mobbing her. As she began, tears streamed down her face, and she said, "I decided to change jobs and quit." Helena gently requested that she begin by telling us a bit more about her present job. Michela clarified that she reported to Dr. Claudio Sanceni, the administrative head of the division, who had recently received a handwritten letter from five members of her ward and called a meeting to discuss their problems with Michela, about whom they had sent a complaint to the hospital's union. In doing this, the group had skipped over the medical administrator, a man Michela consistently referred to using his title and last name, Dr. Orbi, who had been more supportive of her position and who was closer to her status in the hospital hierarchy. Michela described how the meeting had been a series of "insults" directed at her, to which she "shut up [*stata zitta*]" and remained silent. She had documented the meeting and the issues raised, which included the problem of compensating staff for overtime hours and accusations that Michela wrote false disciplinary letters about the staff and that she was being "oppressive" about tardiness. She defended herself, shaking her head and searching for tissues: "They clock in and then they go change. But I can't schedule a patient at 7:00, when they come in at 7:15!" I was sympathetic to her unconcealed pain, yet I also couldn't help but wonder, at least initially, whether Michela's accusation of mobbing was a strategy to defend her own overly strenuous disciplinary techniques.

Helena reminded her that workers required to wear uniforms have the right to change during work hours. Michela nodded, then added: "Another woman goes on vacation in two weeks. I say, 'Exchange shifts between members of your group. Keep one person per hospital ward, so there'll be continuity of therapists. I can substitute you once, even twice, but not three times! The patient has a right!'" She raised her voice and spoke with agitation, as if she were telling one of the therapists directly. Helena nodded gently and met her gaze: "Sometimes, you have to decide whether to be well yourself, or to follow the rules. You can't be so heroic for something that doesn't involve you." Michela read from her notes and cited workers as saying, "I've only learned to justify myself (and my actions)," "I've been here for two years and I've given everything and received nothing," and "It's a difficult work environment. We should have more meetings." Michela felt that the meeting itself represented a collective attempt to coerce her into leaving her position as coordinator. The complaints about Michela suggested to me that these workers, most likely a combination of short-term and long-term workers, were struggling with a more hostile work environment and the anxieties of the new labor regime. Just as Anna had become the embodied target of the male factory workers' precariousness in the film, was Michela being held responsible for the deeply felt insecurity of her staff?

In defense of her writing disciplinary letters or reports to hospital administrators regarding behavioral or administrative problems among the staff, Michela described a recent event. One therapist had been missing for two hours and was then seen reentering the hospital grounds on her moped. When confronted, the employee claimed she was in the bathroom and so, Michela explained, she received a disciplinary letter for her second unjustified absence. She wiped tears from her face and blew her nose: "There are people who don't realize that patients are people. Also, these are people that don't like being controlled, but it's the hospital that wants this. I didn't choose to be the coordinator!" In Michela's narrative of mobbing, she imagines herself as the dutiful subject of hospital regulations: she is the enforcer of norms related to attendance, tardiness, patient treatment, and scheduling. When workers do not abide by hospital policy, Michela, as the unit coordinator, takes on the role of discipliner and enforcer of hospital rules; it is precisely at this moment that mobbing emerges. Michela, in turn, received the brunt of her staff's hostilities because of this position and viewed the hospital administrators as necessarily complicit with her harassment.

Following the meeting, Michela received a letter from a hospital administrator saying she would have to be shadowed (*seguito*), meaning that a psychologist would closely monitor every decision made by Michela and observe her every action with her staff. This represented the pinnacle offense, the one that most humiliated her, the one that she considered the cruelest attack on her competencies as a therapist and manager. Holding the rough draft of her resignation letter in her hand, she said: "I have to get away. Tomorrow, I'm writing them. I'm quitting." Helena leaned forward and, just above a whisper, said: "You need to allow yourself a break. Tomorrow, go and get sick leave and go on vacation. You can't go on like this. But do not quit. Okay, Michela? Do not quit." Helena affirmed that it was not her fault and theorized that her staff's letter of complaint to the hospital trade union had put pressure on administrators to appease the workers and avoid further "political" conflict. In other words, Helena's interpretation was that Michela was being mobbed only as a way for the hospital administrators to discipline and monitor her staff. Deploying this narrative, Helena convinced Michela that the mobbing was not due to her intellectual or emotional weaknesses or failures, but rather due to a macro-institutional practice of conflict aversion and union appeasement. A halfhearted smile brightened Michela's face briefly, and she said there wasn't anyone who would be able to substitute for her while she was gone. Grinning, Helena pointed out that they wouldn't have anyone for a very long time if she decided to quit. Seemingly convinced, Michela nodded again, gathered her belongings, and headed out of the clinic.

Two days later, I discussed Michela's case with Daniele and Helena. Helena said she thought Michela had an "overactive superego" and a "fragile identity" which made her care about hospital regulations to an extreme degree: "She tends towards identifying with the institution." Daniele noted that she seemed to talk about the hospital as if it were another person. Both acknowledged that they tended to side with the workers' point of view, which made Michela's case more difficult as she was the coordinator of the group. I volunteered that it seemed to me she had high standards for the way in which her division should be run. Helena and Daniele smiled at each other, and Helena joked that my opinion reflected my "being American," in that Americans idealize the rules and believe they should be enforced. Many Italians believed that rules and regulations in the United States are legislated and followed, and they viewed Italy as a nation of collective improvisation and creative circumvention of laws and rules. Sighing, Helena concluded, "The public sector is full of calumnies, terrible organizations—[it's] a dump full of mobbing." Cronyism and corruption, whether documented or imagined, augment the validity of mobbing claims because they, too, stem from a similar kind of knowledge: the presupposition that deception and underhandedness rule everyday social relations.

In late April, one week after our first set of meetings, the three of us met again with Michela at the clinic. She had come from a meeting with the medical administrator, her ally Dr. Orbi, and the psychologist who had been asked to shadow her. They had no plans to demote her, and as Helena explained to Daniele and me, in the public sector, one's responsibilities and tasks are legally protected after a three-month period of employment. However, the shadowing would have to continue, in addition to what Michela viewed as intensifying criticism and ostracism by the hospital administrators and her staff. "I said," Michela began, "I'd like time to reflect. He knows that I've always worked for service and for the patient so I would not be disrespected in front of everyone. We are here to discuss this, and I've been crucified." Helena told her that she was mistaken in trying to be "too democratic" and advised: "You didn't show them your iron fist and they hurt you." Helena expressed a growing tendency to expect that workers mobilize tactics of self-defense and aggression as preliminary ways to protect against conflicts and acts of aggression by co-workers. In this way, Helena's understanding of mobbing adhered to a leftist understanding in which precariousness makes workers strike out at one another: *mors tua, vita mea.*

Michela continued, describing how the administrators had reprimanded her and reminded her of the "many opportunities" she had to be more collaborative with workers. Michela was outraged because she felt she had done everything to uphold the regulations of the hospital, only to be punished and then further marginalized and isolated. She began to cry, her words addressing her trusted supervisor, Dr. Orbi: "What did you want from me? Suicide? Not that, not that." It was clear that these events meant extreme pain, sadness, and depression for Michela and that she believed the ineffectiveness of the hospital administration was a technique of malicious sabotage: "They don't do anything. Basically, everyone does whatever they want." She said that one of her staff members had treated seven patients in just three and a half hours, indicative that she had hastily "run through" her client load. Michela was exasperated: "What do I do? I write her up and it doesn't matter. She says, 'Whatever. I'll go on like this because she [Michela] can't do anything.'" No single actor was the mobber, but the collective of practices and people, together with the lack of rule enforcement, constituted aggression against her.

Michela wrote the mobbing clinic regular emails during this time, one of which said:

Hello everyone! . . . I'm quite disoriented. . . . I don't know if I can continue to stay here. . . . I keep having the urge to throw up every time I come to work. . . . I spoke with Dr. Orbi and I don't understand if he knows more than what he's telling me or if he actually can't do more than he's doing. . . . He can't "sell me" or "leave me" in the hands of people who use their power to delegate the faction's privileges or the privileges of acquaintances or friends. We are at a breaking point that is so strong that I am convinced I am truly not able to manage a department that takes as a rule the very absence of rules. Besides that, today I got the confirmation that a physical therapist who shares my work has asked for a transfer and another has retired. Another one will graduate . . . and he'll leave too. . . . maybe it's better that I get out of here before I get blamed for having made the personnel want to escape, as people are already starting to say. I talked with the psychologist. She put her hand on my shoulder, she told me that she understood me, she told me that she was sorry, that I don't deserve this, that everything is horrible, that they've behaved like vultures. But she said she can never say what she thinks or what she has heard out loud because she has to live in this place for many many years to come. (Email communication, April 2005)

Michela deployed the term *faction* for a few of the physical therapists in her division who seemed to be leading the hostile campaign to oust her. Gauging the unstable social terrain within the hospital, she was deeply suspicious of others and the circulation of secret knowledge, and she saw foreboding potentials: the administrators could co-opt workers' resignations as leverage against her, her boss could hide more information, and everyday discourse was a veneer to protect one's public persona. The idea of chaos, "as a rule the very absence of rules," resonates with a much broader underlying Italian ethos of the stateless state (Herzfeld 2009), which was exacerbated by the day-to-day precariousness that Michela felt: nothing was predictable, there were no logical or rational orders. Though we might view her reactions as adapting to this persecutory environment, her psychophysical manifestations and the surrounding conflict prevented Michela from showing herself to be resilient to new work stressors.

A Resolution for Michela

Two weeks later, Daniele, Helena, and I waited for Michela in the comfortable counseling room of the clinic on a Wednesday afternoon. When Michela entered the room, I was surprised at how relaxed and radiant she appeared; tan and smiling, she presented us with some brightly colored marzipan sweets from her stay at her husband's family home in southern Italy. But her calm disposition shifted rapidly, and she tearfully recounted another humiliating meeting with the psychologist: "It's a punishment if I leave now." Unlike her first visit, she now recognized that quitting would put her at a great disadvantage because she would risk losing retirement and health benefits, and she decided to request a transfer within the hospital to be the coordinator of a medical research program largely funded by the European Union. She would never leave her patients, she said, though she regretted leaving Dr. Orbi, who had been an es-teemed supervisor, but she expressed intense sadness at what she framed as his stubborn self-interest: "He always did whatever was in his interests, and never did what he could have done for me." In this claim, she was also critiquing an emergent neoliberal figure, the rational, self-interested actor she saw in him, which, paradoxically, the new labor regime demanded she herself become in creatively orchestrating her administrative transfer and, as it turned out, a pos-sible legal battle.

As Ginsborg has argued, Italian individualism and even clientelism, were we to view Michela's case more cynically, have their origins in a much deeper history of Italian "inefficiency, particularism and bureaucratic discretion" in which favors, flavored with the personal and partial, become a savvy tool for navigating bureaucratic regimes (2003: 217). Michael Herzfeld connects the church's practice of issuing indulgences to the ethos of the Italian state in which citizens, via payments and pardons and personalized permissions, could tailor collective regulations around singular needs and desires (2009: 56–57). I found profound resonance with what Herzfeld witnessed among Romans struggling with eviction in the neighborhood of Monti, which speaks to a greater reso-nance in Italy: "People watch the activities of the supposed civic-minded au-thorities with an eye jaundiced by experience, for they know that bureaucrats, like priests in the confessional, do not always practice what they preach, and that the call for ethic[al] self-examination is no guarantee of compliance" (ibid.: 62). In short, this same self-starting and self-serving circumnavigation is re-warded within institutions and workplaces: it permeates the Italian imaginary of authority and the way in which it is undermined.

Michela also informed us that she had spoken to a lawyer and friend about the possibility of suing for mobbing. Helena responded with a precise strategy: "In the future, if you want to press charges, you have to get a medical certifi-cate from a neurologist, who will prescribe meds, and you must document all of your existing conditions." Assured and steady, Michela nodded: "I have all the certified letters, meeting notes, and I told a university doctor about my health disturbances." Helena helped Michela to make a list of the steps she would need to take in the coming weeks, including asking for a written invitation to ev-ery meeting with the shadowing psychologist; seeking an occupational doc-tor (*medico del lavoro*) who would verify her psychological and physical distur-bances; finding out more about her plan of being a research coordinator; and continuing to write descriptions and to log ongoing and past incidents relating to her case. The next day, Michela wrote us the following letter:

> I hope that this solution to stop working as coordinator and continue to work here will be possible, without having to lose anything financially, [which] is comforting to me. . . . So, when I came to work this morning, I received an official letter from the psychologist, formally stamped, having the object "convocation for first meet-ing for the revision of the organizational-relational model." She listed the objectives: "verify and evaluate the socio-relational model, verify and evaluate the institutional

model, individualization and planning." I don't know what kind of action would be best to take. . . . the letter seemed rather formal and it depressed me a bit.

The bureaucratic language of the letter, the intervention of a specially trained medical expert, the formal rhetoric, the heightened attention to monitoring, accountability—all signatures of audit cultures—had coalesced to produce a greater sense of alienation (Strathern 2000a). The hospital administration also had invoked the discourse of improvement and progress as a frame for creating an ethos of worker self-monitoring and improvement.

I would not see Michela again until mid-July. When Michela came in, even more relaxed than we had seen her previously, she joked that she had "lost all her wrinkles" because she had finally given herself time to rest: she was given twenty days of sick leave, returned to work for two days, and then took an additional twenty days of sick leave with another doctor's note. Michela's mobbing was medicalized not only because of her compromised mental and physical health but also as a defensive strategy that allowed her to retain her position from a safe distance while she solidified other options. With the transfer almost approved, she had returned to train a new staff coordinator, one of the few men in the unit, to take on her role, and she joked that he was the new object of criticism. Hopeful but cautious about her transfer, she said that an off-the-record collaboration between hospital administrators was to blame for the delay. She turned to me and said in the Veneto dialect: "Dogs don't eat other dogs [*Can non magna de can*]." The adage refers to the idea of tightly woven informal networks among high-level people in an economic or political arena: clientelism and cronyism. It applies within this economic framework, conveying the idea that workers are more likely to be exploited because of close personal ties among the corrupt class of politicians, executives, and officials who collectively protect one another from contestation. She was reasserting her own nostalgic moral notion of economic justice: cronyism has no role in the workplace. In August 2005, Michela's new job had not yet commenced though she hoped it would soon. For the time being, she was collecting documents for a possible legal case on her mobbing, though she had put pressing charges on hold.

Consequences for Rule Enforcers

Michela's experience of mobbing began with, but was not limited to, the banding together of the mostly women workers for whom she served as coordinator. Her fairly rigid compliance with institutional regulations, particularly when those regulations had not been consistently enforced at higher administrative levels, seemed capricious to the therapists on Michela's unit. She felt she was doubly endangered because the hospital administrators were the ones who originated this harassment, both in the generation of the rules she felt obliged to enforce and in their inability or unwillingness to reinforce her disciplinary actions for workers. By becoming the agent for institution-wide discipline, Michela embodied the hospital regulations and norms and, accordingly, was positioned to be a target of transgression and disobedience. The neoliberal ideology of independence and autonomy creates the notion that actions should be traceable to single actors; Michela, rather than the faceless structure of labor, became the recognizable agent of neoliberalism. This is where her experience resonates with the film version of mobbing: each of Anna's tasks, as photocopy monitor, as work trainer, and as warehouse supervisor, made her the object of anger and resentment from colleagues. In the high-anxiety and apprehensive labor regime change that dominated the mid-2000s, many workers felt threatened by the potential of corporate restructuring, constantly feared job loss, and longed to secure safeguarded work. Positioning women as rule enforcers is a subversive technique that renders them more vulnerable to others' hostilities and persecution while masking the institution's role: they are positioned as orchestrating others' precariousness even though they are simultaneously made precarious themselves. Perhaps this is a new corporate strategy: situating women as the subject, rather than the object, of surveillance results in their marginalization in ever more subtle and indirect ways.

In Michela's case, she learned not only the futility of applying hospital regulations but, like Anna, the futility of her own productivity. In June, she sent us a document entitled "An Ant's Story" and said it reminded her of her own story. The narrative recounts the life of a "productive and happy" ant who works on his own, without supervision. The general manager hires a supervisor, who hires another, and each new hire produces a new "need" for another position, multiplying the hierarchical divisions within the company. The resulting environment becomes so large that it merits an expensive study to analyze the company's rising costs. When the results of the study conclude that the company is bogged down by a surplus of employees, the general manager fires the ant. Here is the moral to the story:

> Don't ever get it in your head to be the productive and happy Ant. It is preferable to be useless and incompetent. Incompetent people don't need a supervisor, everyone knows. If, despite everything, you are productive, don't ever show you are happy. They'll never forgive you. Occasionally make up some mistake, something that gets you some compassion. If, despite everything, you commit yourself to being the productive and happy Ant, mind your own business, at least you won't have the yellow jackets, roaches, spiders, flies, crickets, suckerfish and owls at your back, and above all, they won't be able to get rid of you with the excuse that what their lack of productivity costs depends on your presence in the production line!!

This fable of neoliberal capitalism and audit culture articulates the constant revision of cultural understandings of bureaucracy, workplace dynamics, and productivity. It is well suited to the ideologies of emergent neoliberalism because workers seem to be learning that productivity can be risky and self-jeopardizing. The story resonates within Italy as it is commonplace to note that workers' lack of skill and their uselessness have become effective shields against increased control and discipline by employers. The "happy and productive" ant becomes relegated to the past in that he represents a moral Fordist imaginary of intense labor as satisfying and rewarding. Within this story is also a call for workers to "own their own businesses," to themselves become capitalists, to self-manage their own labor. This is a different kind of response in that it does not call for collective action or union intervention, but rather marshals workers to adopt strategies to face the market head on, individually. At the same time, the story of the ant is a didactic moment in which worker-citizens learn how to become workers suited not necessarily for neoliberalism but for the heightened apprehension of neoliberal transition: flawed, unassuming workers remain at work while highly skilled workers may be ousted.

A Question of Mental Health

Even though Michela's case of mobbing led to depression, anxiety, and gastrointestinal problems, the veracity of her story was never called into question by Helena or Daniele. However, for Giulia Rossi, a woman in her early forties working as a technical assistant in a university chemistry department, her subjectivity as a rational person and her narrative of mobbing were called into question because of her mental health. Despite the unresolved dimensions of her story, Giulia's case illustrates how gender can further subordinate an already marginalized person: someone living under a diagnosis of mental illness.[5] Like Michela, Giulia had entered the same mobbing clinic at the moment when she found that what she had expected at work no longer seemed to hold true. At the first meeting with Helena and me, Giulia seemed uneasy and nervous, looking down, shifting in the chair, swaying back and forth with her hands grasping under the chair or tucked beneath her legs. Unlike the highly coiffed and groomed Paduan women of her age cohort, Giulia appeared somewhat unkempt: gnawed fingernails, an oversized and slightly ratty dress, uncombed hair.

As a technical assistant, Giulia was in charge of answering telephones, photocopying, file keeping, maintaining office supplies, and general office assistance. Though her work responsibilities were multiple, Giulia was particularly upset that lately she had been "checking the toilet paper, checking the paper towels, watering the plants, replacing toner, and doing photocopies." Poor relations with colleagues whom she felt maliciously forced her to do these less desirable jobs was part of the problem: "The department just wants more *cococo*." Giulia was referring to a new contract that had been passed as part of the Biagi Laws, a "contract of continuing and coordinated collaboration" (*contratto a collaborazione coordinate continuative*), which was designed for ongoing, though not full-time, work by members of professional associations, similar to an American contract for consulting work. From the outset, Giulia framed her case of mobbing in the context of a broadly shifting workspace in which the presence of short-term and semi-permanent workers was a specter of instability for safeguarded workers like Giulia.

In order to obtain a promotion, and therefore be assured of avoiding what she viewed as menial labor, Giulia would have to learn to be proficient in Word and Excel. Giulia told us nervously, "They told me to apply for the next level, but then I have to promise to be able to do those jobs." Giulia viewed the application process as corrupt and backward, seeing the chair's assurance to promote her if she applied as merely an additional "blackmail [*ricatto*]": "it makes sense for them to keep me so they can keep doing whatever they want." It wasn't entirely clear to me how the invitation could be blackmail, however; I believe she meant that the offer was merely an empty gesture: he had no actual intention of promoting her. She insisted that she had overheard the chair say he "did some mobbing [*abbiamo fatto un po' di mobbing*]" and purposefully favored other workers: "It's a real plot. I didn't invent it!" Like other victims of mobbing, her comments revealed a deep mistrust of others, an apprehension regarding her ability to change that bordered on bitter resignation, and an omnipresent fear that she would inevitably be exploited. Though it would allow her to escape her department, the possibility of a new position wasn't a desirable option for Giulia: "I want more autonomy, more flexibility." Paradoxically, Giulia's desire for a flexible position reveals how actors shape and reconstitute the same ideologies that exclude and marginalize them.

At this first meeting, I had no knowledge yet of any mental conditions or illness, but I sensed something unusual about Giulia's manner, speech, and presence. Helena tried to help her strategize and reminded her that she could refuse to complete tasks she found humiliating: "Don't do something. It may help you defend your identity, show that you can still resist and they haven't walked [all] over you." Giulia responded abruptly: "My psychiatrist gives me meds, and I go see a psychologist once or twice a week." In my field notes, I wrote that Giulia's responses seemed to jump unexpectedly from one point to another, and the conversation seemed disjointed. Giulia seemed to have read Helena's suggestion as a coping strategy for her current situation and remarked that, in effect, so too were her medications. After the meeting, Helena explained that she was aware that Giulia had some sort of psychological difficulty; however, she knew of no specific diagnosis.

Within two weeks, Helena had organized a meeting for Giulia and her boss, Antonio Bartali, a professor and the chair of the chemistry department. Before the meeting began, Giulia whispered to me that Antonio had asked her to photocopy a book on mobbing just days prior. Both Helena and Giulia agreed that the boss's request could be read as a direct and hostile threat of mobbing for Giulia, and that his purpose was to peruse the psychological text on mobbing and its effects in order to effectively practice mobbing. He had also written a letter to the university's administrative offices describing Giulia as "unstable" and requesting her transfer from the department. Giulia was content about the transfer, hoping it would offer her additional "guarantees" of better employment and a way to avoid having to acquire new computer skills.

With Antonio's arrival, Helena opened the conversation: "She would like to help build a new path for herself." I scanned Antonio, looking for signals of malice, yet his appearance was fairly gentle: bald, mustached, bespectacled, mild-mannered. He sat down across from Giulia and next to Helena. Giulia cupped her face in her hands and held her oversized handbag on her lap as if it were armor, not making eye contact with Antonio. In a kind voice, Antonio explained that the transfer might actually mean a raise for her, adding: "You were doing fine with us, but . . ." Giulia at once raised her voice: "With Marco and Paola—there's been a little mobbing. Ever since they arrived, it has been the end for me! Answer the phone! And the phone was broken, files are missing. You were all against me and I had no support. Even you said it yourself, ' "Yes, we have been doing some mobbing.' " Antonio's face remained even, though he looked perplexed and cocked his head to one side: "I said this? No." Giulia continued: "They don't give me access to any information. I get no training, no real and actual training. They spy on my cell phone text messages!" She felt that her requests to take vacation days were "always denied, [but] the others get to go," adding, "I am always penalized, always tied to my co-workers' social problems." In addition to being often "by herself," she found the constantly changing personnel to be equally frustrating: "I can't ever manage to be with just long-term [contract] people [*persone fisse*]!" She ended: "I was the last to know the department was moving to another building!"

Once Giulia's voice, trembling and high-pitched, went quiet, the four of us sat in tension-filled silence. It was clear that much of the day-to-day conflict surrounded practices that are characteristic of neoliberal work regimes—guarded information, isolation, high staff turnover—and the situation was exacerbated by what she perceived as intense malice directed at her. After a bit of silence, referring back to his suggestion that she apply for a promotion, Antonio pointed out: "But we gave you a chance for mobility." Giulia rebutted sarcastically: "Changing toilet paper is not a work responsibility!" Antonio explained that her colleagues, those she accused of mobbing her, had either familial or health problems: one had "really big problems," another went "to the psychiatric hospital," and a third saw "a psychiatrist." By emphasizing the emotional and psychological strains upon her colleagues, Antonio underscored the situational dimension of such difficulties. At this point, he asked her, quite kindly, what she wanted to do in terms of her role in the department, or whether she preferred to accept the offer to be transferred. He also proposed a third alternative: managing incoming guests at the front office. Giulia, however, immediately refused, citing "the strain [*pesante*] of so many hours with the public" as her reason. Antonio seemed willing to discuss other solutions, but Giulia became even more nervous and angry, and referred to a raise she had received in the department:

"You told me you helped me with the raise! But I did it all myself, no one helped me! And you dared to hold that against me [*rinfacciarmi*]! You're not professional!" Antonio looked extremely uncomfortable and glanced at Helena, who hastily offered to keep discussing options with Giulia. After they both left, sighing, Helena looked at me relieved: "I was worried she was going to start slapping him."

Precarious Echoes, Staff Conflicts

The sense of apprehension and insecurity in Giulia became externalized as her situation engendered a staff crisis at the mobbing clinic surrounding how Helena had handled her case. While the clinic workers were mostly volunteers, their authority as mobbing specialists was at stake in how the mobbing cases were managed. Much of the anxiety in Giulia's case was due to the fact that Antonio had been called to the clinic and directly challenged. The volunteer staff members, some of whom were precariously employed at the university, had to face fears about their own work: a confrontation between a high-profile university professor and a lower-level assistant could threaten the clinic, their reputations, or, at worst, their employment.

An urgent meeting of the entire clinic staff was called, and Helena personally asked me to attend. I arrived at a formal university meeting room, with wood panels, frescoed ceilings, and an incredibly long wooden table, reminiscent of a medieval banquet. One staff member and leader, Mara, a woman in her fifties, called Giulia "psychotic" and declared that it was widespread university knowledge that Giulia was "unstable," "depressed," and on "psychotropic medication." Helena informed her colleagues that Giulia's use of psychopharmaceuticals did not mean she did not deserve better treatment at work. In the eyes of her colleagues, however, Helena had erred in inviting an esteemed professor to the clinic for talks, especially because Giulia was considered a "mentally unstable" worker. To this, Helena retorted that her colleagues judged Giulia only because of the class differences they perceived between her, in an administrative position, and Antonio, a faculty chair. Denying class as a motivator, the rest of the staff focused on Helena's failure to elicit full staff consent before setting up the meeting. To my surprise, Mara sternly reprimanded me for not having "reminded Helena to follow protocol." Positioned as someone with severe mental illness, Giulia was denied full rational personhood and her illness eclipsed the reasons that Helena or I would aim to assist her. She was less able to fully and convincingly identify as a mobbing victim in part because the harassment claim relies on a sense of sound psychological judgment. Giulia's exclusion from the subject position of adaptable worker was already elusive because of gender, and her illness foreclosed this possibility entirely.

Also evident was that the mobbing industry is itself a gendered field, with women holding positions as psychologists, clinical staff, and consultants, while men are generally mobbing-specialized lawyers, trade union workers, medical doctors, and public health workers. Notably, most mobbing-specialized psychologists and psychiatrists known on the national level, such as Renato Gilioli and Harald Ege, are men. There is a division in the production of knowledge about mobbing, with women centered more as first-responders, while men tend to play a greater role in the production and dissemination of knowledge (medical, state, and legal) about mobbing. In the training meetings I followed with this staff, what was often emphasized was staff consensus, shared goals, and transparency, which Helena did not pursue in organizing the meeting with Antonio. While Helena's actions may have certainly played a role, what struck me was how the figure of the appropriate mobbing clinic worker, like the neoliberal worker more generally, had to work with demands for compliance but also agility in new situations.

Giulia's case of mobbing was framed in terms of her mental instability and confirmed by her pharmaceutical consumption. Mental health was often a primary measurement through which the integrity of mobbing claims was evaluated. This resulted in a process of depoliticizing mobbing, especially when the mobbee was already, or becoming, mentally or physically ill. As was evident in Giulia's discussion with Antonio, the mobbers were also being pathologized, and her alienation was framed as a product of their ongoing mental health struggles. What was less emphasized by the mobbing clinic staff, except Helena, was the extent to which Giulia's rather awkward social persona and psychological pathologies positioned her as a more likely candidate for mobbing to begin with.

Despite these tremendous challenges, it must be recognized that Giulia, like Michela and Anna, was a woman who showed a willingness to work; she desired what she, within a neoliberal labor regime, was incited to desire: autonomy, mobility, flexibility. At the same time, situated between a Fordist and a post-Fordist order, she endeavored to maintain certain safeguards and resisted the disordered aspects of precarious labor that often constitute mobbing: information deprivation, isolation, and surveillance. Much of her suffering was because of the degree to which every practice and initiative at work seemed saturated with undesirable risks and unforeseeable outcomes. For Giulia, the term *mobbing* was a way to name what was undesirable socially, economically, and morally.

The Labor of Mobbing

Is mobbing gender-discriminatory downsizing? To answer in the affirmative would position neoliberal capitalism as a purely rational and logical system. But the stories of mobbing show that flexibility itself is precarious because the terms are constantly shifting; productivity, willingness, rule compliance, and rule enforcement are not necessarily insurance that one might be so proclaimed. The mobbing narratives make mockery of mobbing as a corporate cost-saving measure: the sheer amount of labor that mobbing requires hardly make it an effective means of exclusion. So we must then grapple with the fact that capitalism does not proceed according to fixed and stable logics. Mobbing seems to be generated by the widespread precariousness and ambivalence that pervade Italy's work environment: part Fordist order, part post-Fordist regime. What does appear to be relatively stable, however, is the articulation of the feminine with inflexibility, which is made robust by invoking an authoritative collection of occupational psychology theories, psychiatric models, and prevailing familial orders. The result is the production and naturalization of flawed neoliberal workers as gendered subjects—who suffer severe consequences, in some cases, for being made to stand in as the agents of neoliberal change and, in others, for being asymmetrically excluded from full social recognition as flexible workers.

5   Living It on the Skin

An institution, even an economy, is complete and fully viable only if it is durably objectified not only in things . . . but also in bodies.

—Pierre Bourdieu (1990)

It was the spirit of capitalism made flesh.

—Upton Sinclair (1906)

It seems that Italian offices are, in reality, sick from mobbing.

—Barbara Ardù (1999)

Mobbing's endangerment to health has been foundationally part of its national and transnational circulation, as in Italy's minister of health's proclamation that cigarette smoking and mobbing were among Italy's top national health problems in 2000 (La Repubblica 2000b); and the 2001 European Parliament resolution which called attention to the effect of mobbing on workers' health (Mobbing in the Workplace, A5-0283, 2001). These high-profile political actions reiterated and established a greater legitimacy for the notion that mobbing is indeed imperiling the health of workers, and in quite grave ways. But even though attention focused on mobbing as something that correlates with poor health, mobbing had not been distinguished from other work-induced factors for poor health, such as stress. So when, in 2003, the state occupational insurance agency, INAIL, codified a new illness, organizational coercion pathology (OCP), that resulted from mobbing, the terrain shifted dramatically (INAIL 2003).[1] In less than ten years, mobbing had become not only a salient way of describing a set of vexing practices within the work environment, but also a psychological and physical medical pathology that could be grounds for workers compensation. While there was clear evidence that mobbing has consequences for workers' health, such bare facts did not necessarily mean that it would become an institutionalized and codified way of engaging with the state. Workers' bodily symptoms, bolstered by the robust authority of medical knowledge, allowed subjects to know mobbing, and they became a stable indicator of an otherwise elusively defined labor practice. The mobbing-related occupational illness OCP grants workers new discursive pathways and institutional mechanisms to critique neoliberalism and their own devaluation, while also resulting in both increased state monitoring and demands for biological proof for all claims. Mobbing, already linked to vast neoliberal economic changes and Italy's historical labor protections, has become inextricably tied to bodies and health. The medicalization of mobbing has expanded the potential for workers to receive benefits and resources, even as it produced new structures of state surveillance that limited such possibilities. As workers struggle to define an agent behind their ill health, the body's everyday breakdown becomes a way of knowing one's subjectivity as a worker and a citizen. Quite ironically, then, precisely at a moment when the post-industrial workplace poses less visible physical risks, "health becomes the locus for discourses on civilian versus state rights and responsibilities" (MacEachen 2000: 323). The management of health becomes a vital technique of neoliberal governance, as Nikolas Rose suggests:

> In the name of social and personal wellbeing a complex apparatus of health and therapeutics has been assembled, concerned with the management of the individual and social body as a vital national resource and the management of "problems of living" made up of techniques of advice and guidance, medics, clinics, guides and counselors. (1996: 37)

What this also requires and what has been critical in the making of OCP are a variety of specialized experts who manage the problem of mobbing. These specialized knowledge producers, concentrated in the medical field, play a role in creating the ways in which worker-citizens can interact with the state.

I have so far maintained that mobbing represents a clash, a way of mapping the disjunctures between and complex simultaneity of neoliberal labor reform, precariousness, and welfare state safeguards and protection. But the issue of OCP sheds light on how the duality of the state produces unpredictable and often negative effects for citizens. As neoliberalism becomes intimate and embodied for Italian workers, it requires a renegotiation of the relationship between worker-citizen and state. But neoliberalism is not the only political discourse and ideology in effect here. Cultural understandings about the role of the state in safeguarding the bodies of worker-citizens are informed by a unique friction between neoliberalism, the protectionist welfare state, and Italy's fascist past, which has produced historical conditions and institutional structures in which work is closely related to and measured in terms of bodily health. OCP became a way not just to medicalize forms of work harassment, but also to pathologize what was fast becoming a set of normalized work practices, particularly those characteristic of semi-permanent and flexible labor regimes. OCP, in effect, represents both a bodily and a symbolic critique, simultaneously implicit and explicit, of neoliberal labor regimes. The creation, institutionalization, and contestation of organizational coercion pathology reveal how sweeping transnational economic changes cannot be detached from Italian moral and social orders and bodily realms.

Fascist Histories: Work and Bodies

Organizational coercion pathology may have emerged as a codified psychological and physical illness in Italy, but it was institutionalized specifically as a work-related illness. Its definition rests on a particular articulation between the state, the employer, and the health and bodies of workers. In the age of industrial labor, the primary dangers for the Fordist factory worker were work-related illnesses and accidents related primarily to malfunctioning machines and equipment, falls, fires, and explosions. Preventing and compensating for physical dangers to workers became the basis for building labor protections and insurance programs, and the institutions most significant to OCP were established in the early twentieth century for industrial labor. In 1894, the Industrial Association to Prevent Work-Related Accidents (Associazione degli Industriali d'Italia per Prevenire Gli Infortuni) was founded and set significant institutional precedents (Willson 1985); it was the forerunner of the current SPISAL (Agency for Prevention, Hygiene and Safety at Work), which is responsible for preventing and managing Italy's work-related accidents and illnesses. The first institution in the world dedicated to the study of work-related illness was the Luigi Devoto Work Clinic in Milan, founded in 1902, which has become psychologist Harald Ege's mobbing clinic (Grieco et al. 2003: 98). The fascist state created the Italian Society of Occupational Health (SIML) in 1929 and INFAIL (Istituto Nazionale Fascista per l'Assicurazione contro Gli Infortuni sul Lavoro; National Fascist Institute for Insurance against Work-Related Accidents) in 1933; the latter became INAIL (Istituto Nazionale per l'Assicurazione contro Gli Infortuni sul Lavoro; Workers Compensation Authority), the site of the codification of OCP (Willson 1985: 241). But while the political and legal infrastructure surrounding occupational health was crafted and reorganized, the fascist state mobilized against worker uprisings and, broadly speaking, oppressed the workers movement (Grieco et al. 2003). Workers' health under the fascist regime had a peculiar duality: the agreement between workers and the state was a social agreement, not a direct means for indemnification; rather, as David Horn has argued, "the state intervened in the arena of work accidents in order to defend and strengthen the social organism" (Horn 1994: 40). In other words, the fascist notion of the nation was premised upon its overall productivity and the robust bodies of men as worker-citizens, who worked in order to fulfill their "social duty" to the state (Haider 1969: 269). The health of workers, though momentarily localized in the body, articulated workers' bodies as inherently interconnected with one another—and the nation.

The first case filed as mobbing was from a tribunal court in Turin in 1999, citing legal protections from Article 2087 of the 1942 Civil Code, which declares: "The employer is obliged to adopt measures within the enterprise necessary to safeguard the physical integrity and moral personhood of employees" (Amato et al. 2002: 79).[2] This same obligation legally endorses the interventions of public institutions, work inspectors, prevention institutions, clinics, and human resources personnel in mobbing cases (Lavoro Oggi 2005). But its origins return us to the fascist state, which established the notion of bodily integrity as a fundamental right of labor:

> From the principle that work is a social duty, and that the development of production is an essential element of the life and progress of the Nation, derives the consequence that the bodily integrity, health and physical resistance of the worker constitute a "good" that must be protected, not only and not principally for individual ends, but for the ends of the superior interest of the Nation. (Roberti 1928: 393 in Horn 1994: 41)

Based on this law, workers were able to sue employers for biological damages and, eventually, for psychological and moral damages. Made a separate category in 1986 (Constitutional Court decision no. 184), psychological damage, defined as "an unjust disturbance of the mental equilibrium determined by a permanent or temporary change in mental health and mental health functioning" (Terpolilli 2004: 24), was added to what is protected by Article 2087. Therefore, the Italian state, unlike other nations, has made employers accountable for both the physical and mental health of workers. In addition to the promotion of and funding for mobbing clinics, the law also provides for "socio-health [*socio-sanitari*]" institutions and medical-legal assistance and research (Lavoro Oggi 2005). These significant historical precedents structure cultural values that view work and health as intimately intertwined and create an institutional apparatus in which workplace harassment may be recognized as provoking ill health. But the risks of the neoliberal workplace are not tangible in the same way that machines or fires were visible and recognizable dangers; they are traceable neither to a specific human agent nor to a material object. Without the physical or material cues to indicate where precisely the danger lies, the failures of the body, or the medications prescribed once they are identified, become the signs that can verify the harm caused by mobbing. The historical role of the state in ensuring workers' bodily integrity has been adapted to a modern state teetering toward forms of self-governance and dominated by free market ideologies.

Embodiment and Biopolitics

Over the years in which mobbing has been a recognizable cultural category for Italians, it has garnered much attention from various health agencies in Italy and the rest of Europe. Tracing the medical discourse of mobbing from its emergence to more recent years reveals the underlying cultural notions that tie specific practices within the workplace to good and poor health. This also has entailed the medicalization of labor practices, individualizing worker-citizens by addressing bodily ailments. Medical anthropologists such as Scheper-Hughes and Lock have long cautioned that symptoms of the individual body must be read as always contingent and reverberating into the social body and the body politic (1987: 10); others say that symptoms represent the state's manipulation of bodily suffering (Kleinman 1995). The state's coercion and objectification of human bodies have been widely recognized and debated (e.g., Foucault 1975, 1978; Martin 1987; Aretxaga 2001; Comaroff and Comaroff 1993), but the changing parameters of citizens' management of their own biological vulnerability have been, until recently, underanalyzed. In relation to the explosion of the Chernobyl nuclear reactor in Ukraine, Adriana Petryna (2004) theorizes "biological citizenship" by illuminating how biological claims enable citizens to make demands upon the state, where medical documentation becomes an individualized mechanism to resist and mediate the state's progressive withdrawal.

Nikolas Rose and Carlos Novas have a slightly different understanding of biological citizenship than Petryna, one that is a largely hopeful vision of how citizens, acquiring biological literacy, can enact change (Rose and Novas 2003: 452). While they underscore the importance of biological assumptions and biomedicine in the concept of late modern citizenship, they link these to a global historical reconfiguration of the social and the biological: "the biologization of politics" (ibid.: 440; see also Rabinow 1992). They argue that it is the very pliability of biology that enables differently located citizens to mold biology around the diverse claims, desires, and beckonings of the state. The biological negotiations that take place with mobbing as a work-related illness reveal how this equation is reversed, how an Italian belief that economic exchanges produce and structure biological life changes how Italians conceptualize work. Mobbing-related illness shows how citizenship, when tied to biological epistemologies, may produce unexpected and often negative effects. At the same time, the fractured state, both enabling and opposing biological claims, produces often unpredictable and opposing responses to citizens. Understandings of mobbing, from its inception to the definition of OCP, sit precariously between a sense of somatic disruption and psychological pain. Moreover, that mobbing encompasses both labor and bodily risk forces a revision not only of work-related illness, but also of the articulation between citizen and worker.

Necessarily prior to a medical diagnosis related to mobbing is the conceptualization of mobbing as a form of harassment that is disturbing to both body and mind. Often cited by mobbing-specialized psychologists, doctors, and union workers are the six phases of mobbing as defined by psychologist Harald Ege (1998). Ege is an acclaimed mobbing specialist and the founder of Bologna's clinic Prima: The Italian Association against Mobbing and Psychosocial Stress. His six stages of mobbing show a gradual progression from work harassment to its complex psychophysical escalation: (1) generalized conflict; (2) deterioration of social relations; group acts as if subject does not exist; (3) subject displays mobbing symptoms: insecurity, sleeplessness, depression; (4) subject's professional and private life are attacked; work tasks are often limited, removed, or changed; (5) attacks have a greater effect on subject's mental and physical health; mobbee is often on sick leave, and harassment may continue by repeated visits of legal doctors to check on mobbee's status;[3] (6) mobbee seeks to end job by quitting, early retirement, or, most gravely, suicide (Ege 2002). Ege (1996, 1998) also divides the effects of mobbing into three categories: emotional disturbances (anxiety, depression, irritability); psychosomatic symptoms (headaches, gastrointestinal maladies, backaches, difficulty in concentrating, respiratory and skin-related problems); and behavioral problems (increased use of cigarettes and alcohol, loss of appetite, reduced desire to engage socially, self-isolating behaviors) (see also Bertinaria 2004). While Ege includes certain kinds of practices that are included in mobbing (isolation, marginalization, criticism), for the most part the series of practices and events defining this harassment remains elusive. It is unlike other threats to workers, as it does not represent direct physical danger with visible material injuries and effects. The very nature of post-Fordist labor, which produces mental anguish in workers, forces a reconceptualization of the original labor protections that focused on safeguarding workers' bodies. The manifestations of mobbing, defined by drawing from the notion of a "psychosomatic" body, become more pronounced and important in the latter phases. Mobbing thus becomes retroactively defined by the kinds of mental and bodily symptoms experienced by the victim. The task of defining what constitutes "real" mobbing remains obscure and difficult for workers to accomplish and, in turn, contest.

For the mobbees I met in Italy, it was often difficult to decipher the individual and organizational intentionality of lost files, inconsistent workloads, and unpredictable colleagues: happenstance or calculated hostility? The medical discourse of mobbing has produced a new epistemology of knowledge: the body as a mechanism, and a truthful means, to know one's social and work environment. One question to determine whether or not one is being mobbed, according to an epistemology that focused on work practices, might be: "Are my managers and colleagues mistreating me, overly critical, or ignoring me?" But with health issues more visible and widespread, the condition has been created for different epistemological grounds for mobbing. Workers might now ask, first and foremost: "Am I experiencing depression, sleeplessness, and anxiety related to work?" and then: "Am I being mobbed?" Knowing one's body, then, has become a way to navigate the workplace and one's role within corporate power relations. At the same time, the impetus of change has been placed on the employee to validate her biological claims, rather than on the employer to prevent them. Whether or not specific abusive or persecutory work practices are taking place against the worker seems secondary to the "proof" that bodily suffering is being experienced by the victim. Part of this also relates to how actual mobbers seem to drop out of the mobbing, replaced by pathogens such as isolation, transfers, and unpredictable schedules. Though the effects of mobbing oscillate between physical (gastrointestinal) and psychological (depression) maladies, both are conceptualized as biological responses to and juridical evidence for workplace harassment.

In 2002, the Luigi Devoto Work Clinic in Milan, in collaboration with the ISPESL (Istituto Superiore per la Prevenzione e la Sicurezza del Lavoro)[4] and the European Agency for Security and Health at Work issued a special pamphlet on mobbing, *Mobbing in the Workplace*. Shortly after, the World Health Organization issued *Psychological Violence at Work: Increasing Awareness* (*Violenza psicologica sul lavoro: Accrescere la consapevolezza*) as part of a series on protecting workers' health (Cassitto et al. 2003). The authors, including the famous Italian mobbing psychologist Renato Gilioli, defined mobbing as "repeated and irrational behavior towards one employee or a group such that it creates a health and security risk" (ibid.: 12). Mobbing, then, surfaces as risk behaviors that create health problems for workers—though these behaviors include practices that are increasingly widespread in Italy. The medical model of mobbing, in tandem with an understanding of citizens' bodily integrity, has created the ontological conditions for new political subjectivities to modify not just mobbing but the organization of work.

Mobbing has been positioned as something that provokes ill health, as an immoral consequence of "rational" cost-cutting economic systems. For example, Elena Ferrara describes strategic mobbing for the European Commission's Daphne Project:

> It is a kind of *mobbing* strategically used by organisations in order to dismiss undesirable subjects. They can be subjects belonging to the previous management or assigned to a department to be eliminated, or they are too expensive or no longer meeting the firm's expectations. It often takes place in firms whose staff, after a restructuring, a merger or a change, is redundant and needs to be dismissed. Thus, mobbing becomes a real business strategy. (2004: 6)

In such discourses, mobbing is positioned from a strictly materialist standpoint based on top-down economic logics as a form of cost reduction yet simultaneously as a deviant practice according to welfare ideologies that constitute workers as subjects with rights to bodily integrity. It is this latter sense that legitimates intervention by health authorities. The authors of *Psychological Violence at Work* (Cassitto et al. 2003) make a concerted effort to detail the practices that make up mobbing: damage to personal objects; derision in the presence of colleagues and superiors; diffusion of false information; exclusion; intrusion into one's private life; isolation; instigation from colleagues; continual bad talk; threats of violence; sexual harassment; verbal assaults; provocations; and humiliation (ibid.: 14). What is unusual about this list is that since these actions may be carried out by one individual or many, a focus on the kind of mobber that would likely be demonized, or at least profiled, is entirely absent. There is no kind of manager that emerges as the "perverse mobber"—a popular conceptualization in France, unlike in Italy. Instead, this list offers a generalized set of actions and behaviors with which many workers within Italy's restructured labor regime might identify, at least some of the time. Moreover, situating sexual harassment as a subset of mobbing erases the sexualized dynamics of mobbing and the gendered asymmetries of men both sexually and morally harassing women.[5]

In order to further distinguish mobbing from a turbulent work environment, *Psychological Violence at Work* includes a table that shows what distinguishes "healthy conflicts" from mobbing in the workplace (see table 5.1) (Cassitto et al. 2003: 15).[6] Later, the authors indict the late modern work environment, "a highly flexible work environment, together with downsizing and corporate restructuring," and "horizontal management styles" as key contributing factors to mobbing (ibid.: 23, 25).

Some of the practices included in this table as mobbing are favorable for conforming to flexible work regimes and increasingly the norm in Italy. For example, "ambiguous roles" and "ambiguous interpersonal relationships" have become common for many workers as corporations restructure, shift around responsibilities, and reorganize personnel (Ferrera and Gualmini 2004). "No perspective" and "submerged actions" are part of the generalized unknowing and left-in-the-dark style of management where most workers are not allowed to know about the next steps for closures, layoffs, or off-shore investments (Collins 2003, 2005). Information related to a corporation's off-shore expansions or plant closures has great value, as it may suggest plans to terminate employment contracts. Employees therefore become more suspicious of who has this kind of information, as news that circulates around the workplace has potentially damaging personal consequences: job loss. The neoliberal flexible regime operates by expanding "oblique and evasive communication" and "organizational anomalies," both of which the authors claim are unhealthy. Thus, the practices characteristic of mobbing are emerging as the norm, while the items listed under healthy conflicts represent more of an ideal or nostalgic vision of workplace relations. Rather than an emphasis on a particular pathologized mobber, the World Health Organization authoritatively links a set of organizational practices and the structure of work relations to ill health: the structure of work itself is a pathogen.

Somatic Stories

During my fieldwork, I found that almost every person who had encountered what they defined as mobbing tied their experience to particular bodily reactions, including skin rashes, anxiety, sleeplessness, depression, and vomiting. Fiore suffered from severe back pain; Michela experienced various psychosomatic symptoms, from depression to vomiting, and her sick leave was instrumental in her recovery; and Giulia described her poor health as a result of ongoing harassment at work and taking psychopharmaceuticals. Anna, the film protagonist, was portrayed as having a fainting spell and experiencing depression, and she was bedridden for a period of time. Homing in on how workers react to mobbing, both physically and mentally, allows us to see how mobbing has become linked to embodied experiences and is a means of making demands on the state, without losing sight of how neoliberal economies are chronicled in the somatic registers of a population.

Table 5.1. Healthy Conflicts versus Mobbing

Healthy Conflicts	Mobbing
Clear roles and responsibilities	Ambiguous roles
Collaborative relationships	Uncollaborative behavior, boycotts
Common and shared objectives	No perspective
Clear interpersonal relationships	Ambiguous interpersonal relationships
Good organization	Organizational anomalies
Healthy fights and confrontations	Unethical repeated and systematic actions
Clear and transparent strategies	Equivocal strategies
Open conflicts and discussions	Submerged actions and negation of conflicts
Direct communication	Oblique and evasive communication

In their small office in a large building hosting music schools and various social clubs, Dora Carroni and Lidia Vetri, who both identify as mobbing survivors, since 1997 have co-directed a mobbing clinic funded by the Veneto regional government and nonprofit organizations. Dora is a tall woman in her early fifties with cropped blonde hair, a friendly face without cosmetic adornment, and a genuine smile with prominent front teeth. One afternoon, Lidia, in her early sixties, Dora's shorter and darker-haired work companion, alternated between the desk and the open window, where she flicked the ashes off her cigarette. A middle-aged trade union man had come to the clinic and described how he'd taken a course on mobbing and wanted to do something more, to be involved in preventing it. After his departure and noticing their evident disinterest, I asked why they didn't want the extra help. Lidia glared at me, horrified, and said that, through all the years that she had suffered as a mobbee and gone to every place she could think of: "Every door shut in my face!" "Noelle," Lidia continued, "I've used myself up in this lifetime [*Mi sono consumata in questa vita*]. And I know I will not grow old because it [mobbing] is something I will always carry with me." In one sudden movement, she leaned closer and yanked up the arm of her sweater, swatting the pale skin repeatedly with her other hand and shouting, "I've lived mobbing on this skin! On this skin! [*L'ho vissuto mobbing sulla pelle! Sulla pelle!*]." My eyes fixed on the now-reddened patch on the flesh of her forearm, and I inhaled the cigarette smell of her breath and the desk's ashtray. Then, almost as quickly as her face had become red a moment ago, her entire posture relaxed and she grinned. In her signature raspy voice, she said, "Don't worry, Noelle, this is just how I talk." Lidia's painful experience of being mobbed was measured in terms of permanent bodily trauma. As for the rejection of the man's offer, Dora and Lidia's clinical practices were generally indexed and directed toward their network of psychiatrists and lawyers, revealing their overall mistrust of trade unions, despite their leftist political beliefs. Refusing to collaborate with unions meant keeping the management of mobbing cases away from a site of predominantly men's involvement or, alternatively, keeping the cases on the more medicalized pathways toward compensation for the victims.

Also underpinning Lidia's reaction were cultural understandings of the body. Mobbing "lived on the skin" materializes an embodied subjectivity that mediates between economies and people. The phrase itself, *lived on the skin*, is one that Italians may use to represent life-changing experiences that resonate to the core of the body. The following are some other experiences invoked as lived on the skin: emotional abuse, religion, poverty, a city, political upheaval, and another's death. It can be, therefore, a devastating and rare event, and is surely one that resonates to the core of one's vitality. Links with bodily experiences, and specifically the skin, have surfaced in written materials on the topic of mobbing. The book *Mobbing: Reflections on the Skin* chronicles the mobbing experiences of "R.," a woman who worked as the technical director for a travel agency in Palermo, Sicily, for fifteen years (Ascenzi and Bergagio 2002). R. lost all of her colleagues and staff and remained on the job by herself for over a year until a psychologist was sent from corporate headquarters to observe her. The company made several offers of severance packages for her, but she refused to quit. R. was sent to the northern city of Verona and was forced to leave her husband and son in Sicily to preserve her position. In Verona she suffered serious depression; during her sick leave, the company sent medical professionals to check on her status, reduced her pay, and denied her access to information and job training. Threatened with another transfer to Perugia, she visited Renato Gilioli's clinic in Milan and began building a legal case in 1997: "When everything is done, if I get justice, if I'm right, what we have lived on our skin will be absorbed. And inside of those who are dear to me, it will [be] un-removable, forever" (ibid.: 28). Like Lidia, R. describes mobbing not only as capable of marking the skin, but as something that engages bodies in the process of absorption, leeching the subject's well-being in the process.

Lidia's exclamation of mobbing living on the skin reiterates the permeability of the body, rather than proclaiming the skin as the body's enclosed and protected "end" (Haraway 1991:178; see also Grosz 1994).[7] The experience of mobbees suggests a conceptualization of the body's skin as vulnerable and alterable. Italy's medical history is deeply shaped by humoral medicine, which views the skin and body as highly permeable. According to Elizabeth Whitaker (2003), because of the lasting influence of these humoral traditions, Italians engage in practices that involve drying and covering the skin in order to stave off atmospheric influences that weaken the body. For example, Italians are extremely wary of experiencing a gust of coldness (*prendere freddo*) or a shock of cold air (*colpo d'aria*) because it is believed this will instantaneously block digestion, resulting in various intestinal ailments. People suffering from stomach aches will wrap the stomach in blankets to prevent this type of sudden environmental disturbance. Moreover, one can find Italians putting on sweaters in the summer so that the skin, damp from sweat and susceptible to gusts of air, remains protected. Given how Italians draw from both biomedical and humoral medical frameworks, it is not surprising that living on the skin represents not a surface malady but a deeply embodied experience.

On another occasion, a few months later, I was back at the clinic with Dora and Lidia. Dora was on the phone and Lidia waved me in the door. An article had been published in the newspaper for the Northeast, *Il Gazzettino*, describing a local government official who had reportedly lost his patience with a social worker during a meeting. This was described as mobbing, to the passionate objection of Dora and Lidia. "We're calling the paper," Lidia said firmly, as Dora was waiting on the phone. A single hostile encounter could not be counted as mobbing, they explained to me, not only because it did not encompass long-term harassment and suffering, but also because the victim did not experience any serious health effects. Their own bodily suffering in relation to mobbing, in which poor health and mobbing were deeply articulated, made them highly sensitive to the ways in which media outlets, like newspapers, might co-opt the term. Lidia explained further: "With mobbing, if you've endured it then you think you've done something wrong, and if you've endured it then you understand how you suffer, [how] those people suffer. This is the only way to know if it's mobbing or not." For Lidia, the suffering that mobbees endure, experienced as bodily sensations and psychological and physical ills, are the important measure of knowing it more profoundly. Their practice of calling the newspaper can also be read as an assertion of their epistemological framing of mobbing and serves as a key example of how mobbing experts act to codify, shape, and manage mobbing's media circulation.

Many of their visitors told Lidia and Dora about the biological symptoms they had experienced as a result of mobbing. Pino Arturini, for example, was a forty-seven-year-old municipal police officer, tall and bearded, with bright brown eyes and long-fingered hands. Speaking in the Veneto dialect, Pino recounted that though he had a long career with the police department, trouble began when he was promoted to vice director. Rather suddenly, he was left with neither work assignments to complete nor officers to coordinate. The new title, he explained, was just a "trap" to mob him. Likening himself to "a ghost who wanders the halls of the workplace [*uno spirito che vaga per i corridoi*]," he explained that he was shut up in a room and left only with the civil and penal codes to read. As Lidia had encouraged him, he had collected various medical certificates documenting his trauma, which had included bright red spots that appeared all over his body, anxiety and depression, and the loss of ten teeth in six months. Over the past few years, Pino had taken various sick leaves from work, collected evidence, and began building his legal case of mobbing against the city: Pino was suing for professional demotion and biological damages (*danni biologici*). As biological symptoms refigured the way in which Pino made claims on the welfare state, he adopted a particular self-managing practice of rigid documentation of his day-to-day work life and bodily condition. The responsibility for Pino's welfare as a worker-citizen rested on his individualized capacity and desire to track his body and to navigate public services, like mobbing clinics. Collecting medical certificates had been publicized as a strategic tactic for mobbing cases. According to an "expert in labor rights," a lawyer in Milan: "First thing is that victims must produce medical proof of their state, in order to scientifically validate their psychological status" (Corriere della Sera 2002b). Locally, Lidia and Dora played an important role in the circulation of medical knowledge and the normalization of these self-governing practices. Their work solidified the medical management of mobbing cases on a day-to-day basis, while their practices enacted a form of localized neoliberal governance in which centralized welfare services depended on documentation and intermediaries (Rose 1996; Ong 2006b).

Another client, Maria Crema, a cafeteria worker in her forties, came to the clinic with her husband; both of them were bundled in thick layers and heavy winter coats with hoods trimmed with faux fur. Maria began by describing to Lidia and Dora how she had been given a month and a half of sick leave for a series of health problems resulting from mobbing. Maria's employers, she told us, desiring to coerce her into quitting, had given her impossible tasks to complete. For example, they insisted that she prepare particular dishes without ordering the necessary ingredients, for which she would then be reprimanded. She was transferred to another location, her vacation and overtime hours were taken away, her weekly schedule was reduced, she had received transfer orders via mail without any prior warning or explanation from her employer, and she was hired at a level inferior to her appropriate employment level.[8] Lidia and Dora counseled her to not return to work after the month and a half of sick leave expired, and made sure she had collected a variety of medical certificates documenting her back and arm pain. Suggesting an appointment with their psychiatrist, Dora was sympathetic: "Yes, mobbing is very psychosomatic." They assured Maria that their psychiatrist would be able to give her at least another month of sick leave and necessary medication. This sort of brokering was not unfamiliar: low-grade favors constitute a particular mode of citizen-state encounters in Italy. Though the urging to see their psychiatrist might seem to be a preemptive mode of acquiring legal documentation, Lidia and Dora's explanation was that this was preventive medicine; they hoped to offset and manage severe, even suicidal, depression. Knowing how the problems could escalate, they recommended an early meeting with their collaborating psychiatrist as a precautionary measure for clients.

As the link between health and mobbing has become more explicit, Italian workers share a greater ability to sue their abusive employers—if they can make mobbing show on the skin. While many mobbees clearly recognized the mental and existential pain of what they were experiencing, there were also physical or measurable manifestations—rashes, back pain, teeth loss—that were seen as outgrowths of psychological alienation. The marked skin suggests the effects of a traumatic experience, though it does not necessarily specify the preceding events or cause. For mobbees in Italy, what shows on the body becomes the medium through which they can hold the state responsible for the tangible economic and sometimes intangible social effects that have come with neoliberal change.

Biological symptoms affirm mobbing's existence, but subjects also psychosomaticize large-scale social instability. The subjects of mobbing defy a reading of the body as bounded or passively "inscribed" and reinstate a notion of embodiment as active and socially mediated (Csordas 1994, 2004). The kind of distress experienced by mobbees emerges in the context of a precarious labor market, one shaped by both economic risk and psychic transformation. Precariousness also suggests a workplace in which fear and anxiety about one's future employment are extremely common and the expendability of post-industrial laborers is deeply felt. As workers experience the processes of alienation and exploitation within Italy's neoliberal economic regime, including the devaluation of their labor, they may navigate such changes as embodied experiences: the body becomes an agent through which large-scale social turmoil materializes (e.g., Kleinman 1994; Ong 1988; Obeyesekere 1986). For victims of mobbing in Italy, episodes of illness might also be read as a way in which actors chronicle and furtively critique the violations of a neoliberal workplace and a state-deregulated economy that increasingly undervalues the labor of employees. What self-identified mobbing sufferers register is not only the bodily outcomes of extreme stress and harassment but also a more complex negotiation of their ongoing and intensifying devaluation.

The Workplace as Car Wreck

Local medical doctors' immediate knowledge of mobbing expanded as patients came to them with new symptoms and narratives of turmoil at work. Prior to the diagnosis of OCP, there had already been an ongoing process involving mobbing's institutionalization by Italian health organizations in national and transnational arenas. This is not to suggest that one historical process follows another in seamless chronological succession. As more and more workers had access to the idiom of mobbing as a term for their physical and psychological strain and suffering and as new workplace demands took their toll, it is probable that mobbees turned to their family doctors for help. In multiple ways, then, knowledge about mobbing has become centralized within the medical field. Public authorities like Italy's minister of health have recognized mobbing as an urgent health problem, and some public health agencies have begun to view themselves as key actors in its resolution (La Repubblica 2000b).

The state agency INAIL (Workers Compensation Authority) is responsible for preventing and tabulating occupational illnesses and accidents, and it also insures workers. In September 2001, INAIL began an investigation into the management of reports of "psychological pathologies and psychosomatic disturbances caused by organizational coercion at work" (INAIL 2001). INAIL selected over 200 cases in order to fine-tune and develop its diagnostic agenda;

the scope of the project also included determining if this should be considered a work-related illness (*malattia professionale*). Two years later, INAIL issued a statement that officially created the category of "organizational coercion pathology (OCP)," which marked a significant change in the understanding of work-related illnesses and state responses (INAIL 2003). I visited some INAIL agencies in the Veneto region, and one health official described why he deemed this project necessary: "Doctors used to use the diagnosis 'mobbing.' But saying that someone is suffering from mobbing is like saying that someone has a car wreck. You don't *have* [a] car wreck, the car wreck creates another kind of disturbance." Creating OCP was also a way for INAIL to standardize and script how it would deal with mobbing on an institutional level and how it would manage the growing number of mobbing cases being reported.

Unlike the work-related illnesses of the industrial age, in OCP the critical damage is far more difficult to prove on a legal basis, in large part because of its coding as a trauma-related illness. There are not faulty machines or chemical burns, but rather anxiety or depression, which are only sometimes visible but which are materialized through medical authorities' prescription pads or physical symptoms like skin rashes and weight loss. INAIL detailed precisely how OCP manifests in bodies and behaviors and what kinds of tests would be necessary to diagnose it from early warning signs, including "motor tension, hyperactivity, hypervigilance, and hyperattention" (Terpolilli 2004: 19). Other medical conditions related to OCP include "anxiety, depression, behavioral alteration, emotional and somatic disturbances," post-traumatic stress disorder (*disturbo post traumatico del stress*), and "maladjustment disturbances [*disturbo dell'adattamento*]."[9] To claim that they are experiencing OCP, workers must have "at least one" of the above elements and the behaviors must be "long-lasting, objective and documented" (INAIL 2003). INAIL asserted that its intervention was justified by referring to an Italian court decision stating that mental illness could be legally considered a "work-related illness," entitling workers to insurance protection, provided that work conditions were determined to be the primary cause of injury (Constitutional Court, sent. no. 179/1988; and Decreto Legislativo, no. 38/2000, Article 10, par. 4, 2000).[10] The agency described what caused the pathology as something far more elusive than chemicals or machines, namely, the "organizational structure of work" and clarified: "The imbalances of organizational processes can become mental risk factors for the worker" (INAIL 2001).[11] Practices which are part of this malfunctioning organizational structure of work include "marginalization from work activity, removal of responsibilities, forced inactivity, unjustified and repeated transfers, the assigning of tasks below the qualifications of the employee's professional profile, systematic and structural obstruction to information access and exasperated and excessive exercise of control" (INAIL 2003). Thus, INAIL, a public health institution, did not identify a mobber, and some of these practices do not necessarily result from specific actors; in other words, the pathology stems from broadly conceived neoliberal labor relations. This definition puts the employer at a great disadvantage precisely because they all could be legitimate actions. When Francesco Gallo, a lawyer specializing in mobbing cases, spoke to me about mobbing, he emphasized that mobbing was "an illness caught at work, very often as a consequence of legitimate acts. But even if it is from legitimate acts, then INAIL should still intervene."

By relating organizational coercion to the structure of labor relations, INAIL bypassed the problem of the intentionality of a single person, which was often central to harassment violations based on "intent to harm" (Terpolilli 2004: 18). In other words, it was no longer necessary to prove the pathological action of a colleague or manager. Like the "healthy conflicts" discussed above, INAIL defined, as the antithesis of organizational coercion, what constituted "normal" job-related occurrences, which would not provide workers with insurance relief:

> organizational/management factors tied to the normal occurrences of the work relationship (new assignments, transfers, layoffs); situations influenced by the common psychological-relational dynamic in work and life (interpersonal conflict, relational difficulty and conduct recognizable as purely subjective behaviors, which, in this case, will inevitably be a matter of interpretive discretion). (INAIL 2003)

Such distinctions are enormously slippery as there is no precise measure to determine what may be simply a "relational difficulty" (not insured) and what counts as "excessive exercise of control" (insured). The distinction, importantly, rests on the "interpretive discretion" of INAIL employees and thus expands its domain over workers.

The agency required documentation both for the cause of the illness, which had to be in accordance with its definition of organizational coercion, and for the resulting illness itself. On-site inspections, but only when authorized and carried out by INAIL, were allowed as a measure of proof, in addition to an elaborate illness verification process requiring a neurological exam and psychological diagnostic tests. Thus, the state agency made itself responsible for evaluating co-worker and employer testimonies, as well as determining how much the employer had acted to safeguard workers' health and safety within the company. The process of institutionalization was the foundation upon which a set of procedures to measure mobbing could be mobilized, rendering the complex narratives of employees into quantifiable entities.

Utilizing OCP to show mobbing circumvented the need to show a single subject's malign intent. But INAIL did not dismiss the possibility that certain subjects might experience psychological and physical trauma *and* be able to prove that intent to harm. Thus, INAIL distinguished "strategic mobbing [*mobbing strategico*]" from "organizational coercion" where the former was characterized by the specific aim—strategic and premeditated—to end the worker's position, even though both forms of harassment could result in OCP (Terpolilli 2004: 18). The legal protocol for a case of strategic mobbing requires that the employee garner proof of either corporate or individual intentionality. Most cases of mobbing, however, would be extremely difficult to demonstrate as strategic mobbing. Consider Pino's case: there is nothing illegal about asking a police officer to study the penal code, so finding evidence that this was an intentional and hostile act would be highly unlikely.

Building a legal case around organizational coercion thus became a more viable and practical option for worker-citizens than generating a case of strategic mobbing: psychobiological symptoms were sufficient evidence, and legitimate workplace practices would henceforth, and retroactively, be legally scrutinized as problematic. At the same time, these new parameters moved the resolution of labor conflicts into individual courtroom battles mediated by medical experts, and away from collective bargaining and negotiation. Such a shift is characteristic of the individualizing culture of neoliberalism with its strident motto of "the personal is the only politics there is" (Comaroff and Comaroff 2001: 15). After completing its original investigation in 2003, INAIL announced that only 15 percent of its 200 cases could be defined as OCP and therefore severely limited the number of cases that could be insured (INAIL 2003).[12] Under neoliberal conditions, making and documenting claims based on the individual body has become a new technology of labor reorganization and governance, which, as in this case, allows for greater biological surveillance than compensation.

Managing Biological Claims

The process of medical institutionalization takes place in the everyday: exchanges between actors, localized meaning-making, and various negotiations along the way. On a hot day in early July, I sat in on a meeting with members from SPISAL at an INAIL office in the Veneto region. The newly constructed, multifloor building held research facilities and various medical laboratories and offices: its surfaces and doors gleamed; the furnishings were styled with contemporary clean lines; the purified air was odor-free; and the employees were robed in white. The meeting, in a room distinguished only by a pair of bookcases and a crucifix adorning one bare wall, was to discuss how to organize a protocol on OCP and mobbing cases, possibly to be shared between the two agencies. The cross caught my eye, as it seemed to serve as an implicit reminder of Catholic understandings of the good life and well-being, which both informed and competed with state objectives on health. The attendees began by discussing the distinctive but complementary roles of the two health agencies. Members of INAIL discussed their concern about hiring more psychologists who would be able to conduct the standardized testing required by the OCP mandate. Representatives of both institutions hesitated to include other medical research centers, such as one in Verona, as they would have to pay per patient to have the necessary psychological testing completed. In addition, an INAIL psychologist expressed his concern at the continuing diagnosis of "mobbing" by various physicians who were not yet informed about or had little regard for the newer guidelines. One of the medical doctors from INAIL declared how they should proceed with new cases: "We have to look for counterevidence every time, have objectivity, and we must go to actual companies." The director of INAIL voiced his concern about how time-consuming in-take interviews with workers are for his staff. While the SPISAL director offered to pool resources for this task, the INAIL director maintained that their responsibilities should remain separate.

No specific course of action was set in motion by the end of this meeting. There was only a slight clarification of the roles of each agency. The meeting itself demonstrated a shared institutional investment in the problem of mobbing, but the frequent assertion of their distinct roles was also evident. The meeting ended with this statement by the SPISAL director: "There are no conflicts between us, the work can be shared. . . . we are two entities for different solutions. And this way, we'll avoid any future conflict of interest." I sensed that the men were somewhat wary of one another, and they did not designate explicit pathways of institutional collaboration. It was clear that INAIL worked toward resolving conflicts once they were pronounced, and did not want to transfer activity entirely to SPISAL's primarily preventive goals. While INAIL's OCP codification and its potential effects are certainly significant, the standardization of procedures was going to take a great deal of face-to-face work and institutional change.

It's critical to remember that the conditions of a late capitalist economic regime were also at work in the role of the state health agency: it had to rapidly produce new structures in response to a quickly changing typology of insurance claims. The state institutions, also operating within an increasingly market-driven medical regime and a deregulated labor market, constrained the production of biological claims that could result from neoliberal labor reform: the detailing and defining of the illness and the call for inspections and protocols resulted in diminished eligibility for workers compensation. It is also true that these state agencies needed to rapidly constitute and rearrange organizational energies around interviews, testing, on-site visits, and paperwork. Both workers who requested moneys for mobbing-related suffering or pain and the health institution itself were shifting how they related to one another as part of this ongoing economic restructuring in Italy. Rather than producing a critique of the existing labor market, however, citizens were encouraged by state health agencies to build a more individualized and highly medicalized view of their own political subjectivity. In this sense, the life of OCP casts light upon a dual and paradoxical process: just as workers could utilize bodily suffering for their own material benefits, so too could the state health professionals expand and elaborate their control over verifying these bodily effects, deflecting public attention and resources away from neoliberal reform and critique.

Marked Bodies, Unmarked Capitalisms

Even beyond the contested legal and political pathways for negotiation and interaction with the state and public health institutions, medical understandings altered how mobbing was understood at the most basic levels—who it afflicts and why—often resulting in a changed understanding of mobbees. Medical specialists within Western biomedical traditions, in seeking the reasons that certain subjects become ill, have delved into the preexisting qualities of subjects in order to predict and prevent pathologies. Similarly, in their search to identify such predispositions, medical specialists in Italy have increasingly discussed the individual, health, and behavior inadequacies of those who are mobbed and those who suffer from OCP. Implied in defining the typical OCP sufferer, however, was characterizing mobbing victims as unfit or inflexible workers.

The mobbing specialist and director of a Bologna mobbing clinic, Harald Ege (1998) pinpointed workers' inflexibility as increasing the chances of being mobbed, in addition to workers' envy of other workers, nonconformity, and independence. A trainee of Ege, psychologist Paolo Terpolilli, described the likely mobbee as a "hardly flexible and scarcely malleable" person (2004: 24). Terpolilli also predicted that OCP was more likely in a person who "bases his/ her life on work and takes on a social role contrary to others who identify with family" (ibid.: 19). Similarly, Renato Gilioli said, "[The pathology] manifests itself primarily in weak subjects" (Varese News 2004). These statements conceptualize the sufferer as weak, envious, work-obsessed, and inflexible. Here we see how definitions of an "unfit worker" begin to overlap with and draw from cultural notions of good health as a life balanced between work and family. Ironically, poor health was being defined as "basing one's life on work" right at the moment when Italian citizens seemed most unable to do so. As the labor market was structured to exclude many citizens from building their life around work, those desiring a return to Fordist orders, when one could build a life around long-term employment, became socially devalued. And exclusion from work has been unevenly distributed across the population.

As the metaphor of illness becomes more prevalent for mobbing, the worker who adapts to the demands of the late capitalist workplace will be seen as flexibly bodied, modern, and even morally superior to the victim of mobbing, who will be seen as rigid and traditional. The notion of susceptibility in certain kinds of workers must also be viewed in terms of preventive medicine, which aims to forestall illnesses. Isolating OCP within particular worker populations raises concerns about refashioning the workplace as a site in which to preemptively monitor the bodies of workers. Legitimizing a link between inflexible bodies and the presence of mobbing renders workers' healthy bodies subject to examination and inquiry. As mobbed workers suffer from bodily symptoms, they may be reconfirmed as bodies less elastic under new environmental pressures. Seeking predispositions for mobbing-related illness and confirming the biological inadequacy of certain workers mask the embodied signs of a disrupted economic and moral order within Italian society.

Medicalization depoliticizes mobbees' claims, and only those workers that can make their claims legible by the state are recognized, thereby excluding the mobbees who cannot document their bodily traumas. Paradoxically, this process of medicalization puts workers who remain healthy at a disadvantage. In various ways, being mobbed is an epistemological ambush: it is hard to know if you are being mobbed, as it is the sum of a series of harassing and persecutory actions that are simultaneously normalized as "work" in Italy. Culturally situated knowledge of the body's pain, shaped by scientific and medical epistemologies, changes how people come to know what they call mobbing. On the one hand, institutionalized medicalization changes how people know and document their bodies, placing the focus increasingly on the traumatized body as a critical measure of truth, and less on abusive work practices. Defining an illness as caused by the structure of labor, on the other hand, points toward neoliberal restructuring itself as deviant and pathological. The articulation of the mental and physical wear on workers' bodies with Italy's precarious work regime, distinct from the physical and traceable bodily risks associated with industrial labor, offers a more complex understanding of human illness and bodies under post-industrial labor regimes.

A Fractured State

In July 2005, I was present at INAIL when one of the directors announced an unexpected court decision regarding organizational coercion pathology that was met with surprise, confusion, and outrage by the director and his colleagues. The Tribunale Amminstrativo Regionale (TAR) Lazio, the Regional Administrative Tribunal Court, had nullified INAIL's 2003 codification of OCP and modified the extent to which it could be classified as a legitimate work-related illness (TAR Lazio, no. 5454, July 4, 2005). The ruling came from a suit filed against INAIL and the Ministry of Labor by Confindustria (Confederazione Generale dell'Industria Italiana, General Confederation of Italian Industry), Confagricoltura (Confederazione Generale dell'Agricoltura Italiana, General Confederation of Italian Agriculture), ABI (Associazione Bancaria Italiana, Italian Bank Association), BNL (Banca Nationazale del Lavoro, National Labor Bank), and Nortel Networks. Defining OCP as a work-related illness, according to the court, "was against the juridical sphere of entrepreneurs in that it rendered certain actions immediately punishable"—rendering "poor work organization" a legally actionable offense that would incriminate employers (ibid.). In other words, the court rejected the idea of allowing the generalized (and increasingly normalized) labor conditions to become a recognizable and indictable legal offense and insurable illness.

The court invalidated INAIL's 2003 document, stating that the institution's resolution "lacked essential elements indicating serious and rigorous scientific definitions," thus framing the ruling in terms of jurisdiction and the appropriate exercise of power (TAR Lazio, no. 5454, July 4, 2005). The lack of "scientific" evidence became the authoritative medium through which OCP was rejected by the court, even though INAIL had provided various scientific measures to verify the illness's existence. The court maintained that OCP, caused by work environments, had to include additional physical rather than psychological effects on the worker in order to be officially recognized as an occupational illness, adding: "It is not possible to consider all the dynamics of work relations within a company and the so-called 'organizational coercion.' It is certainly not a worker's 'right' to work in a professional environment that is aesthetic or pleasant." In its mocking tone, the court rhetoric echoed the slipperiness between mobbing and "healthy" workplaces, asserting instead that work environments are necessarily and naturally conflict-ridden. It refused the epistemological premise, proposed by INAIL, that ambivalent and chaotic professional environments could be physically and psychologically endangering to workers. The court framed the ruling in terms of historically available welfare state legal protections: mobbees do not need further protection beyond existing laws that protect the dignity of workers, such as Article 2087 of Italy's Civil Code, which mandates that employers safeguard the "physical integrity and moral personhood" of workers. In short, the state's existing legal protections for workers should be sufficient to safeguard against bodily harm, the court asserted.

This was not the first time that Confindustria, a massive employers organization, had challenged the state on work-related injuries and workers compensation. In 1930, Confindustria, which was established just prior to the fascist period in 1910, claimed that "70 to 75 percent [of accidents] could be attributed to the workers themselves" (Willson 1985: 242). The contemporary case recalls the way in which the state acts as an unsteady mediator between workers and employers, and the differences between the two illuminate the ways in which the configuration between state, laborer, and work has changed. In the age of industrial labor, when bodily trauma was often caused by machines and chemicals, Confindustria sidestepped the fascist state's policy by claiming that workers were themselves responsible. In the age of post-Fordist labor, when psychological trauma is purported to be caused by the organization of labor, Confindustria sidestepped state policy by refuting the medical and scientific grounds of evidence. The court case reveals the state as fractured between safeguarding worker-citizens and advancing capitalist regimes of labor, and also reveals the new notion of workers' individual, as opposed to class-based, risks. Moreover, this court ruling shows a unique historical collision between contemporary neoliberal modalities and the lingering imprint of Italy's fascist past.

The Flesh of Precariousness

While the court's decision did not entirely eliminate OCP as a recognizable illness, as a "psychological and psychosomatic illness due to dysfunction in the organization of work," its legal status as a work-related illness was changed (TAR Lazio, no. 5454, July 4, 2005). The conditions of organizational coercion were changed from "specific" risk factors to "generic" risk factors; that is, in the former version the connection between work activities and psychosomatic symptoms were a "legal assumption," thus not requiring additional evidence (Cantistani 2005). In its revised status, however, the onus would be upon the worker to prove the existence of the illness, its etiological status, and the connection between the illness and the work activity (ibid.). Therefore, the potential for mobbees to bring cases of mobbing and organizational coercion to INAIL remains, for the moment, even more limited. The court ruling only recognized bodily suffering as a result of specific, intentional actors, not as a result of the generalized conditions of labor, and therefore nearly evacuated the potential for workers to trace their faulty health to the broadly defined organization of labor, which, in part, included neoliberalizing forms of rupture, ambivalence, and precariousness. What the state would now recognize was an accountable social actor, a singular body or individual, who injures or causes harm to another worker. This ruling thus stayed within the welfare state tradition of work-related illness and harassment as being traceable to chemicals, equipment, or individuals.

The ruling raises the fundamental question of who should be held accountable for the effects of the precariousness of labor. By nullifying OCP, the court safeguarded the interests of employers because the OCP diagnosis would have rendered employers legally accountable to workers in a new way: they would have been held responsible for the psychophysical effects created by the organization of work. Still, INAIL is also a state organ. Thus, on one hand, the diagnosis by INAIL, a state public health agency, allowed this agency to deflect worker compensation costs to employers who did not adequately protect workers' health. On the other hand, the judicial branch of the state disputed which entity should be held more accountable (state insurance agencies or employers) in compensating workers' ill health and ruled in favor of employers and against the actions of INAIL, the state's own public health institution.

As this ruling unmasked the state as a paradoxical entity, the possibility for subjects to critique neoliberalism was both promoted and curtailed at the same time. Debates about withering or mounting state sovereignty with respect to globalizing orders and economies (Held and McGrew 2003; Strange 2003; Clark 2003; Gilpin 2003) tend to overlook the significance and implications of simultaneous and internal divisions within a single governmental apparatus. How mobbing is managed by the state allows us to see the ongoing friction between the protection and precariousness of labor and bodies. The origins and circulation of mobbing illuminate how the seemingly hegemonic neoliberal mode of production, given Italy's splintered political history and cultural landscape, is not a one-way force opposing workers. Rather, the idea of mobbing reflects the simultaneous and sometimes opposing cultural production of both capitalists and workers, state authorities and citizens.

In order to promote awareness of mobbing, the authors of *Mobbing: Reflections on the Skin* (Ascenzi and Bergagio 2002) include a variety of anti-mobbing slogans in the appendix, including "Mistreating other people is always dangerous. At work, it can be deadly!" (90), and "Mobbing increases the use of drugs, alcohol, smoking, [and the rate of] homicide and suicide" (96). The authors explicitly reference mortality in their discussion of mobbing, illness, and suffering: there is potential for the loss of life. By analyzing how mobbing has become medicalized, we see that multiple kinds of precariousness collapse into the idea of the at-risk body. This is a dynamic meeting point, a traceable fusion between the concrete manifestations of neoliberal capitalism and bodily suffering and mortality. These are processes of cultural legibility and visibility: mental anguish becoming visible on the skin, the perception of the pathological aspects of new workplace regimes, and the recognition of political subjectivities channeled through bodily realms. The duality of OCP in its effects for citizens, allowing new claims yet inviting new controls, is matched by the duality of the Italian welfare state: simultaneously protecting and limiting laborers' rights.

6   The Sex of Mobbing

On the top floor of an old university building on a December day in 2004, the typical northeastern Italian fog hung so low that the windows were obscured by clouds. Inside, unlike the seemingly apathetic fog, I found the mood to be slightly tense. Eight women working in various professional capacities, from student to professor to technical assistant to attorney, were training to become mobbing counselors. Our guest lecturer for the day, a visiting psychologist and mobbing specialist, had distributed a case study for everyone to read and discuss.

Forty-year-old Maria, an assistant professor at a research university, had been collaborating with a full professor, Sandro, on research projects and publications for scientific journals for the past year. A few months after she began, Sandro began complimenting her regarding her physical appearance, calling her "sweetheart [*tesoro*]," and maintaining physical closeness when they worked together. He also made sexual allusions and innuendos while they were together that made Maria feel extremely nervous and uncomfortable. During a weekend conference, Sandro openly sexually propositioned Maria, and she refused his advances. At first he seemed to accept her decision. But upon their return to the university, he began confiding in various colleagues that he had serious doubts about the quality of Maria's work. Aspects of a project that had been handled by Maria were reassigned to other colleagues in their department, and, quite unexpectedly, he removed her name from their joint publication. Maria has begun to worry what she did that provoked him.

On the bottom of the handout were three questions: "(1) What else would you need to know about Maria's case? (2) What kinds of solutions would you propose? (3) How would you act in order to reach the predetermined goals of the staff?"

In this pedagogical moment, the psychologist had positioned us as figures of authority on mobbing. This initially provoked some discomfort in the group. The women present had expressed their commitment to the idea that they were a "listening clinic [*sportello d'ascolto*]" rather than a clinic (*sportello*) in that the former would focus on offering support and professional references for incoming visitors, while the latter suggested a well-trained staff specialized in counseling techniques. In that session, however, we were invited to examine Maria's case and adopt, if temporarily, the subject position of mobbing counselor and its accompanying moral orders, affective dispositions, and responsibilities.

After reading Maria's case, Tina, a woman in her fifties, exclaimed, "How typical [*normale*]! Just today, I saw something like it." The other women nodded and muttered in agreement. The way in which the term *normale* is often evoked in Italian not only means an everyday commonness, but also implies a sense of the expected, as if to say, "Obviously."[1] The discussion revolved around how Maria was being mobbed because of her refusal to agree to a sexual relationship with her colleague. The practices of unwanted sexual attention were distinguished from the later events that resulted in Maria's removal from the project. The women in training discussed various possible solutions that could safeguard Maria's academic career and that would allow her to avoid having to publicly denounce the professor, including requesting a job transfer and initiating a direct but private confrontation with Sandro. Tina commented that whatever Maria decided, it had to be done with "cleverness [*furbizia*]." Tina's proposed strategy of *furbizia* was that Maria's confrontation center on mobbing, rather than on sexual harassment. Cleverness, in this sense, suggested that Maria strategically marshal a valuable piece of cultural knowledge: that mobbing would save her from the stigma and moral scrutiny of a sexual harassment charge. Tina's suggestion became the group consensus with little further debate.

Using this case, we were asked to reframe how women negotiate their rights as workers and citizens, by imagining a collectivity of mobbees, not victims of sexual harassment. The counselors framed mobbing as a viable strategic option to negotiate a woman's role within the workplace and to call upon state and supranational governance in the process. Maria's case was a pedagogical instantiation of how social actors in Italy increasingly view mobbing and sexual harassment as two highly intertwined events. But this commingling of workplace violations is not without a notion of ranking, nor without erasure, both of which are sustained by culturally specific understandings of sexuality, bodies, and gender. Sexual harassment has increasingly been slotted as a precursor or cause of mobbing in mobbing-specialized discourse and in public debates, creating the conditions for Maria's case to be handled as it was. Yet the relationship between sexual harassment and mobbing in Italy is more than simply causal: it is hierarchical and governed by moral and gendered orders that are culturally specific. Unlike sexual harassment (*molestie sessuali*), mobbing has become a political modality that passes as a gender-blind form of harassment, but never fully (La Stampa 1999b). A great deal of social, cultural, and legal work has taken place in Italy for sexual harassment to have become both a separate category on its own and yet still folded within the landscape of mobbing.

Based on the legal histories of sexual harassment and mobbing, workers' bodies were, by and large, understood as physically and mentally endangered by mobbing but not, or at least not as often, by sexual harassment. Even though mobbing was considered a profoundly psychological phenomenon and a morally abject form of harassment, it nonetheless became far more deeply connected to violations of "bodily integrity" than sexual harassment. Claims of sexual harassment expose a basic paradox of social democratic citizenship: they interrupt the apparent seamlessness of the rights of citizenship for workers that were predicated, in the Italian case, on safeguarding male workers' white bodies (Horn

1994; Ginsborg 2003), not female bodies with sexual desires and agency (Bassi 1993; Yanagisako 2002) nor Italy's ethnic and racial minority classes, who were not recognized as full citizens (Cole 1997; Krause 2001; Ardizzoni 2005; Gilbert 2007). It is necessary, then, for mobbing to be both loosely defined and seemingly race- and gender-neutral in order for it to become a privileged site for managing worker-citizenship and navigating the affective apparatus of attending neoliberal regimes. The process of producing a notion of mobbing as free of gender, race, and sex, however, necessarily entails the erasure of dominance over the gendered and racialized bodies of workers (Salzinger 2000; Mascia-Lees and Sharpe 2000; Zippel 2006). Thus, we find a paradox in that mobbing claims, progressive in their aim to correct injustices against workers, nonetheless render forms of structural violence invisible. Still, mobbing, as a discourse that passes as neutral, may indeed create a broader nexus of social support and economic assistance for women and ethnic minorities with respect to sexual harassment. One of the primary ways that mobbing distinguishes itself from sexual harassment is through the attribution of a subject's desire. In cases of mobbing, male and female workers are assumed to fall victim to the greedy desires of others to usurp or eliminate them: they are the victims of complex and sophisticated desires for advancement, capital, and status. Alternatively, victims of sexual harassment, who are almost exclusively female, are seen as producing "natural" male desires: they are cast as the sexualized victims, or occasionally as scheming participants, of an unrestrainable male body. Against the mobber's self-serving and calculated desire to harm and control material resources, the sexual harasser is imagined as willed by his body, which is ungovernable and unmanageable. Desire as an "affective attachment" (Povinelli 2006: 178), or even desiring desire itself, has become a central mode of producing and differentiating subjectivity across numerous contexts (Ahearn 2003; Kulick 2003; Boellstorff 2007; Biehl and Locke 2010). Mobbing, and the way it is stubbornly differentiated from sexual harassment yet covertly sexualized, provides a way to better understand the role of desire in the creation of late capitalist subjectivities.

Sexual Harassment Law in Italy

The history of sexual harassment in Italy has been shaped by the supranational governance of the European Union.[2] The problem of sexual harassment gained greater public attention in Europe in the 1970s and 1980s, coinciding with an increase in female participation in the labor market (Gregory 2000). In this period, member states began to investigate gender relations in the workplace and to devise ways to safeguard women's role in the labor market. The issue became important in both legal and public debates, as more European states published studies and crafted workplace comportment regulations. Visibility for the issue rose in the 1980s: a German women's magazine published a study in 1981 indicating that 59 percent of secretaries said they were sexually harassed; in 1983 the first guidelines, "Sexual Harassment: The Impact of EU Law in the Member States," were published in Britain, and the Belgian state conducted a nationwide survey on the matter in 1984 (Gregory 2000). By 1991, the European Commission had adopted a recommendation to protect "dignity" at work, defining sexual harassment as "unwanted, unreasonable and offensive to the recipient" (ibid.: 180). This marked a political and legal shift as the behavior was defined by the *recipient's* definition of offensive, whereas previous discussion had focused on whether harassers knew that their behavior was offensive. After the 1991 ruling, member states could adopt their own legal codes. But there was not yet urging on the part of the European Union to legally consider sexual harassment with sex equality and discrimination laws; there was only encouragement to pass laws against sexual harassment, which Italy did in 1996 (Zippel 2006: 18).

Within Italy, sexual harassment cases are fraught with cultural understandings of gendered subjectivity because they pivot around the question of sexual desire. Legal decisions frame Italian women as social actors always already desiring sexual attention and Italian men as endlessly battling their uncontainable desire for women.

In 1998, Italy's highest court ruled in favor of a man who had grabbed his female employee and attempted to kiss her lips only to miss and kiss her cheek. The Supreme Court ruled that sexual acts were only those "directed towards an erogenous zone" (Court of Cassation, sent. no. 6651, April 27, 1998) and thus, this act was not accorded recognition as a form of harassment or molestation because only the lips, not the cheeks, are erogenous, regardless of where he originally intended to kiss her (Corriere della Sera 1998). State decisions govern a specific sexualized body, whose predetermined erotic landscape shapes what may be legally punishable by law. Despite the European Union's urging to consider what is offensive to the recipient, the Italian court upheld the importance of the accused harasser's intentions; similar logics extend to cases of violent sexual assault. The Court of Cassation infamously ruled against a woman in a 1998 rape case because she was wearing tight jeans (Zippel 2006: 106). The court proposed that the woman's perpetrator could not have removed her jeans on his own, suggesting that this served as evidence that she could not have been raped: "We must consider that it is a fact of common experience that it is nearly impossible to remove jeans on another person without the wearer's active cooperation" (Court of Cassation, November 6, 1998, in Van Cleave 2005: 448). The case completely foreclosed the possibility that a woman could be raped even if she "voluntarily" removed her own clothing. The state put into effect an ideology of sexual violence based on the presumed and naturalized liability of women's sexual personhood: a woman's dress or comportment, if read by a man as sexual, is likened to her willing desire and thus consent.

Italian courts have a legacy of such rulings, influenced by Catholic and fascist ideologies that have upheld a regime of women's virtuous virginity and the need for men's patriarchal authority and sociosexual decency (Spackman 1996).

Until the 1990s, rape was considered a more serious crime when a woman was married because it was considered an offense to her husband: her body was relegated as secondary, ancillary, to her husband's "honor." Under fascist law, a man who killed his female relatives or wife to save the family honor was eligible for a penalty reduction. Much of the women's movement in the 1970s worked to establish rights for women against the state's control of the reproductive body and familial patriarchal authority (Horn 1994): divorce was legalized in 1970 and abortion was legalized in 1974 (Gregory 2000: 106).

Sexual harassment case law, in many ways, fails to diverge from the pernicious gendered regime present in Italy's state codes. In 2001, Italy's Supreme Court ruled against a woman whose male superior had swatted her on the bottom because the pat was "isolated and impulsive [*isolata e repentina*]" (Court of Cassation, sent. no. 623, January 23, 2001). Calling it "an act of libido," the court's ruling was premised on the supposed voracity of the man's unmediated sexual will rather than the coercive gendered relation between him and his employee (Zippel 2006: 106). Such high-profile rulings mirror and, in turn, generate and reproduce cultural understandings of men's sexuality as driven by unruly desires. Meanwhile, the courts continue to privilege and protect women if they have shown a sense of sexual innocence, while punishing those who exhibit any form of sexual agency and desire. Italy's highest court, for example, ruled in 2003 that molesting a young girl is more serious if she is a virgin (Court of Cassation, sent. no. 12007).[3]

In 2002, the European Union issued a new directive that construed sexual harassment as a form of discrimination in violation of the principle of equal treatment under the law (Directive 2002/73/EC). In addition, corporate agencies or institutions would be held legally responsible to show that all measures had been taken to prevent sexual harassment (Zippel 2006: 83).[4] Thus, the European Commission shifted toward the prevention of sexual harassment rather than simply building sanctions against it. The directive required that member states adopt their own similar legislation by the end of 2005. The Italian version of the equal treatment law considers sexual harassment to be a form of gender discrimination, defining it as "unwanted conduct related to sex that takes place with the purposes or effect of affecting the dignity of the person and creating an intimidating, hostile, offensive or disturbing environment" (Decreto Legislativo 145/2005). Because sexual harassment is variable and centers on the victim's definition of the unwanted behaviors, equal treatment laws can be easily applied to other forms of experience that are equally elusive and hard to define, such as mobbing.

Moral versus Sexual Harassment as Mind versus Body

The unstable divergence of mobbing and sexual harassment has unfolded in two parts, both of which have been sustained in cultural, legal, and institutional realms. The first was the distinction between sexual harassment and mobbing, and the next shift was around the temporal order of the two: sexual harassment is constituted in medical and state discourses as a precursor to mobbing, which can result in its effacement. There has also been a third and simultaneous process, the establishment of a moral hierarchy between the two, where mobbing is seen as both an ethical and physically endangering affront to workers. The cumulative effect of these discursive practices is that mobbing emerges as a morally advanced, superior form of harassment and as suspiciously race- and gender-neutral. Sexual harassment becomes a morally backward practice that shows perpetrators not to have properly contained their natural bodies. The seemingly sex- and race-free discourse of mobbing forecloses the recognition of gendered and racial hierarchies in Italian society, while its neutrality, which is both silencing and enabling, allows the same politically marginalized subjects to denounce labor injustices.

The first phase, then, was ontological separation. Mobbing is a form of harassment and abuse not characterized by, though possibly containing, sexual innuendos or sexualized language. A psychologist quoted in a 1999 news article warned: "Mobbing is a phenomenon that doesn't exclude any work environment and doesn't distinguish between the sexes" (Ardù 1999). Beginning in the late 1990s, the term "moral harassment [*molestia morale*]" was also adopted as a gloss for mobbing by Italians (La Stampa 1999). The term appears to have originated with the work of French psychiatrist Marie France Hirigoyen, who wrote *Moral Harassment: The Perverse Violence of Daily Life* (*Le harcélement moral: La violenze peverse au quotidien*, 1998). Extending mobbing within the French sphere, Hirigoyen defined this harassment as "[a]ll abusive conduct, notably manifesting itself by behavior, words, acts, gestures, or writing that can harm the personality, dignity, or physical and psychic integrity of the person, put their employment at risk, or degrade their work climate" (Hirigoyen 1998, in Saguy 2003: 146). Notably, Hirigoyen emphasized, just as in Italy, the bodily endangerment of workers. In Italy, mobbing as a form of moral harassment is often qualified with definitions such as "psychological violence that produces effects for the health until it creates an authentic work-related illness" (La Stampa 1999a). Mobbing as moral harassment is thus represented as a psychological set of practices that produce physical or psychophysical ailments. In 2002, for example, an Italian newspaper article defined a French woman's "anti-mobbing" struggle as a "battle for the legal acknowledgment of . . . harassment that is not sexual, but a psychological type" (Corriere della Sera 2002a). I consistently found similar discussions of mobbing as mentally and physically disturbing, though not sexualized, in my mobbing and sexual harassment class and among mobbing professionals. Mobbing, unlike sexual harassment, articulates explicitly with morality, with the psyche, and with mental and physical wellness.

Behind this distinction between the moral and the sexual realms lingers not just a Cartesian understanding of the body as split from the mind, but a cultural and distinctly biological understanding that Italian male sexuality is centered in bodily realms. As is clear from Italian legal discourse, sexual harassment in Italy has been repeatedly hailed as an outgrowth—or mishap—of men's naturalized bodily desires. Mobbing thus became its own ontological category, increasingly separate from sexual harassment, and it became more fully associated with the mind, psychology, morality, and rationality. Sexual harassment became mobbing's more animalistic, inferior, and corporeal other.

Hiding within educational literatures on mobbing is also a progress narrative between older types of violence and more advanced forms of workplace violence: traditional versus modern. For example, the violence of mobbing, as compared to sexual harassment, is described as more subtle and sophisticated: "A psychological terror, a nerve war capable of transforming a simple worker into a victim" (Ardù 1999). As we have seen, the discourses of mobbing overlap with a constellation of meanings associated with late capitalism: mobbing discourse marshals the most symbolically drenched signs of white masculinity. Take, for example, the following historical and psychological overview of mobbing:

This phenomenon [of mobbing] is supported by positive images of men—[the] "manager" [or] executive capable of dispassionately managing the drowsiness of jet lag, who speaks English perfectly (actually, who *thinks* in English) and who gives orders from his Palm Pilot from one part of the world to another. Mobbing is the story of subjects who have lost their human identity, who know they are seduced by exciting company "benefits" designed for the customary endpoint of rendering their customary services to whoever pays them; who don't even know who their bosses are because their bosses don't have faces. (Nistico 2003)

The mobber in this passage is masculinized even though the victim of mobbing and the process itself remain, seemingly, gender-neutral. The mobber is figured as a distinctly cosmopolitan subject; the various commodities (Palm Pilots), skills (English speaking), and practices (travel) construct the mobber as white and masculinized: a mobile global citizen who is technologically savvy and commodity wielding. But what this discourse also enables is an identification of mobbers as desirably related to structures of dominance. Like the figure of the mobber, who is represented as a prototypical capitalist manager, the practice of mobbing describes the abusive work practices characteristic of neoliberal regimes of labor. For instance, the mobbee (*mobbizzato*) is "loaded up with marginal tasks [and] the assignment of impossible objectives, [given] useless assignments, drawn up on exaggerated disciplinary actions, [subject to the] declassification of duties, given excessive visits by fiscal agents, excluded from meetings" (Corriere della Sera 2003). Because of the convergence between the imaginaries of the white masculinized manager and the quintessential mobber, we can see how these work experiences, typical of mobbing, might become feminized or even racialized. At the same time that mobbing becomes moral and psychological harassment, it also becomes associated with all that is modern and masculinized, while sexual harassment remains a vestige of a supposedly primitive, female-associated bodily chaos. Mobbing's articulation with forms of historically specific late capitalist "advancement" animates its progress narrative: it has become the masculinized harassment of the neoliberal workplace. Sexual harassment's status as a purportedly lower form of harassment results in its becoming something that can be considered temporally causative and historically as prior to mobbing; in short, we see the archiving of the inferior as symbolic of and entrenched within the past.

Mobbing as Progress

Sexual harassment is considered a precursor of or prior to mobbing not only because of men's "advancement" and the advancement of capital, but also because of women's progress. One of the mobbing counselors at the clinic in Padua wanted me to meet two of her friends who had worked for CGIL, a left-wing trade union. In July 2005, I met Barbara Valentino and Diana Camillo for an informal chat about their impressions of how work had changed. Barbara had worked for over twenty-five years in the hiring department of CGIL; had helped workers in negotiating benefits and contract stipulations; and had also seen many workers who claimed to have been mobbed. I asked what she had seen done to the workers when they were mobbed. Barbara listed changing work schedules, transfers to other office locations, demotion or lower-level work responsibilities, and forced inactivity. But, she added: "Years ago, there was more sexual harassment, but women today are better equipped. Today, they attack your professionalism. Or they force you to take vacation even when you don't want to. . . . It's all psychological criticism, you fall into this [mobbing] mechanism."

Diana adhered to a widely circulated cultural understanding that mobbing was temporally later and higher in complexity than sexual harassment. For her, this seemed to derive from the fact that women would no longer tolerate sexual harassment, while mobbing, aimed at their psychological and moral integrity, could be more pernicious and dangerous.

What also distinguishes the discourse of mobbing from that of sexual harassment is that it can make culturally legible how women undercut other women in the workplace. Sexual harassment, by contrast, has been used almost exclusively to describe men's harassment of women in Italy. Diana told me: "Maybe I'm your boss and you're a woman and I'm a woman. But if you disturb something in me, then I'll do *anything* to eliminate you." Barbara nodded and passionately exclaimed: "Women are just terrible! You end up a hamster that everyone can unload on, everyone can insult. [They] feel . . . authorized to throw themselves onto you." Diana took a more serious tone: "Mobbing lets out the worst that we have inside of us." She added that her male colleagues mobbed people even at the union's office. Trade unions, in other words, were no safe haven. She shook her head, recalling that when she was the head of the sexual harassment division no male colleague would talk to her. Her authoritative position with respect to sexual harassment, at the institutional level, became the excuse for Diana's colleagues to marginalize her. Diana's description of mobbing as letting out the worst provides great insight into how this relatively new way of describing people's comportment resonates with a notion of the human as corruptible by collective forces. The act of collective harassment reflects the idea of an unmediated human interiority that can harm and devastate others, if it is not disciplined and quelled. For Barbara, mobbing is a kind of debasement that transforms the human into the less than human: the hamster.

The Politics of Erasure

Even with the work done to distinguish these two forms of abuse, it is important to be cognizant that this is not in any way a seamless narrative: sex cannot be extracted out of mobbing. In other words, if sexual harassment can purportedly cause mobbing, then it is quite difficult to sustain a narrative of mobbing as a gender-neutral or asexual harassment, yet these are the two dominant discourses. For example, an Italian review of the American film *Secretary* (2002) calls the sadomasochistic love affair between a boss and his secretary "company mobbing between perversion and true love" (Nepoti 2003). Mobbing is overtly sexualized when women are viewed as capable of inciting the desires of their apparently psychologically complex and Machiavellian persecutors.

The majority of articles on this subject do indeed describe mobbing as gender-neutral, yet closer investigation reveals the fragility of this claim (ANSA 2004a). A report may dub mobbing gender-neutral, right before providing additional information that reveals it affects more women than men (ANSA 2004b).[5] One news article states that gender-blind mobbing impacts men and women equally; only later does the article admit that women are actually *twice* as likely to report being mobbed than men, considering their employment levels (ANSA 2005a). Another mobbing study indicated that while only 5 percent of women admit to being sexually harassed, one in three admits to having experienced some form of mobbing, and 55 percent say that sexual harassment is "the worst part of mobbing" (ANSA 2005b). What this reveals is that mobbing as a cultural signifier is just gender-neutral enough to cloak accusations of gendered and sexualized behaviors. Mobbing's sexualized core rests on the idea of deployed sexuality as a means for further marginalization, not on sexuality as part of a worker's subjectivity. It is more morally abhorrent and base in this form because the sexualization is construed as coming not from the spontaneous bodily desires of men, as in sexual harassment cases, but from their precise, mental calculations.

It is precisely because sexualized abuse has come to be viewed as an antecedent of mobbing that subjects are able to adopt mobbing as an overarching cultural term for cases that may have once been named as solely sexual harassment. Scholars who have studied sexual harassment have been troubled by what is behind the popularity of mobbing. Mobbing in Germany creates the conditions for the cultural erasure of "power differentials between men and women" (Zippel 2006: 220). Sociologist Abigail Saguy found that "moral harassment" in France was often represented as "devoid of any discussion of discrimination, sexism or sexuality" (2003: 128). Saguy points out that moral harassment also avoids the trappings of what the French see as the "American excesses" of sexual harassment, a point that holds true in the Italian context as well (ibid.: 13). Saguy explains that European feminists often find American feminists' concern with sexual harassment to be an outgrowth of a puritanical sexual ethos, preventing women from expressing (heterosexual) sexual desire and from claiming sexual agency. Similarly, Italian women would often tell me that sexual harassment in the United States seemed to deny that women may desire to be desired by fellow employees. It seemed that they viewed American definitions of and policies against sexual harassment as something that would forestall compliments about women's beauty or bodies and exchanges that they saw as pleasurable affirmations of their sexual desirability (and, hence, gender identity). In my course on mobbing and sexual harassment at the University of Padua, the sexual harassment instructor quipped that when one of her male employers grabbed her bottom, she realized that she "wasn't half bad-looking." Though this was clearly ironic, this type of humor resonates in Italy because femininity, by and large, is articulated with positioning these actions as desirable, even when their problematic outcomes are recognized.

Women may gain certain social, legal, and economic benefits, however, by deploying the term *mobbing* and by exploiting the many resources dedicated to moral harassment within Italy. Examining sexual harassment and mobbing in Germany, Kathrin Zippel has found that "judges have been more generous to victims of mobbing than to victims of sexual harassment, with significantly higher monetary awards" (2006: 188). According to Zippel, this may be because the mostly male judges find victims of mobbing to be more sympathetic while sexual harassers are assumed to be mistakenly prosecuted. Thus, losing the stigma related to victims of sexual harassment earns mobbees a greater chance of garnering welfare state benefits through the legal system (ibid.: 211). In Italy, mobbing, unlike sexual harassment, also gives worker-citizens an effective way to negotiate settlements with employers and avoid the presumptions about women's sexuality that undergird sexual harassment case law. How precisely this unfolds in Italy is linked to laws that safeguard the worker's body.

The Importance of Erasure and Health

Why mobbing nearly eclipses sexual harassment has much to do with an unusual twist in the laws in Italy protecting bodily integrity and health. Italians increasingly view mobbing as a national health problem. Workers rights center on the protections of bodily integrity, which are predicated on Article 2087 of Italy's Civil Code and, implicitly, upon the historical safeguards erected around the unmarked male industrial worker's body. By contrast, courts in Italy have rarely construed sexual harassment as body endangering. In 1991, as debates about sexual harassment increased in public discourse, one headline shouted, "Sexual Harassment May Have Devastating Effects on One's Health" (Il Sole 24 Ore 1991). In a sexual harassment case in 1993, the male boss had to pay 32 million lira (approximately US$16,000) to his secretary. The unnamed plaintiff's lawyer stated, "It is the first time in Italy that the biological damage [of sexual harassment] gets acknowledged" (La Stampa 1993). Like mobbing, the negativity of sexual harassment has emerged as a sign of disorder within bodily realms. But the subject disrupted by sexual harassment has a distinctly sexed body, unlike the notion of a gender-neutral body in mobbing.

The 1993 case was an exception to a cultural ideology that deems sexual harassment to be insufficient grounds for biological damages. In 1997, the Court of Cassation ruled against a woman suing for biological damages due to sexual harassment because her boss had "profound feelings" for her and thus "would not express violence, petulance or superficiality" (La Stampa 1997). In other words, men's sexual desire and amorousness strongly limited the possibility that actions based on these benevolent feelings could cause biological damage. The courts continue to understand women's sexual subjectivity in sexual harassment cases as necessarily desirous and consensual. It is this persistent conceptualization that makes sexual harassment incompatible with the notion of injured bodies and ill health: how could a subject desire her own injury?

Article 2087, requiring employers to safeguard the physical and psychological integrity of workers, has become the most commonly used law for mobbing cases. Indirectly, it has also altered how courts grapple with sexual harassment. In 1999, in the first legal case about mobbing, a tribunal court in Turin awarded biological damages to the employee (Il Sole 24 Ore 2002c). Importantly, this case, dubbed "a first for moral harassment," included sexual harassment as one of the precursors to full-fledged mobbing. A woman working in a plastic factory in the Turin-bordering city of Borgaro was put to work on a machine in a tightly enclosed space. The worker's boss asked her for sexual favors in exchange for her location transfer, and the factory worker began suffering from agoraphobia, anxiety, and depression (La Stampa 1999a). The judge awarded the plaintiff 10 million lira (US$5,000), recognizing that "the disturbance suffered by the woman provoked a reactive depressive syndrome" (ibid.). The effect of the ruling was to legitimate bodily harm if and only if it exceeds sexual violation and can be framed as mobbing.

The body violated by mobbing is understood as psychosomatic, experiencing psychological distress in tandem with physical effects. Another legal case involving three teachers in the region of Piedmont went up to a third court of appeals (sent. no. 19342, October 25, 2005). The teachers had sued their employer for damages after a year of mobbing and "moral violence" against them that caused severe anxiety and depression and necessitated the use of medical cures, antidepressants, and other pharmaceuticals. The judge upheld the first court's ruling (January 14, 2002) and quantified the degree of moral damage to be 15–18 percent; the teachers were awarded a total of €1,665 in addition to their legal expenses. The ruling extended the definition of mobbing as "harassment . . . with the consequence of gravely affecting the psychic equilibrium of the employee, reducing his/her work capacity and faith in oneself and provoking emotional catastrophe, depression and even suicide" (sent. no. 19342, October 25, 2005).

Mobbing is wholly embedded in a landscape of deep psychological pain and biological and physical trauma. Even as it is portrayed as a psychological form of abuse, its effects are registered on the body.

Mina's Story

I met Mina Zuberi in February 2005 at Fiore Montiglio's equal opportunity office and mobbing clinic. An Egyptian woman in her forties, Mina had been in Italy for over fifteen years and had become an Italian citizen. I saw that she had been living through a great deal of pain—there was a heaviness to her presence and she often wept while she told her story. Mina began by explaining how the hierarchy of the hotel was divided by gender: women at reception and men as bookkeepers, managers, and executives. In 2000, a new manager arrived, Bruno Sgarone, who, in Mina's estimation, wanted to get rid of the "old staff" in order to hire more men or, alternatively, younger women. This was apparent not only in Mina's narrative, but also in the narratives of several colleagues who came to Fiore's office. First, Bruno hired an additional male manager to control the all-female reception staff. Bruno criticized Mina on a daily basis and frequently referred to her as "the dirty Tunisian whore [*la sporca troia tunisiana*]" and sometimes "that black one [*quella nera*]." Even though Fiore pointed out the elements of sexual harassment and racial discrimination in these vicious comments, she eventually adhered to Mina's description of her case as one exclusively of mobbing.

Bruno also immediately cut the additional income that the reception staff made from the commissions they earned by referring clients to certain restaurants or service providers and through the hotel's monetary exchange service. Mina explained that, within the hotel business, various informal earnings were quite normal and mundane. For example, Mina and the other receptionists would add a small percentage to the exchange rate listed by the hotel for clients, a practice understood but apparently not publicly acknowledged by hotel management. For every transaction, they would make a small profit that would be divided among all the receptionists. Many economic transactions at the hotel were under the table (*in nero*), including tips and a variety of services, Mina contended.[6] Mina received additional commissions from transportation services and restaurants when clients arrived via her recommendation. Bruno decided that they would have to end these practices and instructed the other hotel employees to treat Mina and her colleagues at reception, Liza and Gabriela, as if they were "thieves." The marginalization and isolation created a disturbing work climate for Mina. The informal economic transactions between hotel clients and Mina became the basis for the hotel's case against her. The hotel's claim for economic transparency served as a convenient disguise for multiple and pernicious forms of employee abuse and, more gravely, gender and racial discrimination.

A few months after Bruno's arrival, Mina was asked to explain certain aspects of her bookkeeping to Bruno and an assistant manager. She described how Bruno accused her in a persecutory and humiliating way of faulty bookkeeping. The two managers also reminded her, in a way designed to degrade her, that "it takes a good head to manage finances." Mina felt like they were explicitly suggesting that her being a woman made her unable to perform these duties properly. Their threatening and angry accusations upset her greatly and she left work early. The next day, Mina went to the hospital with an acute anxiety attack; she was prescribed antidepressants and obtained permission from INAIL (Workers Compensation Authority) for two months of sick leave. Mina told us that it was INAIL that had first verified that her case was one of mobbing. The hotel, following this event, formally charged Mina with leaving the work premises without permission and accused her of dishonest financial management. Management claimed that her unannounced departure, not following protocol, made her ineligible for sick leave benefits. The hotel also hired lawyers who filed a brief stating that Mina's response was due to the fact that she "already suffered from nervous and emotional disturbances." By seeking to establish Mina as an *already* mentally unstable and weak-bodied individual, the hotel management was trying an additional strategy to make her ineligible for paid sick leave. (Mina won the original case, but the hotel appealed the decision and the case as of August 2010 was still pending.)

Once Mina returned to work after her sick leave, she was no longer permitted to continue her bookkeeping duties. Bruno hired a few young men in their twenties to work at reception, and they would systematically criticize and humiliate her. Mina and her original reception colleagues, all of whom were women, on Bruno's orders had their passwords to the hotel computer deactivated and thus no longer had access to the electronic reservation system or any digital information. Mina told us that she, Gabriela, and Liza were rarely left without one of the new male hires, who would serve as a strict supervisor. Mina was deeply troubled by these events and described deep depression and anxiety. She was only able to endure because of the support of her son and her psychotropic medication. At this point, she began visiting local mobbing centers and asking for advice.

In January 2005, Bruno died suddenly of a stroke. I had heard this news in the local mobbing clinic run by Dora and Lidia months before I actually met Mina, as she had initially visited them. Their initial reaction was jubilation, reflected in Lidia's comment to me that Bruno's horrific treatment of Mina and her colleagues had made him "better dead than alive." But Bruno's untimely death changed the course of Mina's legal action. Since he could no longer be charged personally, the hotel would have to be charged, making the case more complex. But even without Bruno, the daily hostilities continued. In March,

Mina said, one of the new reception managers screamed at her for speaking to a client and accused her of stealing money from the register. She was then fired because one of the reception managers said Mina had "threatened" him after the incident. Sara, a colleague who told Fiore and me her version of the story, heard that Mina had "provoked" the manager. In response to his question asking where she was going, Mina had responded, according to Sara: "To the bathroom. I have my period. Do you want to come?" It was this comment, Sara said, that caused the manager to lose his patience and fire Mina. The day after this episode, Mina received a certified letter immediately terminating her contract and describing her behavior as "threatening, outrageous, and insubordinate." Before coming to the mobbing clinic, Mina had first gone to the trade union CGIL, which sent a letter to the hotel citing her case as mobbing and requesting moral and biological damages.

Mina's lawyer explained that he was still building the case of mobbing because he had to prove the connection between Mina's poor health and her work environment. INAIL had acknowledged Mina's case, in particular based on the documents from her visit to the emergency room, as work-related illness. But, he said, "They changed their minds," though it was not clear to me why her case was deemed ineligible. Her lawyer concluded that, in order to press charges for mobbing and biological damages according to Article 2087 of the Civil Code, he had to first dispute INAIL. Fiore, however, urged him to find sufficient evidence to prove that Mina was mobbed. Thus, Mina's compromised psychophysical integrity became the centerpiece of her legal and political subjectivity as a mobbee. Mobilizing her identification as a victim of sexual harassment would preclude the legal course of action around her health. These processes were highly dependent on the idea of mobbing as body endangering and on the role of INAIL in codifying OCP.

Mina's case is layered with several vectors of structural violence and ongoing and systematic marginalization, rife with situations that could be named as sexual harassment, gender and racial discrimination, and mobbing. But what I found was that Mina and Fiore; Fiore's lawyer, Lina; and Mina's lawyer handled and discussed Mina's case solely as mobbing. One of the primary frames that shaped the way in which the various actors saw this case was health. For Mina, the ongoing stress and persecution at work accumulated and resulted in psychosomatic symptoms, as verified by the state health institution INAIL. The state agency thus played an important role in Mina's case by intervening in the recognition of mobbing vis-à-vis her medically documented biological trauma and the award of sick leave. But Mina also experienced the double violence of being called a "whore" and "the black one" by Bruno and the secondary violence of erasure when these practices were included in the seemingly neutral category of mobbing. Not only did the discourse and precedents hold that racial and sexual harassment are unrelated to health but, more critically, they created a set of conditions in which discrimination failed to be fully recognized. Mina was thus disproportionately and doubly marginalized: both the conditions of cultural legibility and the structure of the local labor law, designed for Italian male bodies, worked against her. That Mina's employment termination followed her candid mentioning of menstruation bears great significance, that is, she was eliminated at the moment when she made visible what her employers and, indirectly, the state rendered either problematic invisible: her sexualized body.

Given the severity of the case, Fiore asked to speak with Mina's colleagues, her lawyer, and the new hotel director. One by one, hotel employees came to speak with me and Fiore over the course of the next several weeks. Overall, I was struck by the consistencies among the various interviewees and the extent to which they attested to Mina's narrative. I will detail a few of the narratives in order to convey the fierce and profoundly gendered hostility present in this workplace and to examine why the case did not become a gender discrimination suit.

Betta Casellato was a waitress in the hotel, working on an indefinite time contract offered by Bruno. When she began working, Bruno asked Betta to bring coffee to his private room where she found him wearing nothing but a bathrobe. He asked her to bring the tray to his bedside and proceeded to compliment her, telling her she was beautiful, that she "drove him crazy [*fa impazzire*]" and that "he could give her things her husband could not." Here, the notion of "driving him crazy" refers to him losing control of his reactions and his emotional responses to her. He touched her, exposing himself. This behavior continued, though Betta said she would steer clear of the bedside, bring his tray, and quickly leave the room. She also felt criticized and humiliated by the head waitress, who seemed to Betta to have been specifically authorized by Bruno to mistreat her. One day, the head waitress pushed a tray into her on purpose and with that, Betta quit. Afterward, Mina told us, Bruno referred to Betta as "the woman who took it in the ass [*la donna che dava il culo*]." Betta had no legal case pending against the hotel.

Gabriela Cumerlato, a woman in her early forties, worked at reception with Mina. After suffering a major back injury, Gabriela could no longer work standing up. One day, Gabriela recounted, the chairs and stools in the reception area had mysteriously disappeared. Bruno told her that he could not put any chairs or stools near the reception desk, as it would look "unprofessional." However, he added, he would be happy to transfer her to Turin, a city on the western coast of Italy, or Sardinia, an island west of mainland Italy. He refused her request to work as a hotel operator, where she could remain seated, and instead hired a twenty-five-year-old woman. Her request for two half-shifts rather than a full eight-hour shift were also denied. Gabriela wrote to SPISAL (Servizio di Prevenzione, Igiene e Sicurezza negli Ambienti di Lavoro; Agency for Prevention, Hygiene and Safety at Work) and requested that it document her physical difficulty and the absence of adequate facilities at the hotel. She rotated through periods of work, sick leave, and vacation time for the next several months. Gabriela, like Mina, confirmed that Bruno had hired young male managers at the reception desk who continually spoke about sex, making them all feel very uncomfortable. Gabriela told us how her male colleagues would talk incessantly about women, saying, "All women are whores," and continuously commenting on women's bodies—"What an ass!" "What tits!" "Nice pussy!"—during their shifts. Gabriela continued to work with intermittent sick leaves until December 2005, when she resigned. Her letter, detailing how her physical condition made it impossible for her to work without proper accommodations, was central to her severance case. After hearing her story, Fiore began to talk about a collective mobbing case, pointing to the compromised bodily integrity of both Mina and Gabriela. A collective gender discrimination case was discussed briefly, but mobbing remained the preferable claim.

Liza Panzini gave an account that paralleled Mina's and Gabriela's, though she remained employed at the hotel. Liza had also experienced what she identified as mobbing in that she felt deeply isolated by the new workers, who refused to speak or collaborate with her, Gabriela, or Mina. She told us: "I was shocked at how soon it began." She even saw certain colleagues reprimanded when they did speak openly with the three women at reception, and Bruno instituted a new rule that no worker would be allowed to speak to anyone at the front office without his official permission. Both Mina and Liza described how their requests for shifts were almost always denied and that they were assigned new shifts that were inconvenient and different from their long-established schedules. The new male colleagues, however, not only had their preferred shifts but also had two consecutive days off. By law, workers must be given at least one day of rest for every seven working days, but Liza told us that she no longer was given consecutive days off. As Liza had requested day shifts so she could care for her ailing mother in the evening, she was forced to use additional leaves of absence to continue to attend to her family. Liza also said that her male colleagues would keep track of every time she went to the bathroom. She claimed that this record included when she had bowel movements, though she did not specify how this information was obtained. She also had a few direct confrontations with Bruno, who repeatedly asked her "why someone like her that made any man's head turn was wasting her time working at a place like this." Fiore pointed out that had the situation been reversed, and a man been propositioned by a woman, she would see that it was an offer for sex: "Such an offer implies a threat." Liza nodded and shrugged. Liza's narrative confirmed what Mina had told us: the hotel's administrators ruled by sexual menace and an overt surveillance of women's bodies. Violations of spatial boundaries, the staging of employer-employee contacts in the private spaces of bedrooms and bathrooms, were transgressions of bodily and moral boundaries.

Over the course of Bruno's management, Liza had obtained multiple prescriptions from her doctor to face the ongoing stress and her intensifying depression, including antidepressants, sleeping pills, and tranquilizers. However, Liza was one of the few that remained in her position and had not taken legal action. When she came to Fiore's office in July, she described how the new director, Luca Palta, had initiated a series of reforms and improvements: "I want to work in peace. I have no intention to press charges now." Her health, as a result, was improving and she was able to stop taking antidepressants but continued with sleeping pills. She said that Luca had joked that he can't even tell her that she has nice hair because she'd call it sexual harassment. Liza laughed: "He told me the hotel is in shit up to here!" holding her hand over her head and referring to his awareness that Mina's case was being investigated and that she had a lawyer. It was clear that Luca was able to obtain workers' loyalty despite highlighting the physical desirability of his female employees. By calling explicit attention to sexual harassment, he differentiated himself from Bruno, while also implying that sexual harassment stems from a man's overreaction to women's natural attractiveness.

Another colleague visited Fiore's office to give her account of what had happened to Mina, even though she had been absent on maternity leave for most of the period. She said: "The directors were happy to eliminate Mina. She was getting in the way, raising her own head." Fiore responded:

> Mina is a woman who didn't bow to others [*abbassare la testa*]. Because of strong jealousy, she was punished by other women. Women can do terrible things and are very jealous of each other on an unconscious level. Instead of admiring a woman like this, they asked: why is she getting ahead? Because she put herself in opposition to patriarchal law [*le leggi del padre*].

Fiore illuminated the deeper process of how Mina's isolation hinged upon gender deviance—a woman's refusal to accept patriarchal authority. Fiore was also pointing to the way in which other women, understood as jealous and competitive, were complicit not only in marginalizing Mina but also in patrolling gendered hierarchies. Even though most of Mina's harassment was by her male colleagues, Fiore was disappointed at Mina's female colleagues, like Liza, who did not openly defend and support Mina.

A Charged Encounter

In July 2005, I was with Fiore Montiglio for her meeting with the new hotel director, Luca, to discuss Mina's case and the ongoing legal suits. Though he had arrived after Mina left, he was now in charge of all hotel operations, including how the hotel would proceed with her case. Fiore and Luca's charged exchange about Mina offers insight into two culturally specific narratives that clash with one another: Fiore's understanding of gendered power, expressed through mobbing rather than sexual harassment, and Luca's mobilization of neoliberal logics and discourses. Workplace conflicts, with mobbing as a prime example, are deeply shaped by cultural understandings of late capitalism and the problem of labor and also undergirded by gender, generational, and racial hierarchies.

Luca Palta, a man in his early forties, entered Fiore's office with shining white teeth, an impeccably tailored, monogrammed suit, and his lawyer. Three of us sat opposite them: Fiore; the lawyer of the equal opportunity office, Lina; and I. After brief introductions, Luca began by saying that Bruno had come to the hotel with the intention to eliminate employees: "He was cutting, wanting fewer employees." Pausing, he reflected: "A hotel doesn't sell a product. Rather, it offers a very particular service." Luca's narrative moved abruptly between the hotel's downsizing and the hotel's relationship with a global economic market, something he did repeatedly throughout the conversation, which I found quite peculiar. Fiore reminded him sternly that there were other "modalities" one could use in order to make such changes, instead of using harassment and mobbing. Luca's lawyer remarked curtly that Mina had been the one who had threatened the reception manager. He then wondered if Mina was consuming some psychotropic medications: "I've lived through some troubles myself, frankly, but if I'm in some form of trouble, I deal with it." Fiore was both cross and serious: "These women don't *have* power." Taking up the framework of Mina's ill health, Luca attempted to make her moral claims about her illness illegitimate by emphasizing her pharmaceutical consumption and supposedly prior instability. He, on the other hand, defined himself in ways characteristic of neoliberal orders, as a man whose health can be self-managed, his body governed by his own autonomous control, not by outside intervention.

Luca said again: "We don't sell screws or armchairs. We have services." I was struck by the sharp disjuncture between Fiore's response and Luca's move toward describing the hotel as an economic entity. Luca viewed Mina as a kind of troubled worker in the context of the hotel's challenging economic position since it produced no material product. It seemed that, for him, giving more information about the challenges of immaterial production worked as a justification for the challenge of managing immaterial labor. It was as if he assumed that, had they produced material objects, then the physical labor of employees would be easier to monitor and measure. Indeed, the manager's remarks only make sense within the logic that economic markets demand particular kinds of mental and affective labor and, undergirding this, certain kinds of calculating subjects. In defensively denying the charges, he was implying that immaterial workers are self-interested tricksters. This defense also works to position Bruno's treatment of Mina not as sexualized, but rather as a complex strategy to reappropriate capital from her. He maintained that his governing practices were subtle, coercive, and indirect, yet he denied they were abusive (which might then make his behavior be recognized as mobbing).

Fiore asked him about the unsupervised and undocumented commissions that Mina earned from recommendations of restaurants, stores, and car rentals to the hotel's clients. Luca responded: "I'm happy if my employees make a commission. It comes back to my hotel and I avoid having to raise salaries—it's an indirect return." By employing a bottom-line logic, Luca seemed to condone her actions, even though, in his next statement, he insisted that such arrangements could not be tolerated because they were not "transparent" financial transactions. Luca reported that Bruno had told him that it was "time to clean things up [*fare pulizia*]," suggesting the removal of "dirty" practices and persons. As Marilyn Strathern (2000b) has argued, transparency has become a uniquely twenty-first-century discourse which seems to promote ethical behavior yet also allows for invasive and highly regulatory policies. By aligning himself with the demand for transparency, Luca established a moral hierarchy between the hotel as an "open" financial establishment and Mina as a deceptive agent, while he also produced a racialized distinction: he was clean; Mina was dirty.

Referring to Mina, he added: "That woman cut us out [*Quella donna ci ha tagliato fuori*]."[7] Indexed specifically as a gendered subject (that woman), Mina, it seemed, had transgressed a field of economic relations reserved for men. Luca mobilized the hotel's main defense in Mina's case as a matter of fiscal responsibility: "Bruno blocked this flow [to her]. We admit he did this in a very harsh way. Naturally, [he was] rule abiding, but harsh. . . . So Mina rebelled against this." The lawyer agreed: "Mina called it abusive in order to do a bit of personal shopping." Luca positioned Mina as falling short of the ideal of open neoliberal labor regimes because of her self-interested deviations from transparency. Reading Mina as a rational and calculating subject, it followed that her mobbing claim was also merely a self-interested project of wealth accumulation. The defense, in short, was that she had to mobilize a workers compensation claim in order to make up for the hotel's having blocked her informal earnings.

Fiore was visibly outraged: "The bullshit is rising." She looked at the lawyer and referenced Luca: "Excuse my language, but there was a new *man* in power and we need to be attentive to this." The lawyer shook his head: "It doesn't matter whether he was a man or a woman—it was the same thing." Fiore, however, was not convinced: "Let's say the new director wanted some of these commissions? He couldn't accept that these women had this power and he tried to find excuses to eliminate them." Within this debate were two contradictory narratives to explain Mina's conflict at work. For Luca and his lawyer, it was a genderless narrative of a disgruntled employee who was morally undeserving of capital, especially considering the obstacles of a pinched service market. This explanation rests on the idea that the worker who shamelessly desires and coercively obtains more than her share deserves punishment—moral, social, economic. Luca was fusing mobbing claims with traditional, backward labor regimes and social practices, which for him were naturally antithetical to the orders of late modern capitalism. For Fiore, on the other hand, the contested behavior derived from gendered relations of power and Mina's transgression of specifically gendered norms: desiring capital, refusing submission. Fiore viewed the workplace as a collective environment that, once damaged and made precarious, alters the consciousness of workers and produces mistrust, fear, and ill health. Luca, on the other hand, seemed to view his employees as morally undeserving subjects in the context of the more important challenge of economic gain in the global service industry.

Fiore urged him to rehire Mina, but Luca firmly insisted that he had no such intentions. Luca maintained that Mina's "dishonesty" in accepting the informal commissions was contrary to the management's expectation to keep "everything in the light of day that beforehand was under the table." Hotel practices, predicated on neoliberal values of transparency and accountability, foregrounded the moral stance of the director against Mina (Best 2005). Revealing, however, that this view was undercut by gender ideologies, he also insisted that the commissions were Mina's way to control her women colleagues: "Forget about it with women [*tra donne non ne parliamo*]." Without an already prevalent gendered emotional regime in which women are cast as jealous and competitive, this comment would have little cultural legibility. He then detailed some of the other problems he faced as an executive of only three months, saying: "With all these legal cases, I'll have to admit to some form of damage. She says it's mobbing, but in my opinion, it's just trendy [*va di moda*]." Fiore told him fiercely: "There was mobbing. And how!" He replied flatly, "Mobbing isn't done [*Il mobbing non si fa*]."[8]

Luca's next statement revealed how the legal and epistemological framework of mobbing as a form of engaging with the state could be recast and devalued. "Employees," he said, "want compensation and it's hard to have them understand that justice doesn't exist. They are used to a tribal justice: workers compensation." Marshaling the notion of "tribal" justice, he framed mobbing as an inferior and lowly activity of the state, but even more significant, it is a term laden with gendered and racialized imaginaries of that which is backward and inferior, paralleling how Bruno had positioned Mina. Additionally, the use of the word *tribal* casts the notion of collective workers rights and the welfare state as traditional and antiquated, and it privileges the neoliberal order, situated between the autonomous subject and the market, as modern and superior. Mobbing cases, if increasingly associated with the tribal justice of undeserving—and mostly female—citizens, risk stigmatization and devaluation. Ironically, mobbing experts and counselors, though advancing the rights of labor and welfare state protections, comply with neoliberal orders by concealing how mobbing preys on already marginalized subjects and silently recreates pernicious social injustices.

The Body of Neoliberal Citizenship

The discursive distinction between mobbing as bodily endangerment and sexual harassment as an expression of the natural body has produced a set of discourses and practices that have altered the ways in which worker-citizens interface with the state and with each other. The kinds of verbal harassment and abusive practices experienced by Mina and her colleagues strongly fit the European Union's definition of sexual harassment as "unwanted conduct related to sex that takes place with the purpose of or effect of affecting the dignity of the person and creating an intimidating, hostile, offensive or disturbing environment" (Decreto Legislativo 145/2005). But the epistemological distinctions and the hierarchy between the two forms of violence in Italy shaped the outcomes and understandings of Mina's case. The uneven ranking of sexual harassment and moral harassment were confirmed and regenerated by various actors, many of them mobbing specialists.

Sexual harassment in Italy is viewed as written on the sexed bodies of citizens—the naturally alluring women and the uncontrollable urges of men—and prosecuting such cases fails to emerge as a way to legitimize workers' rights and their bodily and moral integrity. It is precisely the gender-neutral and race-neutral mythologies of mobbing that create an alternative site around which women can renegotiate their status as sexualized worker-citizens because of how mobbing moves away from the idea of workers as sexual citizens and gendered subjects.

The story of mobbing is a social history of what happens when one form of harassment emerges as something considered ethically superior to another and, in turn, becomes the dominant explanatory model for workplace conflict. Mobbing—moral harassment masquerading as a gender-neutral phenomenon—has become an ethical violation worthy of social support and institutionalization on both state and European levels, its victims worthy of social recognition. But when deploying mobbing as a means to dispute the gendered and sexualized abuses of the labor regime, subjects are called upon to mask their full legal and political subjectivities. Italian legal rulings enforce a regime of bodily endangerment premised upon a critical political imaginary of the citizen's masculinized white body.

Mobbing has gained cultural salience and legitimacy as something that puts male workers, upon whom Italy's social welfare has been built, at risk. At the same time, these discourses reflect and generate normative understandings of gender premised on the notion of citizen-subjects whose desires are dichotomous (men desiring women, women desiring desire). These processes work to maintain a male-dominated engagement with the state. By labeling mobbing victims as backward, traditional, and feminized, the figure of the mobbed worker is cast, legally and discursively, as incapable of surviving neoliberal labor regimes.

As social actors continue to slip sexual harassment under the cloak of mobbing, the narrative of mobbing as free of sexuality and gender may no longer be sustainable. If mobbing claims are cast as weapons of the weak—used by female, immigrant, and racialized workers—then the concept may lose its force as a convincing social, political, and legal modality for confronting the precariousness of neoliberal labor. In unraveling the paradox of the Italian state and, more broadly, other neoliberal modes of governance, we must attend to how what may seem to correct the malign effects of labor regimes may be simultaneously a tool for structural violence.

7   Project Well-Being

Italy never wanted a state. It has always been a land of communes and corporations.

—Umberto Eco (1994)

How does the subjection of desire require and institute the desire for subjection?

—Judith Butler (1997b)

"Protecting the health of the worker must be understood as their well-being [*benessere*] and not just as an absence of pathology" (Lavoro Oggi 2005). In 2005, two years after the official recognition of a mobbing-caused work-related illness, Italy's Workers Compensation Authority (INAIL) publicized a message to health institutions to focus on well-being, not pathology. A concentration on well-being as a key objective for the workplace was not limited to this institution. Rather, there was a more enduring change in the management of mobbing—and labor regimes—in Italy as the focus switched toward the promotion of good health rather than resolution of work harassment or conflicts. In October 2006, for instance, the region of Lazio together with the province of Frosinone co-funded a conference called "Mobbing: Educating Yourself for Prevention." Medical professionals attended panels such as Preventing Mobbing: The Role of the Occupational Doctor, Mobbing's Psychological Damage, Legal Medicine, Mobbing and Safeguards, Organizational Well-Being, and Corporate Conduct Codes.

What kinds of new cultural practices and understandings are generated by a politics of promoting workers' health as opposed to eliminating what is believed to endanger it? The notion of organizational wellness extends medical intervention in the workplace to both "healthy" and "unhealthy" workers; it also positions institutions, not just individuals, as capable of wellness or illness. When occupational psychologist Mariella Mazzuchi told me in early 2005, "Everything's moving toward well-being [*benessere*]," she confirmed my growing sense that the healthy workplace and its ethos of worker wellness had become a new and seductive narrative in the mobbing industry. This suggested that prevention and well-being were the foundational tropes around which a new kind of health risk regime of laboring worker-citizens was being assembled. These notions are also central to the project of creating a class of expert professionals who mediate between worker-citizens and the state and who are authorized to prescribe a healthy workplace. Mobbing prevention programs could enable new structures of power for experts who deploy, as Nikolas Rose has suggested, "know-hows of enumeration, calculation, monitoring, evaluating" and who "manage to be simultaneously modest and omniscient, limited yet apparently limitless in their application to problems" (Rose 1996: 54). Medicalizing individual workers is a step toward applying biomedical expertise, ethics, and knowledge to assess neoliberal work regimes; we find the sanitization of labor relations shifted to the purview of medical experts.

The new illness category of organizational coercion pathology, which refigured cultural understandings and state structures of occupational illness under neoliberal conditions, was itself dependent upon the understanding that the organization of labor was endangering the bodies of workers. When OCP was recognized, mobbing was defined in terms of its potentials and risks in creating psychophysical pathologies in workers. Moreover, the causal conditions for this bodily harm were largely attributable to loosely defined work practices and the organizational conditions created within neoliberal economic regimes. In other words, the generalized workplace and work practices were pathologized rather than a "perverse" individual mobber. The paradox of OCP lies in the fact that worker-citizens, while able to make new claims based on medical evidence of bodily harm from work conditions, were also subject to a new series of medical controls to verify and measure their biological disruptions. These modes of worker regulation were indicative of a form of governmentality in which the Foucauldian notion of biopower, bodily and intimate management, met the neoliberal ethos of risk: "Governing through risk therefore means . . . [that subjects] are encouraged to conduct themselves in the most beneficial ways to their health, wealth and happiness in ways that are rational, self-interested and calculating" (Isin 2004: 220). Though I have examined this mode of governance in relation to the treatment of OCP, I also have resisted reading the process of neoliberalization in Italy as complete and all-encompassing. Rather, I see it as something that subjects anticipate and apprehend as in-process, as something yet-to-be entrenched and normative. Historical and contemporary processes and apparatuses within occupation health continue to interrupt Italy's neoliberal refashioning.

Unlike the containment of OCP, plans to minimize workplace health risks and develop "organizational well-being [benessere organizzativo]" are future-oriented and broad in scope. The promotion of organizational well-being demands that Italian workers imagine how workplaces should be and that they evaluate what may happen tomorrow—a mapping, in other words, not only of risk, but of potentiality. As opposed to risk, which signifies a possible or probable hazard or loss, the term potentiality highlights outcomes and possibilities (Ong 2006b) and the chance of a positive effect, which well-being promises. While there may be a risk of mobbing, there is also the potential for safeguards and health. In turn, safeguards and health suggest the affective possibility of tranquility, happiness, and hope. Unveiling Italian plans to prevent mobbing and promote well-being exposes how social actors imagine and seek to contain anticipated dangers and yet also how they maximize safeguards and promote ease within the neoliberal workplace. The ethics of organizational well-being that have materialized in Italy are also a moral lens through which mobbing, labor, and political subjectivity ought to be viewed.

The apparatus built around promoting well-being, for Italians, relies on the promise of decreasing precariousness (*precarizzazione*), which has become a highly desirable outcome only in the context of its intensifying scarcity. It is not coincidental that stable, lifelong work is promoted as something vital and always already healthful, at the moment it has become something increasingly rare. Precisely as precariousness alienates and devalues labor, the promise of investment in workers seems most persuasive and can command profound compliance. Though the notion of preventing mobbing seems to be a gesture of protection for the worker, the careful monitoring of workers' "risk factors" exploits worker-citizens' desire for and nostalgia about an engaged and centralized welfare state.

From Risk to Potential

Preventive medicine, from its inception, was deeply articulated with Western imperialist projects and capitalist development in diverse cultural and historical localities (Porter and Porter 1988; Doyal 1995; Manderson 1999). Examining the shift toward body vigilance at the level of the population as opposed to individualized care in nineteenth-century France, Foucault emphasized: "Does [medical experience] not involve, because of the special attention it pays to the individual, a generalized vigilance that by extension applies to the group as a whole? It would be necessary to conceive of medicine sufficiently bound up with the state for it to be able . . . to carry out a constant, general, but differentiated policy of assistance" (1973: 19). Foucault showed how medicine switched from a governance of pathology to a governance of normality (ibid.: 35), which "embraced a knowledge of healthy man, that is, a study of non-sick man and a definition of the model man" (34). This insight captures a critical process that applies to the study of contemporary prevention regimes. Italian preventive medicine in the workplace is a fusion of two kinds of normative models: the healthy body and the healthy workplace. The cultural and historical distinction between "model man" and "model worker" may actually help to clarify how certain health and state regimes are created and expanded in the Italian context. It was precisely at the moment when the Italian workplace was deeply pathologized, imagined as something that causes psychological and bodily harm, that a prevention regime could be assembled. Indeed, prevention intensified around the healthy worker just when the "healthy man" seemed most disarticulated from full-time regular employment. While one regulating technique focuses on measuring the sickness, another shifts the analytical center toward the capacity for good health and a good life.

Emergent within Italy are forms of governance that utilize prevention as a way to manage populations through the discourse of future capacities and potentials. Techniques of liberal governmentality mobilize uncertainty: "A characteristic modality of liberal governance [is] that [it] relies both on a creative constitution of the future with respect to positive and enterprising dispositions of risk taking and on a corresponding stance of reasonable foresight or everyday prudence with respect to potential harms" (O'Malley 2000: 461, in Isin 2004: 220). This fusion of medical risk and the state's management of potential good outcomes captures the central dynamic of the Italian health regime in that there is both the economic risk, understood as the increased precariousness of the labor market, and a heightened sense of bodily risk. However, what is obscured in the discourse of potential harms is the desirability of some potential outcomes, the ability of projects to regulate citizens not exclusively through fear and apprehension but also through hopefulness and anticipation.

Ulrich Beck theorizes that the focus on risk prevention is a historical way to manage, on the one hand, capital and labor and, on the other hand, populations. He argues that the problem of wealth distribution that characterized the age of industrial labor was parallel to the ways in which the prevention and circulation of risk have become a central problem of post-industrial labor (Beck 1992: 19). Thus, for Western welfare states, as scarcity waned as a crucial economic and social issue, risk became a new modality of economic and social focus, control, and intervention: the politics of lack were replaced with a politics of possible lack, shifting the form of governance toward estimating and managing future dangers. Unlike the European class-based society of the nineteenth century and early twentieth, a risk society's values center on the social and ethical good of the prevention of catastrophes (ibid.: 49). Risk regimes, therefore, construe differences between subjects based on the probability and severity of foreseeable injury, which means that preventing risk for one group may endanger another. What is less clear in Beck's formulation is how, for worker-citizens, the promise or seductiveness of evading risks within a work regime becomes a new mode of subjectification; the promise of security and the alleviation of distress is perhaps even more persuasive than negative probabilities. The discourse of positive outcomes generates new worker-subject desires that, in and of themselves, are part of crafting self-governing citizen-subjects. The notion of precarious work (*lavoro precario*) reflects a cultural understanding of work as beset with danger and corresponds to a greater desire in worker-citizens to promote projects that control and minimize risk. In this sense, Beck is certainly right in recognizing the "limited controllability of the dangers" of the twenty-first century (1999: 6).

Workplace well-being is thus a site where two forms of risk meet: the risk of economic vulnerability due to precarious labor and the risk of bodily injury due to a stressful and harmful work environment. The emergent prevention re-

gime, premised largely on mobbing, focuses a great deal on the psychobiological risks of the workplace. But in Italian cultural imaginaries, a great deal of
emphasis is placed on the fact that citizens want to imagine an ethical and safe
workplace.

Prescribing Organizational Health: The 626

In Italy, the legislative decree of 1994 (Decreto Legislativo no. 626/1994)
known simply as "the 626" represented a legal shift in how future mobbing
cases could and would be handled. The law was built to protect workers' mental
and physical integrity, often shorthanded as "psychophysical" integrity (Article
2087, 1942; and Law 300, 1970). This piece of legislation prescribed numerous
measures of *tutela* (protection) to safeguard the health and security of working
in both the private and public sectors. The 626 instituted a new workplace figure
to be designated by the employer, the worker representative for safety (*rappre-
sentante dei lavoratori per la sicurezza*), who would be responsible for employee
health measures and would be required to meet periodically with the workforce to discuss topics related to risk prevention and protection. The representative, according to the law, would be "a cardinal point in the new prevention-
ist politics" (Law 626, 1994). One safety representative would be required for
each company with more than fifteen employees, three for companies between
200 and 1,000 employees, and six for all larger entities. The 626 requires that the
safety representative receive 32 hours of training (120 hours for those serving
in larger corporations). In order to ensure that adequate information is given
to the safety representatives, a Service Committee for Prevention and Protection of Risks must be formed either by the company's employees or by an external agency (Law 626, Article 8). The committee must "individuate risk factors,
evaluate risks and seek measures for the security and health of the workplace"
(Article 9).

Employers are obligated to take a number of new measures to secure the
health and security of workers, including expanding access to information, taking certified courses on worker safety with public health institutions or the National Institute of Social Medicine, and promoting the development and participation of state officials with regard to health and safety (Law 626, Article
10). Employers must also have periodic meetings that include the designated
safety representative, the head of the safety committee, a medical doctor, and
all employees (Article 11). Doctors must work together with the employer "for
the specific knowledge of the company organization, both its productive quality
and the risk, for the predisposition of measures that can safeguard [the] health
and psychophysical integrity of workers" (Article 17). The psychophysical is
an essential element of this legal document, not only in that it is premised on
Article 2087 protections, but also as a more comprehensive vision of workers'
health. The 626 requires the calculation of both physical and psychological risks

for workers. It seeks to safeguard the psychophysical body, a complex medical body where the psychological and the physical cannot be easily separated.

Doctors are also required to update and institute workers' health cards, both the national health card with handwritten medical histories and a new "risk" health card to be carried by every worker and held by the employer (Law 626, Article 72). The law states that the doctor must evaluate risks from "biological agents and from working modalities" (Article 78). While the 626 currently emphasizes clear-cut physical and chemical risk factors, Italy's juridical recognition of psychological illness as work-related illness suggests that doctors may use their discretion to note all sorts of risk factors, including organizational and psychological.

Risk has been given a new material and traceable index, a portable object. The future mapping of the inflexible or at-risk bodies of worker-citizens will be managed through the state requirement to make risk visibly presentable—in the form of the risk card—for employers and state actors. Part of this additional legislative function is to measure what employers can be held accountable for in case of legal suits against them—something particularly salient in mobbing cases. For example, employees who enter the workforce with *greater* risks could be less able to hold the employer or the workplace accountable for psychophysical harm or injury (due to mobbing or other work situations). Employers, then, would be able to make workers responsible for managing their own risk factors and for being active in educating themselves about the effects of these risks. In fact, workers' representatives, not employers, are the actors encouraged to become part of the Commission on the Prevention of Work-Related Accidents and Promotion of Hygiene at Work, which is made up of representatives from various national health ministries, institutions, and inspection offices. While employers are legally responsible for these risks, one of the commission's tasks is to design a structure of engagement directly between workers and public health experts.

Law 626 laid the groundwork for the creation of a health risk regime where state actors and worker-citizens meet in a new and unique assemblage of figures, committees, supervisors, and consultants. Workers' right to safeguard their psychophysical integrity has animated an elaborate labor of risk management, labor that includes crafting the books on safety, creating and facilitating worker training, designing the physical and electronic databases of risk cards, and overseeing and expanding the state's prevention and security agencies in workplaces. This law has installed a regime of knowledge about safety, security, and prevention that has become, in turn, the modality through which worker bodily integrity can be achieved. Specific technologies, such as the worker's individualized risk booklet, in addition to creating a written trace of the employer and individual accountability, fashion workers as subjects of risk, inviting them to individualize the project of worker safety as it applies to their psychophysical body. The effect of this, however, is to diminish some of the employers' accountability insofar as workers are empowered to care for and acquire knowledge about their own bodily welfare at work. This prevention regime operates by multiplying the points of contact and the zones of visibility between worker-citizens and the state. There are multiple new political meeting points between workers and visiting doctors, safety specialists and workers, employers and state inspectors, and safety representatives and workers.

As Beck (1992, 1999) anticipated, the problem of job scarcity has been trumped by a focus on the circulation, measurement, and prevention of job risks. Labor market policy in Italy in the 1990s was focused on the privatization of employment and the promotion of flexible job contracts. Not only Italian but also European law continued to expand the mobility and pliability of the labor force. For example, in 1993, Law 221 legalized a new set of temporary contracts; and in 1997, Law 196 lifted the mandate for short-term contracts to "automatically convert" into lifelong contracts (Ferrera and Gualmini 2004: 102). The supranational European and Italian state management of health risks has promised and mobilized an ethical imperative to promote workers' security even as the state simultaneously has increased the means for nonstandard job contracts and, hence, worker insecurity and elimination. Italy's health regime has created an enticing illusion of safeguards and protection for workers even as other laws, such as the 2003 Biagi Laws, have vastly reduced the population of long-term, stable employees. The welfare state seems to expand and contract at the same time: it performs an investment in worker safety while reducing worker longevity by restructuring job contracts. It bears noting that the health risk apparatus *requires* the creation of flexible jobs. The 626 produced a new need for short-term contracts for both private and state workers—psychologists, medical doctors, public health workers—to design trainings, visit workplaces, consult with employers, and operationalize the new law.

The 626 has had a series of consequences for mobbing cases. Mobbees, if tracked by risk cards, enter the workplace with a document of accountability. In other words, if their health is constantly measured, then they may be less likely to be successful in holding employers or workplaces accountable for bodily harm. With the increased vigilance of state inspection agencies and safety representatives, mobbing cases may be more immediately flagged for further investigation. In this ethos of precariousness, prevention and organizational wellness have become the new focuses for the mobbing industry.

Law 626 and Mobbing

The production and dissemination of knowledge about mobbing consistently reiterate the message of prevention, risk, and potentiality. In addition, the discourse of well-being is a narrative mounted on top of risk management which builds upon existing understandings of work as menacing good health and self-fulfillment. In 2003, mobbing specialists in Turin met for a conference, "Preventive Strategies and Techniques of Recovery for Stress-Related Disturbances in the Work World," where they discussed a proposal to have on-site teams of stress specialists, including a psychologist, a medical doctor, and a lawyer: "The need for well-being is rising between computers and desks, in the office. After various companies have opened mini-gyms for their employers . . . they are beginning to worry about the relationships between people" (La Stampa 2003a). While an emphasis on stress-related injury or illness provides the background for a narrative of investment in workers' health and in workers as social actors, psychophysical risks for workers in a society of increasingly nonstandard employment have become less salient than how to promote positive outcomes. In 2006, in the region of the Aosta Valley, there was a similar conference, attended by Italy's Workers Compensation Authority (INAIL), the Office of Equal Opportunity, and local mobbing clinic representatives, entitled "Hardship and Discrimination at Work: What Kind of Prevention? What Kinds of Protections?" whose aim was to "promote and maintain an appropriate level of physical and psychological *well-being* for workers" (ANSA 2006a). Well-being is central to Italy's prevention regime; it is seen as the holistic and morally sound objective for medical management. Well-being departs from healthy in that it reflects the integrated psychosomatic body. *Healthy* refers to a body free of disease, while *well-being* refers more to a condition of healthy existence, consistently healthy choices and practices, and a sense of contentment and ease. It follows that well-being articulates more with worker potentials because it is an imagined condition to be attained if risks are minimized, rather than the elimination or reduction of already-present pathogens.

Well-being can also be found as a keyword within European Union legislation and protocol. The Commission of the European Community, through its legislative recommendations "Adapting to the Transformation of Work and Society: A New Strategy for Health and Safety 2002–2006," urged member states toward a "global imposition of well-being at work, keeping the transformation of work in consideration and the rise of new risks, in particular, psychosocial risks" (EU/2002/118). Workplace risk, prevention, and well-being form the foundation upon which mobbing is managed. In 2004, CRAS (Research Center for Social Affairs) and the European Union's Daphne Project issued a report on mobbing and gender in Italy and in the European Union (CRAS 2006). They prescribed the following to improve "psychosocial labor" and "prevent" mobbing: "(1) Give each worker a chance to choose the modality for executing his/her work; (2) Reduce monotonous and repetitive work; (3) Increase information concerning workers' objectives; (4) Develop a leadership style; (5) Avoid imprecise decisions about roles and responsibilities; (5) Solicit the ethical commitment [*impegno etico*] from employers and workers to create an environment without mobbing." At first glance, such projects align closely with Law 626 in that the goals of prevention and minimizing risk are extended to the project of mobbing, applying the authoritative discourse of risk management. But positioned alongside a new mobilization of workplace prevention and well-being, the politics of eliminating mobbing can also be read as a mapping of the social and moral ideals of capital, labor, and state. In this formulation, the healthy workplace is one in which precision, clarity, and leadership would thrive, and it calls upon and crafts workers as ethical subjects to put in place these values. In the context of Italy's precarious labor market, these visions have particular appeal as they seem to correct the neoliberal corporate ethos of misinformation and apprehension, which is perceived as unethical. The promises and ideals of this highly desirable vision are built upon the lived fears of Italy's precarious workforce, forging public imaginaries of healthy and healed workplaces; worker-citizens are encouraged to craft a wish list for how to refashion the abuses and injustices of neoliberal disorders. The state, in turn, appears to practice an ethics of care and protection of workers as precious social actors, rather than execute policies which abandon and devalue them.

The Rules of Work Doctors

As medicine and health become a lens through which labor organizations are viewed, occupational doctors (*medico del lavoro*) vastly expand their domain of authority. The 626 created a juridico-legal structure for occupational doctors to produce specialized knowledge about workplace risks and to increase their points of contact with both employers and workers. Occupational doctors have also been particularly important figures in containing, preventing, and measuring mobbing. In 2001, a group of physicians representing a number of Italian institutions of occupational medicine published a paper on the new responsibilities of the doctor with respect to "the new risk of moral harassment" (Gilioli et al. 2001 in Di Martino and De Santis 2003: 124). This "consensus document" by over twenty physicians, including mobbing specialist Renato Gilioli of Milan's Work Clinic, was an attempt to standardize a post–Law 626 approach to mobbing and "physical, psychological and social well-being": "Next to traditional health risks (chemical, physical and biological) for workers, psychosocial and organizational risks are becoming one of the principal causes of alterations in health in the workplace. Among these, 'relational risk' or 'interpersonal risk' have received the attention of occupational doctors only recently, but increasingly so" (Gilioli et al. 2001 in Di Martino and De Santis 2003: 125).

That risks are increasingly less traceable insofar as they are "relational" or "interpersonal" does not make the possibility of intervention less robust. On the contrary, relational risks are by definition immaterial and demand the specialized knowledge of a special class, in this case, medical doctors. With respect to Law 626 and the role of the occupational doctor, the document outlines how the doctor is legally responsible to both employee and employer. According to this document, for employees who feel they have been mobbed, the doctor must be able to offer a "diagnosis of pathologies that can recognize the cause(s) at work," proper "medico-legal certification of the endured damage," referrals to other health and insurance agencies, and the creation of a certified report to the Workers Compensation Authority and other "organs of vigilance" (Gilioli et al. 2001 in Di Martino and De Santis 2003: 131–132). The occupational doctor also is authorized by Law 626 to act as a political mediator for possible labor disputes. In short, "the occupational doctor's principal task is to work in prevention, contributing to the diffusion of a prevention culture of the risk of mobbing" (ibid.: 133). Thus, the established importance of mobbing as an undesirable workplace practice has become a vehicle through which the "prevention culture" circulates and advances. And prevention is the modality through which the medical occupation—both in the sense of medical doctors and in the sense of their "occupation" (control) of the workplace—intensifies. The doctor's role in prevention transforms physicians into both ethical figures and leading subjects of the state's governing apparatus.

New training programs organized by various city and regional hospitals have applied the heightened role of the *medico del lavoro* mandated by Law 626 to the prevention of mobbing. One hospital in Turin, for example, echoes the advice of the institutes of occupational medicine that occupational doctors should "(1) Effectively evaluate environmental risks; (2) Conduct health inspections and health checks for workers, in case of health problems connected to mobbing, at the request of the worker or at their own initiative; and (3) Promote initiatives for the company to measure the proper dimension of the risk and to prevent it" (Ospedale 2007). This type of formulation is also the basis of an anti-mobbing legislative proposal drafted by the Italian Labor Union (Unione Italiana del Lavoro) and the organization Woman's Life (Vita di Donna), a Rome-based NGO promoting women's health. The mobbing law proposes that an employer must work effectively with the safety representative and occupational doctors in order to "prevent moral and psychological violence" (UIL 2006). Woman's Life specifies that the occupational doctor should evaluate risks and promote the "psychophysical well-being of workers" (Vita di Donna 2006).

The diffusion of a prevention culture for mobbing hinges upon an understanding of the endangered body. C. Nadia Seremetakis has shown that, within neoliberal economic dynamics, "fast capitalism" in Europe has "inscribed new forms of uncertainty and insecurity in the experience of embodiment" (Seremetakis 2001: 125; see also Holmes 2000). Seremetakis traced these somatic uncertainties through, for example, public fears of disease infection and the aesthetic display of cadavers. In her formulation, the new global order intensifies the body's medical penetration: "the fixation of bodily identity makes use of medically derived optics and deploys medical perspectives in decidedly nonmedical contexts, terrain[s], and situations" (Seremetakis 2001: 125). Thus, a heightened somatic uncertainty and precariousness are precisely the cultural forces that propel medical management of the workplace. The labor of establishing the workplace as dangerous to the body is ongoing and is achieved within the discourse of mobbing. The promotion of well-being centers on the medical endangerment of workers' bodies, creating new optical techniques and technologies of the state within the labor market, but it also works as a kind of symbolic façade of welfare state protection in that it is being assembled as the state retracts labor protections.

Project Well-Being: Policing the Office

In April 2005, I spoke to Mariella Verigni, a psychologist and a specialist in mobbing who worked at one of the Veneto region's projects for the "promotion of psychosocial health" in companies. At a café on a rainy day, Mariella described the Veneto region's multiyear project, the Plan for the Prevention and Promotion of Health in Workplaces (Piano per la Prevenzione e la Promozione della Salute Negli Ambiti di Lavoro, Decree of the Regional Council, no. 3723), a regional extension and specification of Law 626. Drawing from regional and federal funds, the project coordinated state health organizations, including the Workers Compensation Authority (INAIL), the Agency for Prevention, Hygiene and Safety at Work (SPISAL), the Institute for Prevention and Work Safety (ISPESL), and various regional institutes of occupational medicine and centers for occupational medicine located within hospitals. She explained that the project was anchored in workers' psychosocial health generally because mobbing is just "the tip of the iceberg" of their broader campaign to "verify organizational well-being." The multistep plan includes a study of the organizational costs of mobbing, questionnaires, interviews, developing organizational strategies for health, and creating employee focus groups. Objectives of the plan listed in the program materials include "(1) Promote a workplace culture oriented toward assuming safe and responsible lifestyles and behaviors through a cooperation strategy with diverse public institutions, associations and organizations; and (2) Increase the opportunities of worker-citizens [cittadini lavoratori] to have a lifestyle and politics oriented toward health." In this formulation, the notion of health and risk prevention expands to a more global sense of personhood and lifestyle. The narrative of "lifestyle" individualizes the project, such that the individual's routinized habits become the "social reference unit" for the risk regime, which also materializes a symbolic architecture of the space of intimate daily practices and broader social problems. The document includes a section on mobbing and its relation to the fundamental objective "to plan preventive and rehabilitative interventions":

> The mobbing risk [rischio mobbing] is closely tied to the organization of labor that does not sufficiently valorize the human component [of labor] and carries the logic of short-term production with the related lack of interpersonal relationships. . . .
> As long as there is no law precisely on moral harassment one must refer to the legislation related to safeguarding health . . . [which is] protected in the constitutional Article 2087 of the Civil Code.

Workers' right to psychophysical integrity ties the regional legislative platform on mobbing risk to the foundational legal protection of Law 626. Notably, this formulation pledges to "valorize the human component" of labor in ways that "short-term production" has not. In other words, it seeks to remedy the dehumanizing effects of precarious labor and vows to rectify the damage. However, the moral reconstitution of workers as humans and not sellable units relies not only on changes in short-term production, but on the hopefulness of restoration and moral redemption.

Under the regional plan, Mariella and various doctors, psychologists, and inspectors had formed a committee that would deal specifically with mobbing through the measures provided by Law 626. New committees would also offer additional research services on health risks to private corporations; for example, she mentioned that the plan had already been implemented with a large Italian service sector corporation, Zanella. Beginning in January 2004, Project Well-Being outlined all "psychosocial and organizational risk factors" for the benefit of improving workers' health and maximizing organizational efficiency. Collaborating medical doctors and psychologists shared the results of qualitative and quantitative research on the risk factors at Zanella to put together an "intervention plan" for the improvement of worker safety and health. In addition, two biological measures of stress were obtained from Zanella workers, cortisol levels in workers' saliva and twenty-four-hour blood pressure readings. Biological testing results in the creation of a biophysical measure of precariousness, a tangible meeting point between worker-citizens and states. Such tests transform the intangibility of stress and wellness into quantifiable units of bodily output. Prevention plans, premised on workers' right to protected bodily integrity, paradoxically structure collective bodies as vulnerable to experimentation and invasion to ensure the minimization of risk—expanding, then, the biomedical penetration of the state. The essential difference is that preventive medicine casts such projects as nonpolitical and ethical.

Mariella invited me to one of the group's organizational meetings to promote a similar Project Well-Being at another corporate site of Zanella in Veneto. I attended the meeting in April 2005 with medical doctors, psychologists, and a few representatives from the call center of the company. Call centers had been receiving a great deal of publicity in Italy as sites of great stress, mobbing, and worker burnout, and therefore were sites of intense health risk. First, Mariella and her colleagues outlined the idea of Project Well-Being as a way to identify and minimize workers' health risks and to enhance both organizational and individual vitality. Then, the workers described a set of practices that they defined as heightening mental and physical fatigue and illness. Carola, a woman in her mid-sixties, offered: "We are constantly monitored, like a check every five minutes, another kind of check every twenty-five minutes even if you're not with a caller." Francesco, the safety representative of the company, agreed: "The parameters are constantly changed, and you have to keep track of things for the sales rewards. For example, sometimes it was better to deal with a technical problem *without* sending a technician, in order to get the sales reward. But then you don't resolve the problem." Francesco was picking up on one of the irrational aspects of market capitalism, a technique of sales that perpetuates contact with clients, but results in inefficient technical operations. Another colleague, Bettina, added: "That's the problem with the market: to satisfy it, you have to sell something. The instrument through which this happens is the call operator, who always has to sell." Bettina described the company's computer program, which would flash symbols and suggestions of new services and equipment for the operators to offer to phone clients. For the receptive and attentive members of the Project Well-Being committee, the workers identified the increased pressure to sell goods, intense monitoring, and frustration with wavering and obtuse corporate policy. In other words, what I saw were the problems of neoliberal capitalism and labor put on the table for medical managers. There was only a small degree of attention given to physical risk factors, such as the cramped spatial organization or the excessively warm temperatures in the office. In this moment, the Italian state was localized in these institutional actors, who embodied attentiveness and an expression of care and concern for these workers. Unlike the doctor who might diagnose mobbing-related illnesses, these medical practitioners sought the same optimization of workers' lives that the workers themselves desired. The workers were viewed as emotionally complex individuals who deserved to be treated well and with dignity.

Next, the workers described the relational risk factors, including the hostility and condescension of their supervisors. Their complaints included the supervisors' heavy and unnecessary criticism, their constant surveillance, and their continuously raising the minimum requirements for satisfactory work. The staff agreed that this would indeed be an interesting and appropriate place to intervene. One doctor reflected: "Francesco showed us that these are really moral problems." Nodding, Mariella said: "There's no job satisfaction." The underlying cultural assumption guiding this meeting was that the pressure to sell and low job satisfaction were ethically urgent and biomedically resolvable problems. The workers had convincingly performed their own endangerment to the group of professional risk minimizers. In order to access the abundant resources and possible safeguards that the project could offer, the workers had to fashion themselves as precarious subjects, jeopardized by persistent health risks, while the experts marshaled a sense of caring as somewhat paternalistic interventionists. The dynamic between the medical experts and the workers was charged by the allure of positive potentials: the alleviation of hostility and oppressive surveillance by their supervisors, the promise of ease and stability, the humanization of disoriented labor.

The Value of Vigilance

Over the next few months I found that Project Well-Being was, above all, extremely slow-moving. Part of this stemmed from the group's difficulty in planning meetings through the not-yet-established pathways between health and safety state institutions. The occupational doctors, psychologists, and inspectors all had other tasks that had to be accomplished for the state, and this was an additional project. New short-term workers designated to advance the project spent weeks gathering information about mobbing or attending mobbing seminars. Even the letter of acknowledgment to the workers who participated in the initial planning meeting took several hours of meetings, cross-checks, and correspondence between various actors at multiple institutions. Put simply, the structure of state intervention demanded a great deal of labor by multitasking social actors. It also showed the gap between the discursive elements of power and the creation of actual corporate and state practices.

In late May 2005 I attended another meeting where the staff discussed a number of challenges. Though they had asked the company Zanella to participate in their project, the corporation had no explicit legal obligation to do so. If Zanella showed itself to be adequately fulfilling the legal objectives of Law 626, then it did not have to allow access to the research group. Thus, though the group was entirely state-run and state-funded by prevention initiatives, it did not hold any specific legal jurisdiction to oblige companies to be further scrutinized. There was also the problem of how to coordinate with other regions and how they would carry out the project at a variety of Zanella work sites.

At this point, Zanella was interested, as long as there would be press coverage of its collaboration which would ensure its ability to mobilize a publicity campaign of its ethics, transparency, and care for workers, strengthening the social value of Zanella as a corporate brand. Members of the staff were troubled by this extra benefit, but they agreed that the company's compliance with the program would be highly valuable to workers and that the firm's investment in the workers outweighed the fact that Zanella's participation might improve the value and overall worth of the company.

One of the participating physicians, Franco Galetto, concluded the meeting on a positive note: "We are setting off on the right foot. We have a regional and a national program, two different plans, one cultural, the other vigilance. The cultural plan is to hear, talk, and see all the experiences of the company. . . . But the vigilance is local." Franco was articulating an important role of state institutions in this process, as prevention demands a specific kind of watchfulness, a constant and alert readiness. Just as prevention regimes create worker-citizens as subjects of risk and potential, they also fashion local actors, which decentralizes the power of the state to a more diffuse and localized collective body of actors. Medical doctors and worksite surveyors have become a legitimate way for the state to intervene within the work sphere; they are the newest refashioning of the "medical police" within the juridical authority of the neoliberal state. Historically, the double role of physicians as medical police dates to late eighteenth-century Europe (Elmer and Grell 2004; Osborne 1996: 105). Medical police were responsible for various aspects of public health, from sanitation to plague management; at this time, physicians could more seamlessly present themselves as invested in the well-being of the population (Cohen 2009). Within Italy's neoliberal economic regime, occupational doctors are the new medical police for worker well-being. Given the low number of women physicians in Italy, and the even lower number of women who are head physicians and hospital administrators (as low as 3.6 percent in 2000), there is a gendered dimension of power in Italy's medical regime (Vinay 2000: 24). Expanding the authority of the medical police simultaneously generates a male-centered site of knowledge production and authoritative control.

Scientific Management

Mariella introduced me to Dr. Massimo Cannari, head of one of the medical institutes of work in the Veneto region. Massimo is a research specialist and physician, managing various medical projects on mobbing and staffing the hospital's mobbing clinic. "You can't put mobbing under a microscope," he repeatedly told me when I spoke to him in July 2005, explaining the challenge of preventing something as intangible and shifting as mobbing. Massimo's comment reveals why the restructuring of power relations within Italy is not solely biomedical or medicalized, even though it is moving toward a heavy reliance upon scientific authority. Italians view work harassment and the alienation of workers as deeply damaging to health, even though this is not always supported by scientific evidence.

I asked about his participation in Project Well-Being, and he explained there were various advantages to promoting organizational well-being, rather than simply treating the pathology of mobbing and its effects on the body: "How much does poor organization cost? We're putting together some data. Investing in mobbing means wasting a lot of energy and that means disorganization. . . . Now with the Biagi Laws you won't have any more mobbing, but just anxiety and depression caused by work." Promoting organizational well-being, in his view, is also more cost-effective for companies than mobbing, a perspective which summons neoliberal ideologies of efficiency, cost reduction, and organizational excess. He situates well-being as an economically desirable goal, whereas mobbing represents a waste of labor and the breakdown of capitalist objectives. Massimo also envisions a future in which the Biagi Laws, which promote a wide array of short-term, precarious job contracts, will end mobbing. This rationale suggests to me that he believes mobbing derives from economic pressure to reduce long-term labor. This position is contested by Italy's political left wing which, alternatively, views the Biagi Laws as an instigator of mobbing, not the agent of its disappearance. Regardless of these politically divergent opinions about when and how mobbing will cease to trouble the workplace, most people I met in the mobbing industry envisioned workers as facing persistent psycho-physical endangerment. If the post-mobbing neoliberal workplace is beset with health dangers, then it demands the ongoing guarding against risk and medical doctors' presence.

Governing Customer-Citizens

Worker well-being and organizational wellness (*benessere organizza-tivo*) have become prominent themes throughout official state discourse on the workplace. Just as in organizational coercion pathology, the psychophysical disorder attributed to mobbing, the idea of organizational wellness utilizes the term *organizational* to index corporate or industrial firms. In March 2004, Minister of Public Functions Luigi Mazella announced a national initiative for "organizational wellness" in public workplaces. Suggesting that employers keep a close eye on the "perceived levels of physical and mental strain of [their] employees" and "mobbing," he advocated for "fewer hierarchies and a reduction of work bogged down by procedures . . . more creativity and motivation . . . an environment that is not only healthy, but also comfortable and welcoming" (ANSA 2004c). The national project would focus on eliminating health risks for state workers in particular. By promoting the potential outcomes of creativity and comfort, the minister predicated his intervention upon the value of workers; the welfare state, at least momentarily, appeared to be returning. But Mazella's plans also included what he dubbed, using the English, "customer satisfaction," which would systematically promote engagement with "customer-citizens [*cittadino-cliente*]." Mazella's notion of "customer satisfaction" proposed "a model between the [state] administration and citizens based on trust and legitimating public action founded on the capacity to give opportune responses that correspond to *real needs* of citizens and companies" (ibid.). The state, then, was assembling public medical services as something that might satisfy a "market" of the nation's customer-citizens. Welfare, rather than being an intrinsic right of citizens, would become something that customers could "purchase" through decentralized services and programs.

Prevention programs in the workplace are predicated on several central assumptions: the workplace as bodily endangering; an imaginary of the state as a benevolent provider; and employers who share with workers the responsibility for managing risks. What we can glimpse here, however, is also an embedded notion of the neoliberal state as responding to an imagined market of citizen demands. The idea of customer satisfaction for citizens bases state intervention upon certain legible and actionable citizen desires, not inalienable rights. This suggests a rather critical shift between worker-citizens and customer-citizens insofar as governance becomes premised on an idea of citizens as autonomous global clients—consuming the services of the state. In this way, employers play less of a central role in protecting workers. The health risk regime aims to rectify the failings of state policy to adequately protect the labor industry and workers. Workers, however, are indexed as customer-citizens whose engagement means not guaranteed or absolute rights or safeguards, but rather market-driven welfare. A large-scale restructuring of workplaces that advertises state intervention under the guise of promoting health seems to resemble a strengthening, a return, of the welfare state. But health risk regimes are double-sided: the state caters to decentralized techniques of control through medical institutions and promotes the self-monitoring of employers, the protection of employers, and the expansion of institutional "organs of vigilance," such as SPISAL and the Workers Compensation Authority. The Italian state slips between patriarchal protectionism and decentralized governance. At the same time, citizens, through these same processes, become "consumers" (O'Malley 1996: 203) and, as Rose puts it, "purchasers who can choose to buy services from the range of options available to them" (Rose 1996: 54).

Desire and Neoliberal Capitalism

The potential for worker well-being has raised the question of how precariousness and risk incite citizens to desire a stronger state, capable of effectively intervening in the problem of labor and global capitalism, and the effects of this desire. A technique of neoliberal governing, then, is the generation of a desire for order in a labor force characterized by precarity and ambiguity. Worker-citizens' desire for an ethical state capable of resurrecting social and political certainties may compel practices and identifications that will reconstitute the welfare state. My findings of citizens' desires for work and for more robust state management challenge and complicate the revolutionary and utopian potentials that Hardt and Negri predicted and theorized. They imagined "the desire to escape the disciplinary regime and tendentially an undisciplined multitude of workers who want to be free" (2000: 262–263).[1] But in Italy, paradoxically, the response of mobbed and precarious workers was not simply a "mass refusal of the disciplinary regime" (274), but rather a sense of exploitation and persecution at their exclusion from the capitalist mode of production and a turn toward the welfare state. In many ways, the desire for state protection overpowers concerns about whether or not state policy may effectively manage or stabilize the economy (Mann 2003: 139; Rosenau 2003: 228; Gilpin 2003: 354). Italian historian Ginsborg warns that the failure of the Italian state to adequately provide justice for citizens has "increased perforce the desire for summary justice, exercised, if need be, by a single strong and charismatic figure" (2003: 231). In the domain of work, this desire becomes a mode of affective regulation and governance because of the ways in which it preys upon workers' hopes for stability and because of how state involvement can be masked as self-evidently benevolent. These processes begin with the goal of fixed, stable work, and thus they show the importance of labor—secure employment and its demise—in the reconfiguration of the state (Gilpin 2003: 352; Sassen 1988, 1996).

The health risk regime in Italy, in its regulation of workers' psychophysical body, is beset with political contradictions. In this, it bears an affinity to the genealogy of panic disorder in the United States, exposed by Jackie Orr. She calls attention to "psychopower," a normalizing regime of psychological health with a particular feature that both "makes" and "manages" (2006: 14) and both "disciplines" and "produces" (17). Panic disorder is a lucid example of psychopower precisely in how, managed through a pharmaceutical and state alliance, it limits and expands its subjects; it promises healing yet simultaneously creates the conditions for panic. Italy's health risk regime is not dissimilar insofar as health risks are extended and managed, intensified and yet carefully measured. It promises to be the cure for the increase of precariousnes and mobbing, but it also relies on the precariousness of workers and their desire for ease and stability to justify its intervention. Risk relies on workers' fear of their own endangerment and their trust in the state to rectify this state of panic. In a landscape of hope-saturated safeguards, preventive medical management and the alluring promise of well-being regulate Italy's increasingly precarious and discontented workforce, even as the opportunities for stability vanish.

Notes

Introduction

1. In Padua, local parts of the city are designated "the Casbah," "the Bronx," and "Africa," indexing where many immigrants sell goods or live (Colatrella 2001: 326). Many Paduan youth who attend the university and commute to the city talk openly about their disgust or fear of the train station, a visible contact point for ethnic Italians and immigrant communities.

2. Still, there have been publications in English that adopt the term *mobbing* (e.g., Davenport, Schwartz, and Elliott 1999; Spindel 2008; Westhues 2008; Atkinson 2009).

3. Neoliberalism, understood as a global historical process shaped by specific market-oriented economic policies, has become increasingly dominant since the 1970s (Barry et al. 1996; Comaroff and Comaroff 2001; Sandbrook et al. 2007). Beginning in the 1970s, "free market fundamentalists" Milton Friedman and Friedrich von Hayek helped to disseminate notions of radical neoliberalism in Europe and the United States (Sandbrook et al. 2007: 213; Berend 2006: 275). Neoliberalism ideologies, which oppose most forms of state intervention, regulation, and ownership (Berend 2006: 275), sustain a view that "self-regulating" markets will "resolve problems of destitution, joblessness and insecurity" (Sandbrook et al. 2007: 15).

4. The two-tier phenomenon is shaped by what Saskia Sassen has called "bipolarity" in employment regimes: "a demand for highly specialized and educated workers alongside a demand for basically unskilled workers whether for clerical, service, industrial service, or production jobs" (1998: 146). Long-term workers, however, do not always fall within Sassen's first category.

5. In the early 1990s, championing the ideology of family and hard work and positioned against notions of southern indolence and criminality, the party initially began as a movement for the independence of northern Italy as the Republic of Padania. Refashioned as Italy's pro-federalist party rather than a separatist party, the Northern League opposes heavy taxation, support for southern Italy, and immigration (Colatrella 2001: 316; Tambini 1996; Ardizzoni 2005: 515). Party leader Umberto Bossi's speeches often construct the North as more "European" than "backward" and "bureaucratic" Rome (Tossutti 2001: 69).

6. Hardt and Negri refer to "informatization" as a process including the use of new technologies, the robust growth of the service sector, and the expansion of immaterial labor (see Castells 1996). Though I draw from radical political theorists such as Hardt and Negri, I do not impute to capital its own intentionality or, more critically, inevitability. The state, theorized by anthropologists as only appearing to be a distant and distinctive entity, is shaped by and part

of daily practices and the production of meaning (e.g., Scott 1985; Steinmetz 1999; Mitchell 1999; Edelman 1999; Gledhill 2000; Gill 2000).

7. The word *mobber* was used in these instances, though the proper Italian word is *mobbizzatore*.

8. Biopolitics includes new forms of self-governance deployed to modulate bodily well-being and health (Collier and Ong 2005; Ong 2006b; Rose 2007), the biological need to control risk (Beck 1992), "ontological security" (Turner 2001), and the biological basis of citizenship (Heath et al. 2002; Rose and Novas 2003; Petryna 2002, 2004).

9. I have used pseudonyms for all of the names and companies in this book.

10. My daily practice in Padua was to take field notes in small notebooks and then extend these notes into full-length descriptions on my computer; in the end, I collected over 500 single-spaced pages as a record of my fieldwork. I also gathered a variety of written documents throughout the months of fieldwork: (1) corporate documents (newsletters, conduct codes, etc.) from human resources or personnel workers that deal with interpersonal relationships in the workplace in general and (if available) with mobbing in particular; (2) published legal bulletins of the European Union and local institutions; (3) news articles primarily from two main newspapers: *Corriere della Sera*, a national newspaper based in Milan, and *Il Gazzettino di Padova*, Padua's main daily newspaper; (4) union pamphlets, brochures, conference materials, and books on mobbing; and (5) legal and archival materials related to mobbing, labor law, and Italy's economic development.

1. Toward Neoliberalism

1. I will use either "indefinite time contract" or "lifelong contract" to refer to these contracts.

2. Italy allowed temporary employment for the first time after two European Court of Justice rulings obligated the country to do so (Ferrera and Gualmini 2004: 100). Implementing European recommendations, employment placement centers were to implement a "preventive" approach to the labor market, providing highly trained consultants and electronic data banks in order to "get the unemployed into the labour market as soon as possible" (ibid.: 99).

3. CGIL was founded in 1906 and grew to over 2 million members by 1920. Under fascist rule, union organizations were abolished, but CGIL was reconstituted at the end of World War II in 1944. In the late 1940s a series of schisms within the union created Italy's two other major trade unions, CISL (Confederazione Italiana Sindicato Lavoratori) and UIL (Unione Italiana del Lavoro).

4. Books dedicated to precariousness include Platania 2006; Ferracuti 2006; Roggla 2005; Bajani 2006; and Nove 2006.

5. Italy has over 90,000 laws on record as opposed to France's 7,325 and Germany's 5,587 (Ginsborg 2003: 217).

6. Employers cannot simply convert to short-term contracts, as Italian and European law prescribes that an employee will default to an indefinite time contract

after two or more short-term contracts with the same employer (EU Directive 1999/70/Ce; Cirioli 2006). Forty percent of full-time workers with short-term contracts become long-term employees after one year, but this still leaves 60 percent whose next contract is short term.

7. Among individuals between twenty-five and twenty-nine, men also lived with their parents more than women did (71 percent compared to 52.7 percent; ISTAT 2006).

8. Unfortunately, since the worker had already left the company, I was not able to contact the woman who had accused Elenora of mobbing her. Later, I found out that Lidia and Dora had handled the case against Elenora, which was still pending.

2. The Politics of Precariousness

1. Gianni, for example, would receive a cut from Contax if he lost more than 8 percent of his total client base, so he, in turn, demanded that his agents aim for a loss of no more than 12 percent.

2. "Leave someone at home [*lasciare a casa*]" is a common gloss for firing workers. Davide also used a version of this expression when he fired someone: "Va a casa [She's going home]."

3. Even women able to adopt an identity as a freelance professional seemed to do so with greater complications. Twenty-eight-year-old Angelina had graduated with a degree in liberal arts and had, for the moment, found work as a research assistant at a chemical research laboratory and plant. Her boss assured her that her freelance contract would be renewed each year and added that she would "freely" be able to take on other jobs at the same time. She discussed the benefits of the job with me and her cousin Giacomo: "With the freelance contract, it's nice because I can always leave." Giacomo laughed: "That's actually the one thing that all workers always have the right to do—leave." The flexibility to depart was, in Angelina's view, a value of freelance work.

4. Being clever (*furbo*) is a description used often in Italy; it may also be represented nonverbally by using the thumb to draw a line from the outer corner of one eye diagonally toward the corner of the mouth. "Cleverness" is only one possible gloss, as being *furbo* entails both sneakiness and savvy. What it almost always implies is some sort of premeditation or intentionality of action.

3. Existential Damages

1. The colonial context, particularly in terms of the interests of Christian missionaries, enables a relatively clean division between imperialist outsiders and the indigenous peoples, but this does not fully model what is under way in Italy.

2. Rose's interest in how souls are governed has been influenced by Foucault's theorizing on the soul. Along with technologies of production, signs, and power, Foucault defined technologies of the self as those "which permit individuals to effect by their own means or with the help of others a certain number of operations on their own bodies and souls . . . so as to transform them-

selves in order to attain a certain state of happiness, purity, wisdom, perfection, or immortality" (1988: 18). Thus, subjects were positioned as entangled in regulatory operations designed toward their interiorities, including the soul. Unraveling how the reporting of sexual offenses in Christian confession serves as a mode of intervening with and shaping sexuality, he focused on soul shaping as a form of Christian practice and ideology in particular, in which he distinguished between "hermeneutics of the self" and "theologies of the soul" (ibid.: 16). While the former operates as a type of "care and self-knowledge" (21), the latter hinges upon a divine notion of "self-renunciation [as] the condition of salvation" (22), and both share a technology based upon "the truth of oneself" (48). What remains salient within Christian epistemology and across these Foucauldian logics is that the individual has a self-referential epistemology: one must know oneself in order to disclose one's interiority to others (40).

3. As Lazzarato (1996) suggests, "what is 'productive' is the whole of the social relation," but this nonetheless becomes represented in certain material symbols within a juridical system.

4. See also Meucci 2006: 494.

5. Among the reasons that he might not identify his experience as mobbing as readily as other workers, it is worthwhile to note that mobbing specialists such as Renato Gilioli have argued that most men are mobbed following corporate mergers—a time when economic constraints seem most evident—while women are victims of "emotional mobbing," which are assumed to be brought on by women's affective sensibilities.

6. See also Atanasio 2004.

4. Feminizing the Inflexible

1. Similarly, Carla Freeman pursues the question of "how gendered notions of work [are] connected to these 'reclassifications' of labor" as she traces the emergent subjectivity and class consciousness of women data entry workers in Barbados (2000: 55).

2. The verb conquer (*conquistare*) may translate more naturally into English here as "winning," but this use of the verb has important implications.

3. The Latin phrase *ab divinis* means "from the divine": something spiritual or from the heavens.

4. The use of film analyses in ethnographic practice and writing has become increasingly common as anthropologists track discourses, images, meanings, new desires, and practices, revealing "how media enable and challenge the workings of power and the potential of activism, the enforcement of inequality and the sources of imagination; and the impact of technologies on the production of individual and collective identities" (Ginsburg, Abu-Lughod, and Larkin 2002: 3). In her analysis of a film about Chinese rural society, Judith Farquhar suggests that what we find in film are "manifestations of very material, if diverse, social technologies. Technology practically materializes complex sys-

tems of knowledge and institutional networks, and it serves to alter the efficacy of users in the context of ordinary practices" (Farquhar 1999: 156). Louisa Schein deploys what she calls an "ethnotextual approach" to anthropological media analysis, tracing "intertextual interpretations . . . locating them in the wider play of cultural signification that exceeds the video medium" (2004: 436). Schein's methodological approach combines situated viewing, interviews about media involvement, and mapping of the consumption of an entire genre of film.

5.   I use this phrase after Emily Martin's *Bipolar Expeditions* (2007) in which she refers to "those living under the description of bipolar disorder" as a way to designate a particular set of people indexed by this diagnosis and the cultural meanings surrounding this term at a particular historical moment. I view it as a way to bracket, but not undermine, the question of a "real" diagnosis and to focus instead on the label and the experience of people grouped as such.

5. Living It on the Skin

1.   A more literal translation of *disturbi psichici da costrittività organizzativa sul lavoro* would be "psychological disturbances from organizational coercion at work." INAIL refers to both "psychological and psychosomatic pathologies," so I have retained the more general gloss of "pathology."

2.   "L'imprenditore è tenuto ad adottare nell'esercizio dell'impresa le misure . . . necessarie a tutelare l'integrità fisica e la personalità morale dei prestatori di lavoro."

3.   A "legal doctor" in Italy refers to a medical professional who is authorized by the state to verify medical claims for legal proceedings. Sometimes, they are referred to as "occupational doctor" (*medico del lavoro*) or "fiscal doctor" (*medico fiscale*). Anna in the film was visited by a legal doctor.

4.   Established in 1980, ISPESL is an organ of the national health care apparatus that evaluates whether health norms and regulations are enforced. It conducts research to prevent work-related accidents and illnesses, develops new health requirements, and assesses risk for new materials, technologies, tools, and machines. ISPESL develops projects to prevent accidents and protect workers, standardizes the methods used to evaluate health risks, enhances safety measures, performs technical and scientific consulting for the conformity of products and procedures, and certifies health safeguards. In addition, the institution promotes public awareness campaigns and organizes educational courses for employers and health representatives.

5.   *Mobbing* is often glossed as *molestie morale* (moral harassment), making it parallel in structure to *molestie sessuale* (sexual harassment).

6.   The pamphlet, which treats mobbing as anomalous, describes the psychological and physical effects of this allegedly unlikely work situation on the worker. Symptoms are divided into psychopathological (e.g., mood changes, apathy, flashbacks), psychosomatic (e.g., asthma, headaches, heart problems), and behavioral (e.g., drug or alcohol consumption, smoking, sexual dysfunction) (Cassitto et al. 2003: 16).

7. Within the field of anthropology of the body, the notion of the "social skin" (Turner 1980) has been a starting point for delving into the ways that social practices and discourses interact with bodily experience. Andrew Strathern recognized, "The skin is the immediate point of contact with the physical world outside . . . and can also conveniently symbolize the point of contact between [people] and the social forces that surround them" (1977: 101). Feminist theorists have pointed toward understanding the skin less as a barrier and more as a porous entity across which mutual exchange occurs—between machine and organism (Haraway 1991).

8. An employee's contract lists a specific hierarchical level which corresponds with work assignments and minimum salary.

9. Though used in the great majority of cases, PTSD, according to the DSM-IV, includes specific criteria, such as the presence of persistent flashbacks and intrusive thoughts related to the trauma, an increased state of arousal, and hypervigilance. Maladjustment syndrome (*la sindrome da disadattamento*) or maladjustment disturbances (*disturbo dell'adattamento*) manifest as "clinically significant emotional and behavioral symptoms in response to one or more identifiable (non-extreme) stress factors" (INAIL 2001). According to DSM-IV, maladjustment disturbances must develop within three months of the determining stress factors and the reaction must surpass the prevalent response to the given stress factors. The most common symptoms, diagnosed as either acute or chronic, are depressed mood, anxiety, and psychosomatic manifestations. *Acute* refers to symptoms persisting for a period of six months or less.

10. Article 13 (Decreto Legislativo, no. 38/2000) states: "the worker is protected by obligatory insurance against work-related accidents and illness, which includes biological damage such as harm to the psychophysical integrity of the worker as evaluated by a legal doctor. The rate of indemnity does not depend on the capacity to produce by the damaged person." This right is also recognized by the Worker's Statute (Article 5 of Law 300/70), which prohibits repeated visits by doctors to check on the sick leaves of employees. The Constitutional Court (sentence no. 184/1986) had ruled that psychological damage would be considered part of biological damage.

11. This document maintained that OCP was a "psychological and psychosomatic illness caused by dysfunction of a work organization" (*malattie psichiche e psicosomatiche da disfunzioni dell'organizzazione del lavoro*).

12. INAIL published another report regarding reports of mobbing or "psychopathologies related to organizational coercion at work." This report included 482 cases between 1999 and 2004, ranging from 1 percent of the cases in 1999 to 55 percent of the cases reported in 2003–2004. The average mobbee was more likely to be male (60 percent of cases), between the ages of forty-one and fifty (35.3 percent), a mid-level employee (56.2 percent), and from a northeastern region (28.8 percent of cases). INAIL's report was one of the few that showed more men than women, as other studies have tended to report women in the service sector as the most likely mobbees (Ege 2002). It is also important to consider the employment rate gap: 40 percent of the cases come from around only a 30 percent employment rate for women.

6. The Sex of Mobbing

1. For example, one might say one was tied up in traffic on a holiday weekend, and an interlocutor will respond, "Typical! [*Normale!*]."

2. A 2006 study estimated 900,000 reports by women of sexual coercion, or quid pro quo sexual harassment, at work (ISTAT 2006).

3. In 2006, the court ruled that the rape of a female virgin would not be penalized more than the rape of a non-virgin (Court of Cassation, sent. no. 6329, 2006). It reversed an older law that made the sexual assault of virgins more punishable because it was understood as a greater disgrace to her and her family.

4. See also Il Sole 24 Ore 2002c.

5. See also La Stampa 2004b.

6. The phrase *in nero* literally translates as "black" economy, but means the informal economy.

7. The use of "that" as a modifier is as derogatory as it would be in English.

8. His comment uses an impersonal form, but it could also be translated as "no one does mobbing."

7. Project Well-Being

1. At the same time, Hardt and Negri also promote a "citizenship income," which is "a political demand of the multitude: a social wage and guaranteed income for all" (2000: 403). While they tie this desire to something beyond the state, it is important to recognize that citizens' desire for a stable income nonetheless recognizes and produces the state as a legitimate and desired apparatus. I aim not to "harbor any nostalgia for the powers of the nation-state" (ibid.: 336), but I must recognize the ways in which the state creates the conditions around which its regulation is still desired.

Bibliography

Abu-Lughod, Lila. 1990. "The Romance of Resistance: Tracing Transformations of Power through Bedouin Women." *American Ethnologist* 17: 41–55.

Accornero, Aris. 2006. *San Precario lavora per noi: Gli impieghi temporanei in Italia.* Rome: Rizzoli.

Adam, Frane. 1994. "After Four Years of Democracy: Fragility and Stability." *Druzboslovne Razprave* 15–16: 35–50.

Agamben, Giorgio. 1993. *The Coming Community.* Minneapolis: University of Minnesota Press.

Agnew, John. 2002. *Place and Politics in Modern Italy.* Chicago: University of Chicago Press.

Ahearn, Laura. 2001a. *Invitations to Love: Literacy, Love Letters, and Social Change in Nepal.* Ann Arbor: University of Michigan Press.

———. 2001b. "Language and Agency." *Annual Review of Anthropology* 30: 109–137.

———. 2003. "Writing Desire in Nepali Love Letters." *Language and Communication* 23: 107–122.

Ahmed, Sara. 2004. *The Cultural Politics of Emotion.* New York: Routledge.

Alonso, Ana Maria. 2005. "Territorializing the Nation and 'Integrating the Indian': 'Mestizaje' in Mexican Official Discourses and Public Culture." In Thomas Blom Hansen and Finn Stepputatat, eds., *Sovereign Bodies: Citizens, Migrants and States in the Postcolonial World.* Pp. 39–60. Princeton, N.J.: Princeton University Press.

Altmann, Stuart A. 1956. "Avian Mobbing Behavior and Predator Recognition." *Condor* 58(4): 241–253.

Amato, Fabrizio, Maria Valentina Casciano, Lara Lazzeroni, and Antonio Loffredo. 2002. *Il Mobbing: Aspetti lavoristici: Nozione, responsibilità, tutele.* Milan: Giuffré.

Ambrosini, Murizio. 2001. "The Role of Immigrants in the Italian Labour Market." *International Migration* 39(3): 61–83.

Anagnost, Ann. 1994. "The Politicized Body." In Angela Zito and Tani E. Barlow, eds., *Body, Subject and Power in China.* Pp. 131–156. Chicago: University of Chicago Press.

———. 2004. "The Corporeal Politics of Quality (Suzhi)." *Public Culture* 16(2): 189–208.

Ankarloo, Bengt, and Stuart Clarke. 1999. *Witchcraft and Magic in Europe.* Philadelphia: University of Pennsylvania Press.

ANSA Notiziario Generale in Italiano. 2004a. "Mobbing: CISL in Europa 13 milioni di vittime." *ANSA Notiziaro Generale in Italiano*, November 24.

———. 2004b. "Mobbing: CondMariato capo produzione." *ANSA Notiziaro Generale in Italiano*, May 14.

———. 2004c. "PA: Mazzella travet no passacarte." *ANSA Notiziaro Generale in Italiano*, March 24.

———. 2004d. "Ricerca: Bertinotti 15 Maggio in piazza per lotta precariato." *ANSA Notiziaro Generale in Italiano*, May 11.

———. 2005a. "Censis: Decelera mercato lavoro, Italiani pigri d'Europa." *ANSA Notiziaro Generale in Italiano*, December 2.

———. 2005b. "Governo: Ricerca tre quarti Italiano vogliono donna premier." *ANSA Notiziaro Generale in Italiano*, October 17.

———. 2005c. "Lavoro: Allarme CGIL, troppi precari e poche garanzie." *ANSA Notiziaro Generale in Italiano*, June 28.

———. 2005d. "Lavoro: Bassolino, flessibilità non sia sinonimo precarieta." *ANSA Notiziaro Generale in Italiano*, December 16.

———. 2005e. "Lavoro: Buffo, bene Prodi, precariato problema numero uno." *ANSA Notiziaro Generale in Italiano*, October 28.

———. 2005f. "Psichiatria: Fino a 18% lavoratori vittime del mobbing." *ANSA Notiziaro Generale in Italiano*, February 23.

———. 2006a. "Convegno, mostra e progetto su discriminazione nel lavoro." *ANSA Notiziaro Generale in Italiano*, May 9.

———. 2006b. "Lavoro: Bonanni (CISL) da fisco risorse per occupazione donne." *ANSA Notiziaro Generale in Italiano*, July 12.

———. 2006c. "Lavoro: Movimenti e sindacati a governo." *ANSA Notiziaro Generale in Italiano*, July 8.

Antonietta, Maria C. 2007. "La Cassazione sul mobbing: 'Non é reato.'" *Corriere della Sera*, August 30.

Appadurai, Arjun. 1990. "Disjuncture and Difference in the Global Economy." *Public Culture* 2(2): 1–24.

Appadurai, Arjun, ed. 1986. *The Social Life of Things: Commodities in Cultural Perspective*. Cambridge: Cambridge University Press.

Arcidiacono, Caterina. 1999. "Donne e madri: Dalla madre all'amore con l'altro." In *Saperi femminili nella scienza e nella società*. Pp. 63–77. Milan: Francoangeli.

Ardizzoni, Michela. 2005. "Redrawing the Boundaries of Italianness: Televised Identities in the Age of Globalization." *Social Identities* 11(5): 509–530.

Ardù, Barbara. 1999. "Ecco il mobbing: Veleni in ufficio." *La Repubblica*, July 24. http://www.repubblica.it/online/sessi_stili_mobbing/mobbi/mobbi.html (accessed March 2003).

Aretxaga, Begoña. 1997. *Shattering Silence: Women, Nationalism, and Political Subjectivity in Northern Ireland*. Princeton, N.J.: Princeton University Press.

———. 2001. "The Sexual Games of the Body Politic: Fantasy and State Violence in Northern Ireland." *Culture, Medicine and Psychiatry: An International Journal of Comparative Cross Cultural Research* 25: 1–27.

Aronowitz, Stanley, Dawn Eposito, William DiFazio, and Margaret Yard. 1997. "The Post-Work Manifesto." In Stanley Aronowitz, ed., *Post-Work*. Pp. 31–80. London: Routledge.

Arrighi, Giovanni. 1994. *The Long Twentieth Century*. London: Verso.

Ascenzi, Antonio, and Gian Luigi Bergagio. 2002. *Mobbing: Riflessioni sulla Pelle*. Turin: Giappichelli.

Associazione contro Mobbing. 2006. "Il Mobbing." www.helpmobbing.it/il_mobbing.html (accessed June 21, 2010).

Atanasio, Riccardo. 2004. "Indennizzo Inail e responsabilità civile, tribunate ordinario di Milano, sezione lavoro, udienza del 29 Giugno 2004, N. 1142/01 RG." http://www.altalex.com/index.php?idnot=9463 (accessed November 9, 2009).

Atkinson, Valerie J. J. 2009. *Mobbing: Sophisticated Bullying in the Workplace.* New York: Mellen.

Austin, J. L. 1975. *How to Do Things with Words.* Cambridge, Mass.: Harvard University Press.

Bajani, Andrea. 2006. *Mi spezzo ma non m'impiego: Guida di viaggio per lavoratori flessibili.* Turin: Einaudi.

Bakhtin, M. M. 1981. *The Dialogic Imagination.* Austin: University of Texas Press.

Balibar, Etienne. 2004. *We, the People of Europe? Reflections on Transnational Citizenship.* Princeton, N.J.: Princeton University Press.

Ballarino, Gabriele. 2005. "Strumenti nuovi per un lavoro vecchio." *Sociologia del Lavoro* 97: 174–189.

Banfield, E. 1958. *The Moral Basis of Backward Society.* New York: Free Press.

Baranski, Z., and S. Vinall, eds. 1991. *Women and Italy: Essays on Gender, Culture and History.* New York: St. Martin's.

Baranski, Z., and R. West. 2001. *Modern Italian Culture.* Cambridge: Cambridge University Press.

Barca, Fabrizio, and Marco Becht, eds. 2001. *The Control of Corporate Europe.* Oxford: Oxford University Press.

Barca, Fabrizio, Katsuhito Iwai, Ugo Pagano, and Sandro Trento. 2001. "Divergences in Corporate Governance Models: The Role of Institutional Shocks." In Andrea Boltho, Alessandro Vercelli, and Hiroshi Yoshikawa, eds., *Comparing Economic Systems: Italy and Japan.* Pp. 15–37. London: Palgrave.

Barry, Andrew, Thomas Osborne, and Nikolas Rose. 1996. "Introduction." In Andrew Barry, Thomas Osborne, and Nikolas Rose, eds., *Foucault and Political Reason.* Pp. 1–17. Chicago: University of Chicago Press.

Bassi, Tina L. 1993. "Violence against Women and the Response of Italian Institutions." In M. Cicioni and N. Prunster, eds., *Visions and Revisions: Women in Italian Culture.* Pp. 199–213. Providence, R.I.: Berg.

Bauman, R., and C. L. Briggs. 1990. "Poetics and Performance as Critical Perspectives on Language and Social Life." *Annual Review of Anthropology* 19: 58–88.

Bauman, Zygmunt. 2003. *Liquid Love.* Cambridge: Polity.

Beck, Ulrich. 1992. *Risk Society: Towards a New Modernity.* London: Sage.

———. 1999. *World Risk Society.* Oxford: Blackwell.

———. 2000. *The Brave New World of Work.* Cambridge: Cambridge University Press

Beck, Ulrich, and Elisabeth Beck-Gernsheim. 1995. *The Normal Chaos of Love.* Cambridge: Polity.

Bedani, Gino. 1995. *Politics and Ideology in the Italian Workers Movement.* Oxford: Berg.

Belussi, Fiorenza. 1996. "Local Systems, Industrial Districts and Institutional Networks: Towards a New Evolutionary Paradigm of Industrial Economies?" *European Planning Studies* 4(1): 1–15.

Ben-Ghiat, Ruth. 2001. "The Italian Cinema and the Italian Working Class." *International Labor and Working-Class History* 59: 36–51.

Berardi, Franco "Bifo," ed. 2009. *The Soul at Work: From Alienation to Autonomy.* Translated by Francesca Cadel and Giuseppina Mecchia. Los Angeles, Calif.: Semiotext(e).

Berend, Ivan T. 2006. *An Economic History of Twentieth-Century Europe: Economic Regimes from Laissez-Faire to Globalization.* Cambridge: Cambridge University Press.

Berezin, Mabel. 1999. "Political Belonging: Emotion, Nation and Identity in Fascist Italy." In George Steinmetz, ed., *State/Culture: State-Formation after the Cultural Turn.* Pp. 355–377. Ithaca, N.Y.: Cornell University Press.

Bergeron, Suzanne. 2001. "Political Economy Discourses of Globalization and Feminist Politics." *Signs* 26(4): 983–1006.

Bernardi, Fabrizio. 2000. "The Employment Behavior of Married Women in Italy." In H. Blossfield and S. Drobnic, eds., *Careers of Couples in Contemporary Society.* Pp. 121–145. Oxford: Oxford University Press

Bernardi, Ulderico. 2005. *Veneti.* Treviso: Canova.

Bertinaria, Sabina. 2004. *Gli esami strumentali nella valutazione del danno da mobbing: L'Accertamento psicodiagnostico.* Rome: Assocazione Italiana Psicologia Giurdica.

Best, Suzanna. 2005. *The Limits of Transparency: Ambiguity and the History of International Finance.* Ithaca, N.Y.: Cornell University Press.

Bianchi, M., M. Bianco, and L. Enriques. 2001. "Pyramidal Groups and the Separation between Ownership and Control in Italy." In Fabrizio Barca and Marco Becht, eds., *The Control of Corporate Europe.* Pp. 154–187. Oxford: Oxford University Press.

Biehl, João, and Peter Locke. 2010. "Deleuze and the Anthropology of Becoming." *Current Anthropology* 51(3): 317–351.

Bigioni, Paul. 2005. "The Real Threat of Fascism." In his *Common Dreams.* New York: Global Policy Forum.

Bignotti, Gigi. 2005. "Mobbing: Incubo per centomila: A tutte le età." *Il Gazzettino,* January 9: 3.

Bini, Paolo C. 2003. "The Italian Welfare System between the European Unification and the Globalization Process: A Suggested Interpretation." In Matteo Di Matteo and Paolo Piacentini, eds., *The Italian Economy at the Dawn of the 21st Century.* Pp. 334–350. Farnham, England: Ashgate.

Black, Christopher F. 2001. *Early Modern Italy: A Social History.* London: Routledge.

Blim, Michael. 1990. "Economic Development and Decline in the Emerging Global." *Politics and Society* 18(1): 143–164.

———. 2000. "What Is Still Left for the Left in Italy? Piecing Together a Post-Communist Position on Labor and Employment." *Journal of Modern Italian Studies* 5(2): 169–185.

———. 2002. "The Italian Post-Communist Left and Unemployment: Finding a New Position on Labor." In W. Lem and B. Leach, eds., *Culture, Economy, Power: Anthropology as Critique, Anthropology as Praxis.* Pp. 136–149. Albany: State University of New York Press.

Boddy, Janice. 1997. "Womb as Oasis: The Symbolic Context of Pharaonic Circumcision in Rural Northern Sudan." In Roger Lancaster and Michaela di Leonardo, eds., *The Gender/Sexuality Reader: Culture, History, Political Economy.* Pp. 309–324. New York: Routledge.

Boellstorff, Tom. 2007. *A Coincidence of Desires: Anthropology, Queer Studies, Indonesia.* Durham, N.C.: Duke University Press.

Boeri, Tito, and Pietro Garibaldi. 2005. "Regimi di protezione dell'impiego: Implicazioni teoriche e indicazioni alle riforme in atto in Italia." *Sociologia del Lavoro* 90: 42–65.

Bohle, Dorothee. 2005. "Neoliberal Hegemony, Transnational Capital and the Terms of the EU's Eastward Expansion." *Capital and Class* 88: 57–86.

Boltho, Andrea. 2001. "Foreign Trade Performance: From Early Similarities to Present Diversity." In Andrea Boltho, Alessandro Vercelli, and Hiroshi Yoshikawa, eds., *Comparing Economic Systems: Italy and Japan*. Pp. 107–134. London: Palgrave.

Boltho, Andrea, Alessandro Vercelli, and Hiroshi Yoshikawa. 2001. "Introduction." In Andrea Boltho, Alessandro Vercelli, and Hiroshi Yoshikawa, eds., *Comparing Economic Systems: Italy and Japan*. Pp. 1–15. London: Palgrave.

Bondanella, Peter E. 2001. *Italian Cinema: From Neorealism to the Present*. New York: Continuum.

Borneman, J., and N. Fowler. 1997. "Europeanization." *Annual Review of Anthropology* 26: 487–514.

Borselli, Edmondo. 2001. "The Crisis and Transformation of Italian Politics." *Daedalus* 130(3): 85–95.

Bosia, Michael J. 1990 [1980]. *The Logic of Practice*. Stanford, Calif.: Stanford University Press.

———. 2005. "'Assassin!': AIDS and Neoliberal Reform in France." *New Political Science* 27(3): 291–308.

Bourdieu, Pierre. 1990. *The Logic of Practice*. Cambridge: Polity.

Bramezza, Ilaria. 1996. *The Competitiveness of the European City and the Role of Urban Management in Improving the City's Performance*. Amsterdam: Thesis Publishers.

Brennan, Denise. 2004. *What's Love Got to Do with It? Transnational Desires and Sex Tourism in the Dominican Republic*. Durham, N.C.: Duke University Press.

Brenner, Neil. 2004. *New State Spaces: Urban Governance and the Rescaling of Statehood*. Oxford: Oxford University Press.

Buci-Glucksmann, Christine. 1980. *Gramsci and the State*. London: Lawrence and Wishart.

Buffone, Giuseppe. 2005. "Danno esistenziale: Il neo bipolarismo costituzionale della responsabilità civile." *Altalex: Quotidiano d'informazione giuridica*. http://www.altalex.com/index.php?idnot=196 (accessed May 25, 2010).

Burawoy, Michael. 1979. *Manufacturing Consent: Changes in the Labor Process under Monopoly Capitalism*. Chicago: University of Chicago Press.

———. 2000. "Introduction." In Michael Burawoy, ed., *Ethnography: Forces, Connections, and Imaginations in a Postmodern World*. Berkeley: University of California Press.

Burchell, Graham. 1996. "Liberal Government and Techniques of the Self." In Andrew Barry, Thomas Osborne, and Nikolas Rose, eds., *Foucault and Political Reason*. Pp. 19–36. Chicago: University of Chicago Press.

Butler, Judith. 1990. *Gender Trouble: Feminism and the Subversion of Identity*. New York: Routledge.

———. 1993. *Bodies That Matter: On the Discursive Limits of "Sex."* London: Routledge.

———. 1997a. *Excitable Speech: A Politics of the Performative*. New York: Routledge.

———. 1997b. *The Psychic Life of Power*. Stanford, Calif.: Stanford University Press.

———. 2004. *Precarious Life*. London: Verso.

Cafruny, Alan W. 2003. "The Geopolitics of U.S. Hegemony in Europe: From the Breakup of Yugoslavia to the War in Iraq." In Alan W. Cafruny and Magnus Ryner, eds., *A Ruined Fortress? Neoliberal Hegemony and Transformation in Europe*. Pp. 95–122. Lanham, Md.: Rowman and Littlefield.

Cafruny, Alan W., and Magnus Ryner. 2003. "Introduction: The Study of European Integration in the Neoliberal Era." In Alan Cafruny and Magnus Ryner, eds., *A*

Ruined Fortress? Neoliberal Hegemony and Transformation in Europe. Pp. 1–13. Lanham, Md.: Rowman and Littlefield.

Caldwell, Lesley. 1991. "Italian Feminism: Some Considerations." In Z. Baranski and S. Vinall, eds., *Women and Italy: Essays on Gender, Culture and History.* Pp. 95–116. New York: St. Martin's.

Cameron, David R., Gustav Ranis, and Annalisa Zinn. 2006. *Globalisation and Self-Determination: Is the Nation-State under Siege?* London: Routledge.

Cameron, Deborah. 1997. "Performing Gender Identity: Young Men's Talk and the Construction of Heterosexual Masculinity." In Sally Johnson and Ulrike Meinhof, eds., *Language and Masculinity.* Pp. 47–64. Oxford: Blackwell.

Cameron, Deborah, and Don Kulick. 2003. *Language and Sexuality.* Cambridge: Cambridge University Press.

Canguilhem, Georges. 2008. "Health: Crude Concept and Philosophical Question." Translated by Todd Meyers and Stefanos Geroulanos. *Public Culture* 20(3): 474.

Cani Sciolti. 2006. "Bertinotti: É la precarietà il vero cancro." http://www.canisciolti.info/modules.php?name=News&file=article&sid=7160 (accessed March 12, 2007).

Cantistani, Daniela. 2000. *La dimostrazione giuridica del mobbing.* Bologna: Prima.

———. 2005. "Mobbing e INAIL: Prima e dopo la sentenza del Tar Lazio N. 5454/2005 che ha annullato la Circolare N. 71/0203." *Prima.* http://www.mobbing-prima .it/dan.htm (accessed March 2006).

Carboni, Carlo. 2005. "Nuova economia, nuova società." *Sociologia del Lavoro* 98: 43–67.

Caritas di Roma.1998. *Immigrazione dossier statistico 1998.* Rome: Anterem.

Carnazza, Paolo, Alessandro Innocenti, and Alessandro Vercelli. 2001. "Small Firms and Manufacturing Employment." In Andrea Boltho, Alessandro Vercelli, and Hiroshi Yoshikawa, eds., *Comparing Economic Systems: Italy and Japan.* Pp. 158–176. London: Palgrave.

Carta. 2005. "La Relazione di Fausto Bertinotti, VI Congresso Nazionale, Partito della Refondazione Communista, relazione introduttiva, 4 Marzo 2005." http://www .carta.org/articoli/2590 (accessed October 15, 2006).

Carter, Bob. 2006. "The Restructuring of States in the Global Economy." In Peter Fairbrother and Al Rainnie, eds., *Globalisation, State and Labour.* Pp. 136–150. London: Routledge.

Cassitto, Maria Grazia, Emanuela Fattorini, Renato Gilioli, and Chiara Rengo. 2003. *Violenza psicologica sul lavoro: accrescere la consapevolezza.* Geneva: World Health Organization.

Castel, Robert. 1997. "Diseguaglianze e vulnerabilità sociale." *Rassegna Italiana di Sociologia* 1: 41–56.

———. 2003. *From Manual Workers to Wage Laborers.* London: Transaction.

Castells, Manuel. 1996. *The Rise of the Network Society.* Vol. 1 of *The Information Age: Economy, Society, Culture.* Oxford: Blackwell.

———. 1997. *The Power of Identity.* Oxford: Blackwell.

Cavalli, Alessandro. 2001. "Reflections on Political Culture and the 'Italian National Character.'" *Daedalus* 130(3): 119–137.

Cavanaugh, Jillian R. 2006. "Little Women and Vital Champions: Gendered Language Shift in a Northern Italian Town." *Journal of Linguistic Anthropology* 16(2): 194–210.

Chase, Jacquelyn. 2002. "Introduction: The Spaces of Neoliberalism in Latin America." In Jacquelyn Chase, ed., *The Spaces of Neoliberalism: Land, Place and Family in Latin America.* Pp. 1–21. Bloomfield, Conn.: Kumarian.

Cherubini, Arnaldo. 1977. *Storia della prevadenza sociale in Italia (1860–1960)*. Rome: Riuniti.

CGIL Foggia. 2006. "Non ti scordar di me." http://www.cgilfoggia.it/public/guidadoc/878a.pdf (accessed June 21, 2010).

Cirioli, Daniela. 2006. "Illegittima la riassunzione a termine." *Italia Oggi*, May 7: 45.

Clark, Ian. 2003. "The Security State." In David Held and Anthony McGrew, eds., *The Global Transformations Reader: An Introduction to the Globalization Debate*. Pp. 177–188. Cambridge: Polity.

Cohen, Ed. 2009. *A Body Worth Defending: Immunity, Biopolitics, and the Apotheosis of the Modern Body*. Durham, N.C.: Duke University Press.

Colatrella, Steven. 2001. *Workers of the World: African and Asian Migrants in Italy in the 1990s*. Trenton, N.J.: Africa World Press.

Cole, Jeffrey. 1997. *The New Racism in Europe: A Sicilian Ethnography*. Cambridge: Cambridge University Press.

Collier, Stephen, and Andrew Lakoff. 2005. "On Regimes of Living." In Aihwa Ong and Stephen Collier, eds., *Global Assemblages*. Pp. 22–39. Oxford: Blackwell.

Collier, Stephen, and Aihwa Ong. 2005. "Global Assemblages, Anthropological Problems." In Aihwa Ong and Stephen J. Collier, eds., *Global Assemblages*. Pp. 3–21. Oxford: Blackwell.

Collins, Jane. 2002. "Mapping a Global Labor Market: Gender and Skill in the Globalizing Garment Industry." *Gender and Society* 16(6): 921–940.

———. 2003. *Threads: Gender, Labor, and Power in the Global Apparel Industry*. Chicago: University of Chicago Press.

———. 2005. "Deterritorialization and Workplace Culture." In Marc Edelman and Angelique Haugerud, eds., *Anthropology of Development and Globalization*. Pp. 250–261. Oxford: Blackwell.

Comaroff, Jean, and John L. Comaroff. 1989. "The Colonization of Consciousness in South Africa." *Economy and Society* 18(3): 267–296.

———. 1993. "The Diseased Heart of Africa: Medicine, Colonialism, and the Black Body." In Jean Comaroff, Shirley Lindenbaum, and Margaret Lock, eds., *Knowledge, Power and Practice: The Anthropology of Medicine and Everyday Life*. Pp. 305–329. Berkeley: University of California Press.

———. 2001. "Millennial Capitalism: First Thoughts on a Second Coming." In J. Comaroff and J. Comaroff, eds., *Millennial Capitalism and the Culture of Neoliberalism*. Pp. 1–56. Durham, N.C.: Duke University Press.

———. 2006. "Colonizing Currencies: Beasts, Banknotes and the Color of Money in South Africa." In P. Geschiere and W. van Binsbergben, eds., *Commodification: Things, Agency, and Identities: The Social Life of Things Revisited*. Pp. 43–53. Munster, Germany: LIT.

Comencini, Francesca, dir. 2004. *Mi Piace Lavorare: Mobbing [I Like to Work: Mobbing]*. Rome: BIM.

Conboy, Katie, Nadia Medina, and Sarah Stanbury, eds. 1997. *Writing on the Body: Female Embodiment and Feminist Theory*. New York: Columbia University Press.

Constable, Nicole. 2003. *Romance on a Global Stage: Pen Pals, Virtual Ethnography, and "Mail Order" Marriages*. Berkeley: University of California Press.

Coronil, Fernando. 1997. *The Magical State: Nature, Money and Modernity in Venezuela*. Chicago: University of Chicago Press.

Corriere della Sera. 1998. "Anche il bacio sulla guancia può essere violenza sessuale." *Corriere della Sera,* June 9.

———. 2002a. "Denunciata dai dipendenti l'eroina anti-mobbing." *Corriere della Sera,* April 12.

———. 2002b. "Mobbing: Malattia da 20 miliardi di euro." *Corriere della Sera,* September 1.

———. 2003. "Un milione di lavoratori maltrattato dai capi." *Corriere della Sera,* January 18.

———. 2006. "Cambieremo la Legge 30." *Corriere della Sera,* November 11.

Cox, R. W. 1987. *Production, Power, and World Order: Social Forces in the Making of History.* New York: Columbia University Press.

Craighero, Ambra. 2008. "Mobbing: Quando il lavoro fa ammalare." *Corriere della Sera,* January 23. CRAS (Centro Ricerche Affari Sociali). 2006. *Mobbing: Raising Awareness of Women Victims of Mobbing.* Rome: CRAS.

Crehan, Kate. 2002. *Gramsci, Culture and Anthropology.* Berkeley: University of California Press.

Crouch, Colin. 1997. "Italy since the 1996 Elections: A Special Case with General Lessons." *Political Quarterly* 68(1): 23–30.

Csordas, Thomas. 2004. "Health and the Holy in Afro-Brazilian Cambomblé." In Helen Thomas and Jamilah Ahmend, eds., *Cultural Bodies: Ethnography and Theory.* Pp. 241–259. Oxford: Blackwell.

Csordas, Thomas, ed. 1994. *Embodiment and Experience: The Existential Ground of Culture and Self.* Cambridge: Cambridge University Press.

Curtis, Debra. 2004. "Commodities and Sexual Subjectivities: A Look at Capitalism and Its Desires." *Cultural Anthropology* 19(1): 95–121.

Das, Veena. 2006. *Life and Words: Violence and the Descent into the Ordinary.* Berkeley: University of California Press.

Davenport, Noa, Ruth D. Schwartz, and Gail Pursell Eliot. 1999. *Mobbing: Emotional Abuse in the American Workplace.* Ames, Iowa: Civil Society Publishing.

Davis, Mike. 1999. *Ecology of Fear: Los Angeles and the Imagination of Disaster.* New York: Vintage.

De Grazia, Victoria. 1993. *How Fascism Ruled Women: Italy 1922–1945.* Berkeley: University of California Press.

Della Sala, Vincent. 2003. "D'Alema's Dilemmmas: Third Way, Italian Style." In Oliver Schmidtke, ed., *The Third Way Transformation of Social Democracy.* Pp. 103–130. Farnham, England: Ashgate.

De Martino, Ernesto. 1959. *Sud e Magia.* Milan: Feltrinelli.

Derrida, Jacques. 1977. "Signature, Event, Context." *Glyph* 1: 172–197.

Desiati, Mario. 2006. *Vita precaria e amore eterno.* Milan: Mondadori Strade Blu.

Diamanti, I. 1993. *La Lega: Geografia, Storia e Sociologia di un Nuovo Soggetto Politico.* Rome: Donzelli.

di Leonardo, Michaela. 1991. "Introduction: Gender, Culture, Political Economy: Feminist Anthropology in Historical Perspective." In M. di Leonardo, ed., *Gender at the Crossroads of Knowledge: Feminist Anthropology in the Postmodern Era.* Pp. 1–51. Berkeley: University of California Press.

Di Martino, Vittorio, and Roberto De Santis. 2003. *Mobbing: La Violenza al lavoro.* Troina, Italy: Oasi.

Di Matteo, Massimo, and Hiroshi Yoshikawa. 2001. "Economic Growth: The Role of Demand." In Andrea Boltho, Alessandro Vercelli, and Hiroshi Yoshikawa, eds., *Comparing Economic Systems: Italy and Japan.* Pp. 41–63. London: Palgrave.

Di Matteo, Matteo, and Paolo Piacentini, eds. 2003. *The Italian Economy at the Dawn of the 21st Century.* Farnham, England: Ashgate.

Di Tacco, Gianni. 2008. "Storie di ordinari soprusi." http://www.cosechenonvanno.com/lavoro/storie-di-ordinari-soprusi (accessed April 25, 2010).

Doyal, Lesley. 1995. *What Makes Women Sick: Gender and the Political Economy of Health.* New Brunswick, N.J.: Rutgers University Press.

Drake, Richard. 1989. *The Revolutionary Mystique and Terrorism in Contemporary Italy.* Bloomington: Indiana University Press.

Dunant, Sarah, and Roy Porter. 1996. *The Age of Anxiety.* London: Virago.

Dundes, Alan. 1992. *The Evil Eye: A Casebook.* Madison: University of Wisconsin Press.

Dunn, Elizabeth C. 2004. *Privatizing Poland: Baby Food, Big Business and the Remaking of Labor.* Ithaca, N.Y.: Cornell University Press.

Edelman, Marc. 1999. *Peasants against Globalization: Rural Social Movements in Costa Rica.* Stanford, Calif.: Stanford University Press.

Edelman, Marc, and Angelique Haugerud. 2005. "Introduction." In Marc Edelman and Angelique Haugerud, eds., *Anthropology of Development and Globalization.* Pp. 1–74. Oxford: Blackwell.

Ege, Harald. 1996. *Mobbing.* Bologna: Pitagora.

———. 1998. *I Numeri di mobbing.* Bologna: Pitagora.

———. 2002. *La valutazione peritale del danno da mobbing.* Milan: Giuffrè.

Ege, Harald, ed. 1997. *Il Mobbing in Italia.* Bologna: Pitagora.

Ehrenreich, B., and A. Hochschild. 2003. *Global Woman: Nannies, Maids and Sex Workers in the New Economy.* New York: Metropolitan.

Elmer, Peter, and Ole Peter Grell. 2004. *Health, Disease and Society in Europe 1500–1800.* Manchester: Manchester University Press.

Engels, Friedrich. 1972. *The Origin of the Family, Private Property and the State.* New York: Pathfinder.

Esposito, Roberto. 2008. *Bìos: Biopolitics and Philosophy.* Minneapolis: University of Minnesota Press.

Ettlinger, Nancy. 2007. "Precarity Unbound." *Alternatives* 32: 319–340.

European Agency for Safety and Health at Work. 2002. "Fact Sheet 23: Il mobbing sul posto di lavoro." http://osha.europa.eu/it/publications/factsheets/23/view (accessed November 5, 2010).

Faculty of Education of the University of Verona. 2007. "1st Level University Master in Mobbing and Organizational Stress." http://www.formazione.univr.it/fol/main?ent=cs&id=169&lang=en (accessed March 8, 2007).

Fairbrother, Peter, and Al Rainnie. 2006. "The Enduring Question of the State." In Peter Fairbrother and Al Rainnie, eds., *Globalisation, State and Labour.* Pp. 1–11. London: Routledge.

Falconi, Mario. 2006. "Contro il mobbing per tutelare i medici e salvaguardare i cittadini." *Bollettino: Mobbing Patologia Professionale Stress Correlata ai Conflitti nei Luoghi di Lavoro* 58(4): 1.

Fargion, Valeria. 2003. "Half Way through the Ford: The Italian Welfare State at the Start of the New Century." In Neil Gilbert and Rebecca A. Von Voorhis, eds., *Changing Patterns of Social Protection.* Pp. 309–338. London: Transaction.

Farmer, Paul. 1990. "Sending Sickness: Sorcery, Politics, and Changing Concepts of AIDS in Rural Haiti." *Medical Anthropology Quarterly* 1(4): 6–27.

Farquhar, Judith. 1999. "Technologies of Everyday Life: The Economy of Impotence in Reform China." *Cultural Anthropology* 14(2): 155–179.

———. 2002. *Appetites: Food and Sex in Post-Socialist China.* Durham, N.C.: Duke University Press.

Fassin, Didier. 2001. "The Biopolitics of Otherness: Undocumented Foreigners and Racial Discrimination in French Public Debate." *Anthropology Today* 17(1): 3–7.

Ferguson, James, and Akhil Gupta. 2002. "Spatializing States: Toward an Ethnography of Neoliberal Governmentality." *American Ethnologist* 29(4): 981–1002.

Ferguson, Ronnie. 2003. "The Formation of the Dialect of Venice." *Forum for Modern Language Studies* 39(4): 450–464.

Fernandez-Kelly, Maria Patricia. 1983. *For We Are Sold, I and My People: Women in Industry in Mexico's Frontier.* Albany: State University of New York Press.

Ferracuti, Angelo. 2006. *Le Risorse umane.* Milan: Feltrinelli Serie Bianca.

Ferrara, Elena. 2004. "Raising Awareness of Women Victims of Mobbing: The Italian Contribution." *Daphne Programme: Preventive Measures to Fight Violence against Children, Young People and Women.* http://ec.europa.eu/justice/funding/daphne3/funding_daphne3_en.htm (accessed November 5, 2010).

Ferrera, Maurizio, and Elisabetta Gualmini. 2004. *Rescued by Europe? Social and Labour Market Reform in Italy from Maastricht to Berlusconi.* Amsterdam: Amsterdam University Press.

Fielding, A. J. 1994. "Industrial Change and Regional Development in Western Europe." *Urban Studies* 31(415): 679–705.

Filippini, Carlo, and Giampaolo Arachi. 2003. "The Fiscal Decentralization and the Autonomy of the Local Government." In Matteo Di Matteo and Paolo Piacentini, eds., *The Italian Economy at the Dawn of the 21st Century.* Pp. 261–286. Farnham, England: Ashgate.

Filippone, Bruno. 2002. "Mobbing: Cos'è?" *Fogli* 4: 16–31.

Fiorii, Flavia. 2006. "Mobbing: Vittima un lavoratore su 10." *Corriere della Sera*, July 10. http://www.corriere.it/Rubriche/Salute/Diritto_alla_salute/2006/07_Luglio/02/ART_mobbing×020706.shtml (accessed August 5, 2006).

Fishback, Price V., and Shawn Everett Kantor. 1996. "The Durable Experiment: State Insurance of Workers' Compensation Risk in the Early Twentieth Century." *Journal of Economic History* 56(4): 809–836.

Foner, Eric. 2001. "Italy's House of Freedoms." *Nation*, May 31.

Foucault, Michel. 1973. *The Birth of the Clinic.* New York: Vintage.

———. 1975. *Discipline and Punish: The Birth of the Prison.* New York: Random House.

———. 1978. *The History of Sexuality*, vol. 1. New York: Vintage.

———. 1980 [1972]. *Power/Knowledge: Selected Interviews and Other Writings, 1972–1977.* New York: Pantheon.

———. 1983. "The Subject and Power." In Hubert L. Dreyfus and Paul Rabinow, eds., *Michel Foucault: Beyond Structuralism and Hermeneutics.* Pp. 208–226. Chicago: University of Chicago Press.

———. 1988. *Technologies of the Self.* Edited by Luther H. Martin, Huck Gutman, and Patrick H. Hutton. Amherst: University of Massachusetts Press.

———. 1997. "The Abnormals." Translated by Robert Hurley. In Paul Rabinow, ed., *Ethics: Subjectivity and Truth.* Pp. 51–52. New York: New Press.

Freeman, Carla. 2000. *High Tech and High Heels in the Global Economy: Women, Work and Pink-Collar Identities in the Caribbean*. Durham, N.C.: Duke University Press.

———. 2001. "Is Local:Global as Feminine:Masculine? Rethinking the Gender of Globalization." *Signs: Journal of Women in Culture and Society* 26(4): 1007–1037.

———. 2002. "Designing Women: Corporate Discipline and Barbados's Off-Shore Pink-Collar Sector." In Jonathan Xavier Inda and Renato Rosaldo, eds., *The Anthropology of Globalization: A Reader*. Pp. 83–99. Oxford: Blackwell.

Friedman, Jonathan. 2005. "Globalization, Dis-integration, Re-organization: The Transformations of Violence." In Marc Edelman and Angelique Haugerud, eds., *Anthropology of Development and Globalization*. Pp. 160–168. Oxford: Blackwell.

Gabaccia, D., and Franca Iacovetta, eds. 2002. *Women, Gender and Transnational Lives: Italian Workers of the World*. Toronto: University of Toronto Press.

Gal, Susan. 1995. "Language, Gender and Power: An Anthropological Perspective." In K. Hall and M. Bucholz, eds., *Gender Articulated: Language and the Socially Constructed Self*. Pp. 169–182. New York: Routledge.

———. 2003. "Movements of Feminism: The Circulation of Discourses about Women." In Barbara Hobson, ed., *Recognition Struggles and Social Movements: Contested Identities, Agency and Power*. Pp. 93–120. Cambridge: Cambridge University Press.

———. 2005. "Language Ideologies Compared: Metaphors of Public/Private." *Journal of Linguistic Anthropology* 15(1): 23–57.

Gallo, F., and H. Birgit. 2003. "Italy: Progress behind Complexity." In W. Wessels, A. Maurer, and J. Mittag, eds., *Fifteen into One? The European Union and Its Member States*. Pp. 271–297. Manchester: Manchester University Press.

Galt, Anthony. 1991. "Magical Misfortune in Locorotondo." *American Ethnologist* 18: 735–750.

Garelli, Franco. 2007. "The Public Relevance of the Church and Catholicism in Italy." *Journal of Modern Italian Studies* 12(1): 8–36.

Genda, Yuju, Maria Grazia Pazienza, and Marcello Signorelli. 2001. "Labour Market Performance and Job Creation." In Andrea Boltho, Alessandro Vercelli, and Hiroshi Yoshikawa, eds., *Comparing Economic Systems: Italy and Japan*. Pp. 134–157. London: Palgrave.

Ghezzi, Giorgio, and Daniele Ranieri. 2006. *Danni da mobbing e loro risarcibilitá*. Rome: Ediesse.

Gibson-Graham, J. K. 1996. *The End of Capitalism as We Knew It*. Oxford: Blackwell.

Giddens, Anthony. 1990. *The Consequences of Modernity*. Cambridge: Polity.

———. 1992. *The Transformation of Intimacy: Sexuality, Love and Eroticism in Modern Societies*. Cambridge: Polity.

———. 1998. *The Third Way: The Renewal of Social Democracy*. Cambridge: Polity.

Gilbert, Mark. 2007. "Italy: Red, Black, and Blue." *World Policy Institute* (Summer): 34–38.

Gilbert, Neil, and Rebecca A. Von Voorhis, eds. 2003. "Introduction." In Neil Gilbert and Rebecca A. Von Voorhis, eds., *Changing Patterns of Social Protection*. Pp. 1–7. London: Transaction.

Gilioli, Alessandro, and Renato Gilioli. 2001. *Cattivi capi, cattivi colleghi*. Milan: Mondadori.

Gilioli, Renato, et al. 2001. "Documento di Consenso: Un nuovo rischio all'attenzione della medicina del lavoro: Le Molestie morali (mobbing)." *La Medicina del Lavoro* 92(1): 61–69.

Gill, Lesley. 2000. *Teetering on the Rim: Global Restructuring, Daily Life, and the Armed Retreat of the Bolivian State.* New York: Columbia University Press.

Gilpin, Robert. 2003. "The Nation-State in the Global Economy." In David Held and Anthony McGrew, eds., *The Global Transformations Reader: An Introduction to the Globalization Debate.* Pp. 349–358. Cambridge: Polity.

Ginsborg, Paul. 1990. *A History of Contemporary Italy: Society and Politics 1943–1988.* London: Penguin.

———. 2003. *Italy and Its Discontents: Family, Civil Society, State 1980–2001.* London: Palgrave Macmillan.

Ginsburg, Faye, Lila Abu-Lughod, and Brian Larkin. 2002. "Introduction." In Faye Ginsburg, Lila Abu-Lughod, and Brian Larkin, eds., *Media Worlds: Anthropology on New Terrain.* Pp. 1–38. Berkeley: University of California Press.

Giroux, Henry A. 2004. *Proto-Fascism in America.* Bloomington, Ind.: Phi Delta Kappa Education Foundation.

———. 2005. "The Terror of Neoliberalism: Rethinking the Significance of Cultural Politics." *College Literature* 32(1): 1–19.

Gledhill, John. 1995. *Neoliberalism, Transnationalization, and Rural Poverty: A Case Study of Michoacán, Mexico.* Boulder, Colo.: Westview.

———. 2000. *Power and Its Disguises: Anthropological Perspectives on Politics.* London: Pluto.

———. 2005. "'Disappearing the Poor?': A Critique of the New Wisdoms of Social Democracy in the Age of Globalization." In Marc Edelman and Angelique Haugerud, eds., *Anthropology of Development and Globalization.* Pp. 382–390. Oxford: Blackwell.

———. 2006. "Resisting the Global Slum: Politics, Religion and Consumption in the Remaking of Life Worlds in the Twenty-First Century." *Bulletin of Latin American Research* 25(3): 322–339.

Gobbetti, D. 1996. "La Lega: Regularities and Innovation in Italian Politics." *Politics and Society* 24(1): 57–82.

Goddard, Victoria. 1996. *Gender, Family and Work in Naples.* Oxford: Berg.

Goldstein, Daniel. 2004. *The Spectacular City: Violence and Performance in Urban Bolivia.* Durham, N.C.: Duke University Press.

———. 2005. "Flexible Justice: Neoliberal Violence and 'Self-Help' Security in Bolivia." *Critique of Anthropology* 25: 389–411.

Good, Byron. 1994. *Medicine, Rationality, and Experience: An Anthropological Perspective.* Cambridge: Cambridge University Press.

Goodwin, Charles, and Marjorie Goodwin. 2000. "Emotion within Situated Activity." In Nancy Budwig, Ina C. Uzgiris, and James V. Wertsch, eds., *Communication: An Arena of Development.* Pp. 33–54. Stamford, Conn.: Ablex.

Goodwin, Jeff, James M. Jasper, and Francesca Polletta. 2001. *Passionate Politics: Emotions and Social Movements.* Chicago: University of Chicago Press.

Gordon, Avery. 2008. *Ghostly Matters: Haunting and the Sociological Imagination*, 2nd ed. Minneapolis: University of Minnesota Press.

Gordon, C. 1991. "Governmental Rationality." In G. Burchell, C. Gordon, and P. Miller, eds., *The Foucault Effect.* Pp. 1–52. Hemel Hempstead, England: Harvester Wheatsheaf.

Graeber, David. 2005. "The Globalization Movement: Some Points of Clarification." In Marc Edelman and Angelique Haugerud, eds., *Anthropology of Development and Globalization*. Pp. 169–172. Oxford: Blackwell.

Gramsci, Antonio. 1971. *Selections from Prison Notebooks*. Edited by Quintin Hoare and Geoffrey Nowell Smith. London: Lawrence and Wishart.

———. 1977. *Antonio Gramsci: Selections from Political Writings 1921–1926*. Edited by Quintin Hoare. London: Lawrence and Wishart.

Grazie a Legge Biagi Avanza Flessibilità. 2005. http://www.uonna.it/biagi-legge-precariato -flessibilita.html (accessed June 21, 2010).

Gregory, Jeanne. 2000. "Sexual Harassment: The Impact of EU Law in the Member States." In Mariagrazia Rossilli, ed., *Gender Policies in the European Union*. Pp. 175–193. New York: Peter Lang.

Grewal, Inderpal. 2005. *Transnational America: Feminisms, Diasporas, Neoliberalisms*. Durham, N.C.: Duke University Press.

Grieco, A., A. Porro, G. Bock Berti, and G. Marri. 2003. "The Origins of the Italian Occupational Health Society." In A. Grieco, D. Fano, T. Carter, and S. Iavicoli, eds., *Origins of Occupational Health Associations in the World*. Pp. 93–107. Amsterdam: Elsevier.

Grillo, Richard. 2002. "Immigration and the Politics of Recognizing Difference in Italy." In R. Grillo and J. Pratt, eds., *The Politics of Recognizing Difference: Multiculturalism Italian-Style*. Pp. 1–24. Farnham, England: Ashgate.

Grosz, Elizabeth. 1994. *Volatile Bodies: Toward a Corporeal Feminism*. Bloomington: Indiana University Press.

Guano, Emanuela. 2006. "Fair Ladies: The Place of Women Antique Dealers in a Post-Industrial Italian City." *Gender, Place and Culture: A Journal of Feminist Geography* 13(2): 105–122.

Gundle, Stephen. 2000. *Between Hollywood and Moscow: Italian Communism and the Challenge of Mass Culture, 1943–1991*. Durham, N.C.: Duke University Press.

Habermas, Jurgen. 2003. "The Postnational Constellation." In David Held and Anthony McGrew, eds., *The Global Transformations Reader: An Introduction to the Globalization Debate*. Pp. 542–547. Cambridge: Polity.

Hacking, Ian. 1998. *Rewriting the Soul: Multiple Personality and the Sciences of Memory*. Princeton, N.J.: Princeton University Press.

Haider, Carmen. 1969. *Capital and Labor under Fascism*. New York: AMS.

Hall, Kira. 1995. "Lip Service on Fantasy Lines." In Kira Hall and Mary Bucholz, eds., *Gender Articulated: Language and the Socially Constructed Self*. Pp. 183–216. New York: Routledge.

Haraway, Donna. 1991. "A Cyborg Manifesto: Science, Technology, and Socialist-Feminism in the Late Twentieth Century." In her *Simians, Cyborgs and Women: The Reinvention of Nature*. Pp. 149–181. London: Routledge.

———. 1992. "The Promises of Monsters: A Regenerative Politics for Inappropriate/d Others." In Lawrence Grossberg, Cary Nelson, and Paula A. Treichler, eds., *Cultural Studies*. Pp. 295–337. New York: Routledge.

Hardt, Michael. 1999. "Affective Labor." *Boundary 2* 26(2): 89–100.

Hardt, Michael, and Antonio Negri. 2000. *Empire*. Cambridge, Mass.: Harvard University Press.

Harney, Stefano. 2006. "Programming Immaterial Labour." *Social Semiotics* 16(1): 75–87.

Harrap's Italian Dictionary. 1990. New York: Prentice Hall.

Harrison, Bennett. 1994. "The Italian Industrial Districts and the Crisis of the Coopera-tive Form: Part II." *European Planning Studies* 2(2): 159–175.

Hartley, P. H. T. 1950. "An Experimental Analysis of Interspecific Recognition." *Sympo-sium for the Society of Experimental Biology* 4: 313–336.

Harvey, David. 1989. *The Constitution of Postmodernity.* Oxford: Basil Blackwell.

———. 2001. *Spaces of Capital: Towards a Critical Geography.* London: Routledge.

———. 2005. *A Brief History of Neoliberalism.* Oxford: Oxford University Press.

———. 2006. "Neoliberalism as Creative Destruction." *Geografiska Annalier, Series A, Physical Geography* 88(2): 145–158.

Hassner, Pierre. 1980. "PCI: Eurocommunism and Universal Reconciliation: The Inter-national Dimension of the Golden Dream, 1975–1979." In Simon Serfaty and Lawrence Gray, eds., *The Italian Communist Past: Yesterday, Today and Tomor-row.* Westport, Conn.: Greenwood.

Hauschild, Thomas. 2002. *Magie und Macht in Italien: über Frauenzauber, Kirche und Politik.* Gifkendorf, Germany: Merlin.

Heath, Deborah, Rayna Rapp, and Karen-Sue Taussig. 2002. "Genetic Citizenship." In David Nugent and Joan Vincent, eds., *Companion to the Handbook of Political Anthropology.* Pp. 152–167. Oxford: Blackwell.

Hedetoft, Ulf. 2003. *The Global Turn: National Encounters with the World.* Aalborg, Den-mark: Aalborg University Press.

Held, David. 2003. "The Changing Structure of International Law: Sovereignty Trans-formed?" In David Held and Anthony McGrew, eds., *The Global Transforma-tions Reader: An Introduction to the Globalization Debate.* Pp. 147–161. Cam-bridge: Polity.

Held, David, and Anthony McGrew. 2003. "The Great Globalization Debate: An Intro-duction." In David Held and Anthony McGrew, eds., *The Global Transforma-tions Reader: An Introduction to the Globalization Debate.* Pp. 1–50. Cambridge: Polity.

Held, David, and Anthony McGrew, eds. 2002. *Governing Globalisation: Power, Au-thority and Global Governance.* Cambridge: Polity.

Helg, Rodolfo. 2003. "Italian Districts in the International Economy." In Matteo Di Mat-teo and Paolo Piacentini, eds., *The Italian Economy at the Dawn of the 21st Cen-tury.* Pp. 236–245. Farnham, England: Ashgate.

Herzfeld, Michael. 1985. *Poetics of Manhood: Contest and Identity in a Cretan Mountain Village.* Princeton, N.J.: Princeton University Press.

———. 2006. *Anthropology: Theoretical Practice in Culture and Society.* Oxford: Black-well.

———. 2009. *Evicted from Eternity.* Chicago: University of Chicago Press.

Heyman, Josiah M., and Alan Smart. 1999. "States and Illegal Practices: An Overview." In their *States and Illegal Practices.* Oxford: Berg.

Hirsch, Jennifer. 2003. *A Courtship after Marriage: Sexuality and Love in Mexican Trans-national Families.* Berkeley: University of California Press.

Ho, Karen. 2005. "Situating Global Capitalisms: A View from Wall Street Investment Banks." *Cultural Anthropology* 20(1): 68–96.

———. 2009. *Liquidated: An Ethnography of Wall Street.* Durham, N.C.: Duke Univer-sity Press.

Hochschild, Arlie. 1983. *The Managed Heart: Commercialization of Human Feeling.* Berke-ley: University of California Press.

———. 2003. *The Commercialization of Intimate Life: Notes from Home and Work.* Berkeley: University of California Press.

Holmes, Douglas. 1999. *Cultural Disenchantments: Worker Peasantries in Northeast Italy.* Princeton, N.J.: Princeton University Press.

———. 2000. *Integral Europe: Fast Capitalism, Multiculturalism, Neofascism.* Princeton, N.J.: Princeton University Press.

Holston, James. 2000. "Alternative Modernities: Statecraft and Religious Imagination in the Valley of the Dawn." *American Ethnologist* 26(3): 605–631.

Horn, David. 1994. *Social Bodies: Science, Reproduction and Italian Modernity.* Princeton, N.J.: Princeton University Press.

Illouz, E. 1997. *Consuming the Romantic Utopia: Love and the Cultural Contradictions of Capitalism.* Berkeley: University of California Press.

Il Sole 24 Ore. 1991. "Donne: Eva al Lavoro: Più Tutela dalle Cee." *Il Sole 24 Ore*, July 11.

———. 2002a. "Esordio del 'mobbing.'" *Il Sole 24 Ore*, December 17.

———. 2002b. "Il Ritratto dell'Uomo Flessibile." *Il Sole 24 Ore*, May 31.

———. 2002c. "Norme e Tributi." *Il Sole 24 Ore*, April 18.

INAIL. 2001. *Deliberal del Consiglio di Amministrazione n. 473 del 26 luglio 2001: Definizione di percorsi metolodologici per la diagnosis eziologica delle patologie psichiche e psicosomatiche da stress e disagio lavorativo.* Rome: INAIL.

———. 2003. *Disturbi psichici da costrittività organizzativa sul lavoro: Rischio tutelato e diagnosi di malattia professionale: Modalità di trattazione delle pratiche.* Rome: INAIL.

Innocenti, Alessandro. 2003. "Production Outsourcing in Italian Manufacturing Industry." In Matteo Di Matteo and Paolo Piacentini, eds., *The Italian Economy at the Dawn of the 21st Century.* Pp. 212–232. Farnham, England: Ashgate.

Irvine, Judith. 1990. "Registering Affect: Heteroglossia in the Linguistic Expression of Emotion." In Catherine Lutz and Lila Abu-Lughod, eds., *Language and the Politics of Emotion.* Pp. 126–161. Cambridge: Cambridge University Press.

Irvine, Judith T., and Susan Gal. 2000. "Language Ideology and Linguistic Differentiation." In Paul Kroskrity, ed., *Regimes of Language.* Pp. 35–84. Santa Fe, N.M.: School of American Research Press.

Ishay, Micheline. 2005. "The Socialist Contributions to Human Rights: An Overlooked Legacy." *International Journal of Human Rights* 9(2): 225–245.

Isin, Engin F. 2004. "The Neurotic Citizen." *Citizenship Studies* 8(3): 217–235.

ISTAT. 1999. *Rapporto Annuale: La situazione del paese nel 1998.* Rome: Istituto Poligrafico e Zecca dello Stato.

———. 2003. *Il Mercato del lavoro in provincia di Padova nel 2002: 05 Marzo 2003.* Rome: Istituto Poligrafico e Zecca dello Stato.

———. 2006. *Strutture familiari e opinioni su famiglia e figli.* Rome: Istituto Poligrafico e Zecca dello Stato.

Jain, S. Lochlann. 2006. *Injury: The Politics of Product Design and Safety Law in the United States.* Princeton, N.J.: Princeton University Press.

———. 2010. "The Mortality Effect: Counting the Dead in the Cancer Trial." *Public Culture* 2(1): 90.

Jamieson, Mark. 2000. "Compassion, Anger and Broken Hearts: Ontology and the Role of Language in the Miskitu Lament." In Joanna Overing and Alan Passes, eds., *The Anthropology of Love and Anger: The Aesthetics of Conviviality in Native Amazonia.* Pp. 82–96. London: Routledge.

Jessop, Bob. 1977. "Theories of the Capitalist State." *Cambridge Journal of Economics* 1: 353–373.

———. 1999. "Narrating the Future of the National Economy and the National State: Remarks on Remapping Regulation and Reinventing Governance." In George Steinmetz, ed., *State/Culture: State-Formation after the Cultural Turn.* Pp. 378–405. Ithaca, N.Y.: Cornell University Press.

Jewkes, Stephen. 1997. "Pedaling for Profits." *Europe* 368 (July–August): 18–20.

Kendall, Laurel. 1996. *Getting Married in Korea: Of Gender, Morality and Modernity.* Berkeley: University of California Press.

Keohane, Robert O. 2003. "Sovereignty in International Society." In David Held and Anthony McGrew, eds., *The Global Transformations Reader: An Introduction to the Globalization Debate.* Pp. 147–161. Cambridge: Polity.

Keough, Leyla J. 2006. "Globalizing 'Postsocialism': Mobile Mothers and Neoliberalism on the Margins of Europe." *Anthropological Quarterly* 79(3): 431–461.

Kideckel, David. 2008. *Getting By in Post-Socialist Romania: Labor, the Body, and Working Class Culture.* Bloomington: Indiana University Press.

Kierzkowski, Henryk. 2002. "Introduction." In Henryk Kierzkowski, ed., *Europe and Globalization.* Pp. 1–10. London: Palgrave Macmillan.

King, Russell, and Jacqueline Andall. 1999. "The Geography and Economic Sociology of Recent Immigration to Italy." *Modern Italy* 4(2): 135–158.

Klein, Naomi 2002. *No Logo: No Space, No Choice, No Jobs.* New York: Picador.

Kleinman, Arthur. 1985. "Somatization: The Interconnections among Culture, Depressive Experiences, and the Meanings of Pain: A Study in Chinese Society." In A. Kleinman and B. Good, eds., *Culture and Depression.* Pp. 132–167. Berkeley: University of California Press.

———. 1995. *Writing at the Margin: Discourse between Anthropology and Medicine.* Berkeley: University of California Press.

———. 2000. "The Violences of Everyday Life: The Multiple Forms and Dynamics of Social Violence." In Arthur Kleinman and Veena Das, eds., *Violence and Subjectivity.* Pp. 226–241. Berkeley: University of California Press.

Koenig-Archibugi, Mathias. 2003. "National and European Citizenship: The Italian Case in Historical Perspective." *Citizenship Studies* 7(1): 85–109.

Kondo, Dorinne K. 1990. *Crafting Selves: Power, Gender and Discourses of Identity in a Japanese Workplace.* Chicago: University of Chicago Press.

———. 1999. "Fabricating Masculinity: Gender, Race, and Nation in a Transnational Frame." In Caren Kaplan, Norma Alarcón, and Minoo Moallem, eds., *Between Woman and Nation: Nationalisms, Transnational Feminisms, and the State.* Pp. 296–319. Durham, N.C.: Duke University Press.

Kopytoff, Igor. 1986. "The Cultural Biography of Things: Commoditization as Process." In Arjun Appadurai, ed., *The Social Life of Things.* Pp. 64–94. Cambridge: Cambridge University Press.

Krause, Elizabeth. 2001. "'Empty Cradles' and the Quiet Revolution: Demographic Discourse and Cultural Struggles of Gender, Race, and Class in Italy." *Cultural Anthropology* 16(4): 575–611.

———. 2006. "Encounters with the 'Peasant': Memory Work, Masculinity and Low Fertility in Italy." *American Ethnologist* 32(4): 593–617.

Kulick, Don. 1998a. *Travesti.* Chicago: University of Chicago Press.

———. 1998b. "Anger, Gender, Language Shift and the Politics of Revelation in a Papua New Guinean Village." In Bambi B. Schieffelin, Kathryn A. Woolard, and Paul V. Kroskrity, eds., *Language Ideologies: Practice and Theory.* Pp. 87–102. Oxford: Oxford University Press.

———. 2003. "No." *Language and Communication* 23: 139–151.

———. 2005. "The Importance of What Gets Left Out." *Discourse Studies* 7(4–5): 615–624.

Kulick, Don, and Charles H. Klein. 2003. "Scandalous Acts: The Politics of Shame among Brazilian Travestí Prostitutes." In B. Hobson, ed., *Recognition Struggles and Social Movements: Contested Identities, Agency and Power.* Pp. 215–238. Cambridge: Cambridge University Press.

Lamphere, Louise, Helena Ragoné, and Patricia Zavella, eds. 1997. *Situated Lives: Gender and Culture in Everyday Life.* London: Routledge.

La Repubblica. 1999a. "Mobbing: I Comportamenti di vittime e aggressori." *La Repubblica,* July 24. http://www.repubblica.it/online/sessi_stili/mobbing/mobbi1/mobbi1 .html (accessed June 21, 2010).

———. 1999b. "Persecuzione in ufficio Torino, corso anti-mobbing." *La Repubblica,* October 25. http://www.repubblica.it/online/societa/gobbe/mobby/mobby.html (accessed January 9, 2008).

———. 2000a. "Dopo 3 anni di ingiustizie ho fondato l'associazione." *La Repubblica,* February 8.

———. 2000b. "Il mio decalogo per vivere bene." *La Repubblica,* December 13. http://www.repubblica.it/online/cronaca/regole/regole/regole.html (accessed January 9, 2008).

———. 2001. "Il mobbing prospera nella new economy." *La Repubblica,* March 26. http://www.repubblica.it/online/societa/mobbing/convegno/convegno.html (accessed June 21, 2010).

———. 2005. "L'Europa non tema il modello anglosassone." *La Repubblica,* June 28.

La Stampa. 1993. "Trentadue milioni per un bacio." *La Stampa,* February 20.

———. 1997. "L'amore assolve le molestie." *La Stampa,* August 20.

———. 1999a. "A Borgaro il primo caso giudizario per molestie morali." *La Stampa,* December 11.

———. 1999b. "Seminario del comune." *La Stampa,* October 26.

———. 2003a. "CGIL in piazza a settembre." *La Stampa,* July 3.

———. 2003b. "Spettacolo e tempo libero a Torino." *La Stampa,* November 22.

———. 2004a. "Donna Vessate: Una precarietà che fa paura." *La Stampa,* February 12.

———. 2004b. "L'Identikit delle vittime." *La Stampa,* March 2.

Lavoro Oggi. 2005. "Le Legge regionale sul mobbing." *Lavoro Oggi,* April 14: 51.

Lazzarato, Maurizio. 1996. "Immaterial Labor." In Paolo Virno and Michael Hardt, eds., *Radical Thought in Italy: A Potential Politics.* Pp. 133–147. Minneapolis: University of Minnesota Press.

Lee, Benjamin, and Edward LiPuma. 2002. "Cultures of Circulation: The Imaginations of Modernity." *Public Culture* 14(1): 191–213.

Lefkowitz, Daniel. 2003. "Investing in Emotion: Love and Anger in Financial Advertising." *Journal of Linguistic Anthropology* 13(1): 71–97.

Lentner, Howard H. 2004. *Power and Politics in Globalization: The Indispensable State.* New York: Routledge.

Lerner, Wendy. 2000. "Neoliberalism: Policy, Ideology and Governmentality." *Studies in Political Economy* 63: 5–25.

Levinas, Emmanuel. 1996. "Peace and Proximity." In Emmanuel Levinas, Adrian T. Peperzak, Simon Critchley, and Robert Bernasconi, eds., *Basic Philosophical Writings.* Pp. 161–170. Bloomington: Indiana University Press.

Lindholm, Charles. 2005. "An Anthropology of Emotion." In Conerly Casey and Robert B. Edgerton, eds., *A Companion to Psychological Anthropology: Modernity and Psychocultural Change.* Pp. 30–44. Oxford: Blackwell.

Livia, A., and K. Hall. 1997. "'It's a Girl!': Bringing Performativity Back to Linguistics." In A. Livia and K. Hall, eds., *Queerly Phrased: Language, Gender, and Sexuality.* Pp. 3–18. Oxford: Oxford University Press.

Lock, Margaret. 2002. "Medical Knowledge and Body Politics." In Jeremy MacClancy, ed., *Exotic No More.* Pp. 190–208. Chicago: University of Chicago Press.

Lock, Margaret, and Patricia A. Kaufert. 1998. *Pragmatic Women and Body Politics.* Cambridge: Cambridge University Press.

Lo Giudice, Calogero. 2004. *Danno biologico INAIL e danno differenziale del lavoratore.* http://www.francocrisafi.it/web_secondario/varie%202004%201/danno%20biologico.pdf (accessed November 5, 2010).

Luhrmann, Tanya M. 2006. "Subjectivity." *Anthropological Theory* 6(3): 345–361.

Lutz, Catherine. 1985. "Depression and the Translation of Emotional Worlds." In her *Culture and Depression: Studies in the Anthropology and Cross-Cultural Psychiatry of Affect and Disorder.* Pp. 63–100. Berkeley: University of California Press.

———. 1988. *Unnatural Emotions: Everyday Sentiments on a Micronesian Atoll and Their Challenge to Western Theory.* Chicago: University of Chicago Press.

———. 2002. "Making War at Home in the United States: Militarization and the Current Crisis." *American Anthropologist* 104(3): 723–735.

Lutz, Catherine A., and Lila Abu-Lughod, eds. 1990. *Language and the Politics of Emotion.* Cambridge: Cambridge University Press.

MacEachen, Ellen. 2000. "The Mundane Administration of Worker Bodies: From Welfarism to Neoliberalism." *Health, Risk and Society* 2(3): 315–327.

MacLeod, Dag. 2004. *Dismantling the State: Privatization and the Limits of Neoliberal Reform in Mexico.* State College: Pennsylvania State University.

Mamdani, Mahmood. 2002. "Good Muslim, Bad Muslim: A Political Perspective on Culture and Terrorism." *American Anthropologist* 104(3): 766–775.

Manderson, Lenore. 1999. "Public Health Developments in Colonial Malaya: Colonialism and the Politics of Prevention." *American Journal of Public Health* 89(1): 102–107.

Mann, Michael. 2003. "Has Globalization Ended the Rise and Rise of the Nation-State?" In David Held and Anthony McGrew, eds., *The Global Transformations Reader: An Introduction to the Globalization Debate.* Pp. 127–134. Cambridge: Polity.

Marazzi, Christian. 2007. "Rules for the Incommensurable." *SubStance* 36(1): 11–36.

Marcus, G. E. 1993. *Elites: Ethnographic Issues.* Albuquerque: University of New Mexico Press.

———. 1995. "Ethnography in/of the World System: The Emergence of Multi-sited Ethnography." *Annual Review of Anthropology* 24: 95–117.

Marcus, George, and Michael Fischer. 1986. *Anthropology as Cultural Critique: An Experimental Moment in the Human Sciences.* Chicago: University of Chicago Press.

Martin, Emily. 1987. *The Woman in the Body*. Boston: Beacon.

———. 1992. "The End of the Body?" *American Ethnologist* 19(1): 121–140.

———. 1994. *Flexible Bodies*. Boston: Beacon.

———. 1999. "The Woman in the Flexible Body." In Adele E. Clark and Virginia L. Olsen, eds., *Revisioning Women, Health and Healing*. Pp. 97–115. London: Routledge.

———. 2007. *Bipolar Expeditions*. Princeton, N.J.: Princeton University Press.

Martineli, A., A. Chiesi, and S. Stefanizzi. 1990. *Recent Social Trends in Italy 1960–1995*. Montreal: McGill-Queen's University Press.

Marx, Karl. 1976. *Capital*, vol. 1. London: Penguin.

Mascia-Lees, Frances E., and Patricia Sharpe. 2000. "Interpreting Charges of Sexual Harassment: Competing Discourses and Claims." In Frances E. Mascia-Lees and Patricia Sharpe, eds., *Taking a Stand in a Postfeminist World: Toward an Engaged Cultural Criticism*. Pp. 167–190. Albany: State University of New York Press.

Massumi, Brian. 1993. "Everywhere You Want to Be: Introduction to Fear." In Brian Massumi, ed., *The Politics of Everyday Fear*. Pp. 3–37. Minneapolis: University of Minnesota Press.

Maurer, William. 1999. "'Forget Locke': From Proprietor to Risk-Bearer in the New Logics of Finance." *Public Culture* 11(2): 47–67.

———. 2003. "Comment: Got Language? Law, Property, and the Anthropological Imagination." *American Anthropologist* 105(3): 775–781.

McElhinny, Bonnie S. 2002. "Language, Sexuality and Political Economy." In K. Cambell-Kibler, R. J. Podesva, S. Roberts, and A. Wong, eds., *Language and Sexuality: Contesting Meaning and Practice*. Pp. 111–134. Stanford, Calif.: CSLI.

Melossi, Dario. 2003. "'In a Peaceful Life': Migration and the Crime of Modernity in Europe/Italy." *Punishment and Society* 5(4): 371–397.

Meucci, Mario. 2006. *Danni da mobbing e loro risarcibilità*. Rome: Ediesse.

Migliavacca, Mauro. 2005. "Lavoro atipico tra famiglia e vulnerabilità sociale." *Sociologia del Lavoro* 97: 105–120.

Migliore, Sam. 1997. *Mal'uocchiu: Ambiguity, Evil Eye, and the Language of Distress*. Toronto: University of Toronto Press.

Miller, Peter, and Nikolas Rose. 1990. "Governing Economic Life." *Economy and Society* 19: 1–31.

Mills, Mary Beth. 1999. *Thai Women in the Global Labor Force: Consuming Desires, Contested Selves*. New Brunswick, N.J.: Rutgers University Press.

———. 2003. "Gender and Inequality in the Global Labor Force." *Annual Review of Anthropology* 32: 41–62.

———. 2005. "From Nimble Fingers to Raised Fists: Women and Labor Activism in Globalizing Thailand." *Signs* 31(1): 117–144.

Mitchell, Timothy. 1999. "Society, Economy, and the State Effect." In George Steinmetz, ed., *State/Culture: State-Formation after the Cultural Turn*. Pp. 76–97. Ithaca, N.Y.: Cornell University Press.

———. 2002. *Rule of Experts: Egypt, Techno-Politics, Modernity*. Berkeley: University of California Press.

Mitchell, Timothy J. 1990. *Passional Culture: Emotion, Religion and Society in Southern Spain*. Philadelphia: University of Pennsylvania Press.

Modaffari, Luigi. 2008. "Danni esistenziali: Genesi, ratio, orientamenti e parabola della dibatututa figura giurisprudenziale." hwww.overlex.com/leggiarticolo.asp?id=1913 (accessed June 24, 2010).

Molé, Noelle J. 2004. "Literacy Practices in the Piazza: An Analysis of Graduation Rituals in Northern Italy." In Wai Fong Chiang, Elaine Chun, Laura Mahalingappa, and Siri Mehus, eds., *SALSA 11 Proceedings*. Pp. 109–122. Austin: Texas Linguistic Forum.

———. 2007a. "Labor Precariousness in Italy." *Anthropology News* 49(1): 52–53.

———. 2007b. "Protection and Precariousness: Workplace Mobbing, Gender, and Neoliberalism in Northern Italy." Ph.D. diss., Department of Anthropology, Rutgers University.

———. 2008. "Living It on the Skin: Italian States, Working Illness." *American Ethnologist* 35(2): 189–210.

———. 2010. "Precarious Subjects: Anticipating Neoliberalism in Northern Italy's Workplace." *American Anthropologist* 112(1): 38–53.

Moore, Henrietta L. 2006. "The Future of Gender or the End of a Brilliant Career." In P. Geller and M. Stockett, eds., *Feminist Anthropology*. Pp. 23–42. Philadelphia: University of Pennsylvania Press.

Morgen, Sandra. 2001. "The Agency of Welfare Workers: Negotiating Devolution, Privatization and the Meaning of Self-Sufficiency." *American Anthropologist* 103(3): 747–761.

Mudu, Pierpaolo. 2004. "Resisting and Challenging Neoliberalism: The Development of Italian Social Centers." *Antipode* 36: 917–941.

Muehlebach, Andrea. 2007. "The Moral Neoliberal: Welfare State and Ethical Citizenship in Contemporary Italy." Ph.D. diss., Department of Anthropology, University of Chicago.

———. 2009. "*Complexio Oppositorum*: Notes on the Left in Neoliberal Italy." *Public Culture* 21(3): 495–515.

———. (n.d.). "On Affective Labor in Post-Fordist Italy." Unpublished manuscript, Department of Anthropology, University of Toronto.

Mullin, Molly. 2001. *Culture in the Market Place: Gender, Art and Value in the American Southwest*. Durham, N.C.: Duke University Press.

Musi, Emanuela. 2008. "La Travagliata storia del danno esistenziale." *Il Denaro* 57: 22.

Mussolini, Benito. 1932. "Fascismo: Dottrina." In *Enciclopedia italiana*, vol. 14. Rome: Istituto della Enciclopedia Italiana.

Nader, L. 1972. "Up the Anthropologist: Perspectives Gained from Studying Up." In D. Hymes, ed., *Reinventing Anthropology*. Pp. 284–311. New York: Random House.

Nardini, Gloria. 1999. *Che Bella Figura: The Power of Performance in an Italian Ladies' Club in Chicago*. Albany: State University of New York Press.

Nassimbeni, Guido. 2003. "Local Manufacturing Systems and Global Economy: Are They Compatible? The Case of the Italian Eyewear District." *Journal of Operations Management* 21: 151–171.

Nepoti, Roberto. 2003. "Al cinema il mobbing aziendale tra perversione e amore vero." *La Repubblica*, April 5. http://www.repubblica.it/online/cinema_recensioni/secretary/secretary/secretary.html (accessed April 16, 2003).

Newitz, Annalee. 2006. *Pretend We're Dead: Capitalist Monsters in American Pop Culture*. Durham, N.C.: Duke University Press.

Nistico, Fausto. 2003. "In Corso di Pubblicazione su 'Informazione Previdenziale': Mob, Mobber, Mobbing." www.unicz.it/lavoro/NISTICOMOBBING (accessed April 16, 2003).

Nove, Aldo. 2006. *Mi chiamo Roberta, ho quarant'anni, guadagno 250 euro al Mese.* Turin: Einaudi.

Obeyesekere, Gananath. 1986. *Medusa's Hair.* Chicago: University of Chicago Press.

Ochs, Elinor. 1992. "Indexing Gender." In her *Rethinking Context: Language Acquisition and Language Socialization in a Samoan Village.* Pp. 335–358. New York: Cambridge University Press.

———. 1996. "Norm-Makers, Norm-Breakers: Uses of Speech by Men and Women in a Malagasy Community." In Donald Brenneis, ed., *The Matrix of Language.* Pp. 99–116. Boulder, Colo.: Westview.

Ochs, E., C. Pontecorvo, and A. Fasulo. 1996. "Socializing Taste." *Ethnos* 1–2: 7–46.

OECD. 1997. *Globalization and Small and Medium Enterprises (SMEs).* Paris: OECD.

———. 2001. *Territorial Reviews: Italy.* Paris: OECD.

Ogasawara, Yuko. 1998. *Office Ladies and Salaried Men: Power, Gender and Work in Japanese Companies.* Berkeley: University of California Press.

O'Malley, Pat. 1996. "Risk and Responsibility." In Andrew Barry, Thomas Osborne, and Nikolas Rose, eds., *Foucault and Political Reason.* Pp. 189–207. Chicago: University of Chicago Press.

———. 2000. "Uncertain Subjects: Risks, Liberalism and Contract." *Economy and Society* 29: 460–484.

Ong, Aihwa. 1987. *Spirits of Resistance and Capitalist Discipline: Factory Women in Malaysia.* Albany: State University of New York Press.

———. 1988. "The Production of Possession: Spirits and the Multinational Corporation in Malaysia." *American Ethnologist* 15(1): 28–42.

———. 1990. "State versus Islam: Malay Families, Women's Bodies, and the Body Politic in Malaysia." *American Ethnologist* 17: 258–276.

———. 1999. *Flexible Citizenship.* Durham, N.C.: Duke University Press.

———. 2006a. "Experiments with Freedom: Milieus of the Human." *American Literary History* 18(2): 229–244.

———. 2006b. *Neoliberalism as Exception: Mutations in Citizenship and Sovereignty.* Durham, N.C.: Duke University Press.

Orloff, Ann S. 1993. "Gender and the Social Rights of Citizenship: The Comparative Analysis of Gender Relations and Welfare States." *American Sociological Review* 58(3): 303–328.

Orr, Jackie. 2006. *Panic Diaries: A Genealogy of Panic Disorder.* Durham, N.C.: Duke University Press.

Ortner, Sherry. 2005. "Subjectivity and Cultural Critique." *Anthropological Theory* 5: 31–52.

Osborne, Thomas. 1996. "Security and Vitality: Drains, Liberalism and Powers in the 19th Century." In Andrew Barry, Thomas Osborne, and Nikolas Rose, eds., *Foucault and Political Reason.* Pp. 99–121. Chicago: University of Chicago Press.

Osgood, Robert E. 1980. "The PCI, Italy and NATO." In Simon Serfaty and Lawrence Gray, eds., *The Italian Communist Past: Yesterday, Today and Tomorrow.* Pp. 143–157. Westport, Conn.: Greenwood.

Ospedale, Regina-Margherita. 2007. "Mobbing: Azione medico." www.oirmsantanna.piemonte.it/web/news/eventi/mobbing/azione_medico.asp (accessed January 2007).

Pace, Enzo. 2007. "A Peculiar Pluralism." *Journal of Modern Italian Studies* 12(1): 86–100.

Pagano, Ugo, and Sandro Trento. 2003. "Continuity and Change in Italian Corporate Governance: The Institutional Stability of One Variety of Capitalism." In Matteo Di Matteo and Paolo Piacentini, eds., *The Italian Economy at the Dawn of the 21st Century.* Pp. 177–211. Farnham, England: Ashgate.

Pandolfi, Mariella. 1990. "Boundaries within the Body: Women's Suffering in Southern Peasant Italy." *Culture, Medicine, and Psychiatry* 14: 255–273.

Patel, Rajeev, and Philip McMichael. 2004. "Third Worldism and the Lineages of Global Fascism." *Third World Quarterly* 25(1): 231–254.

Pellegrini, L. 1996. *La Distribuzione commerciale in Italia.* Bologna: Il Mulino.

Perramond, Eric. 2005. "Downsizing the State: Privatization and the Limits of Neoliberal Reform in Mexico." *Latin American Politics and Society* 47(3): 169–173.

Petryna, Adriana. 2002. *Life Exposed: Biological Citizens after Chernobyl.* Princeton, N.J.: Princeton University Press.

———. 2004. "Biological Citizenship." *Osiris* 19: 250–265.

Phillips, D., and M. Bull. 1996. "The Dilemmas of Post-Communism in Contemporary Italy." *Problems of Post-Communism* 43(4): 62–70.

Piore, Michael, and Charles Sabel. 1984. *The Second Industrial Divide: Prospects for Prosperity.* New York: Basic.

Pitt-Rivers, Julian. 1954. *The People of the Sierra.* Chicago: University of Chicago Press.

Platania, Federico. 2006. *Buon lavoro: 12 Storie a tempo determinato.* Ravenna, Italy: Fernandel.

Plesset, Sonia. 2006. *Sheltering Women: Negotiating Gender and Violence in Northern Italy.* Stanford, Calif.: Stanford University Press.

Pogliotti, Giorgio. 2006. "La Legge Biagi sarà rivista." *Il Sole 24 Ore,* May 19.

Polanyi, Karl. 1957. *The Great Transformation.* Boston: Beacon.

Pollard, John. 2008. *Catholicism in Modern Italy: Religion, Society and Politics since 1861.* London: Routledge.

Porter, Dorothy, and Roy Porter. 1988. "The Politics of Prevention: Anti-Vaccinationism and Public Health in Nineteenth Century England." *Medical History* 32: 231–252.

Povinelli, Elizabeth. 2006. *The Empire of Love: Towards a Theory of Intimacy, Genealogy, Carnality.* Durham, N.C.: Duke University Press.

Price, Janet, ed. 1999. *Feminist Theory and the Body: A Reader.* London: Routledge.

Prima. 2005. "Prima: Associazione Italiana contro Mobbing e Stress Psicosociale." http://www.mobbing-prima.it/princ_it.htm (accessed November 12, 2005).

Procoli, Angela. 2004. "Introduction." In Angela Procoli, ed., *Workers and Narratives of Survival in Europe.* Albany: State University of New York Press.

Putnam, Robert. 1993. *Making Democracy Work: Civic Traditions in Modern Italy.* Princeton, N.J.: Princeton University Press.

Rabinow, Paul. 1992. "Artificiality and Enlightenment: From Sociobiology to Biosociality." In J. Crary and S. Kwinter, eds., *Incorporations: Zone 6.* Pp. 234–252. New York: Urzone.

Rajan, Kaushik Sunder. 2006. *Biocapital: The Constitution of Postgenomic Life.* Durham, N.C.: Duke University Press.

Rebhun, L. A. 1994. "Swallowing Frogs: Anger and Illness in Northeast Brazil." *Medical Anthropology Quarterly* 8(4): 360–382.

———. 1999. *The Heart Is Unknown Country: Love in the Changing Economy of Northeast Brazil.* Stanford, Calif.: Stanford University Press.

Reddy, William. 1999. "Emotional Liberty: Politics and History in the Anthropology of Emotions." *Cultural Anthropology* 14(2): 256–288.

———. 2001. *The Navigation of Feeling: A Framework for the History of Emotions.* Cambridge: Cambridge University Press.

Reyneri, Emilio. 2005a. "Flessibilità: Molti significati, alcune contraddizioni." *Sociologia del Lavoro* 90: 21–26.

———. 2005b. *Sociologia del mercato del lavoro: Le forse dell'occupazione.* Bologna: Il Mulino.

Rifkin, Jeremy. 1995. *The End of Work: The Decline of the Global Labor Force and the Dawn of the Post-Market Era.* New York: Penguin.

Rizza, Roberto. 2005. "La costruzione sociale del mercato del lavoro: Forme di embeddedness del lavoro mobile." *Sociologia del Lavoro* 97: 56–79.

Robinson, William I. 2005. "Gramsci and Globalization: From Nation-State to Transnational Hegemony." *Critical Review of International Social and Political Philosophy* 8(4): 1–16.

———. 2007a. "Beyond the Theory of Imperialism: Global Capitalism and Transnational State." *Societies without Borders* 2: 5–26.

———. 2007b. "Theories of Globalization." In George Ritzer, ed., *Blackwell Companion to Globalization.* Pp. 125–143. Oxford: Blackwell.

Röggla, Kathrin. 2005. *Noi non dormiamo: L'insonnia dei precari di successo.* Milan: Isbn.

Rondinelli, Dennis A., and G. Shabbir Cheema. 2003. *Reinventing Government for the Twenty-First Century: State Capacity in a Globalizing Society.* Bloomfield, Conn.: Kumarian.

Rosaldo, Michelle. 1980. *Knowledge and Passion: Ilongot Notion of Self and Social Life.* Cambridge: Cambridge University Press.

———.1982. "The Things We Do with Words: Ilongot Speech Acts and Speech Act Theory in Philosophy." *Language and Society* 11: 203–237.

Rose, Nikolas. 1994. *Governing the Soul, Shaping the Private Self.* London: Free Association Press.

———. 1996. "Governing 'Advanced' Liberal Democracies." In Andrew Barry, Thomas Osborne, and Nikolas Rose, eds., *Foucault and Political Reason.* Pp. 37–64. Chicago: University of Chicago Press.

———. 2007. *The Politics of Life Itself.* Princeton, N.J.: Princeton University Press.

Rose, Nikolas, and Carlos Novas. 2003. "Biological Citizenship." In Aihwa Ong and Stephen Collier, eds., *Global Anthropology.* Pp. 439–463. Oxford: Blackwell.

Rosenau, James N. 2003. "Governance in the New Global Order." In David Held and Anthony McGrew, eds., *The Global Transformations Reader: An Introduction to the Globalization Debate.* Pp. 223–233. Cambridge: Polity.

Rosenberg, Justin. 2005. "Globalization Theory: A Post Mortem." *International Politics* 42: 2–74.

Sacconi, M., and M. Tiraboschi. 2006. *Un futuro da precari? Il lavoro dei giovani tra rassegnazione e opportunita.* Milan: Mondadori.

Safa, Helen. 1981. "Runaway Shops and Female Employment: The Search for Cheap Labor." *Signs* 7(2): 418–433.

Saguy, Abigail. 2003. *What Is Sexual Harassment?: From Capitol Hill to the Sorbonne.* Berkeley: University of California Press.

Salce, Luciano, dir. 1975. *Fantozzi.* Italy: Rizzoli Films.

Salzinger, Leslie. 2000. "Manufacturing Sexual Subjects: 'Harassment,' Desire and Discipline on a Maquiladora Shopfloor." *Ethnography* 5(1): 67–92.

———. 2003. *Genders in Production: Making Workers in Mexico's Global Factories.* Berkeley: University of California Press.

Sandbrook, Richard, Marc Edelman, Patrick Heller, and Judith Teichman. 2007. *Social Democracy in the Global Periphery: Origins, Challenges, Prospects.* Cambridge: Cambridge University Press.

Santoro, Lara. 1997. "Pocketful of Efficient Entrepreneurs Powers Italy's Wealthiest Corner." *Christian Science Monitor* 89(68): 1.

Sassen, Saskia. 1988. *The Mobility of Labor and Capital: A Study of International Investment and Labor Flow.* Cambridge: Cambridge University Press.

———. 1996. *Losing Control? Sovereignty in an Age of Globalization.* New York: Columbia University Press.

———. 1998. *Globalization and Its Discontents.* New York: New Press.

———. 2003. "The State and Globalization." In Oliver Schmidtke, ed., *The Third Way Transformation of Social Democracy.* Pp. 59–72. Farnham, England: Ashgate.

———. 2005. "Globalization after September 11." In Marc Edelman and Angelique Haugerud, eds., *Anthropology of Development and Globalization.* Pp. 173–176. Oxford: Blackwell.

Sasso, Cinzia. 2002. *Donne che amano il lavoro e la vita.* Milan: Sperling & Kupfer.

Saunders, George R. 1995. "The Crisis of Presence in Italian Pentecostal Conversion." *American Ethnologist* 22(2): 324–340.

Schein, Louisa. 2000. *Minority Rules.* Durham, N.C.: Duke University Press.

———. 2004. "Homeland Beauty: Transnational Longing and Hmong American Video." *Journal of Asian Studies* 63(2): 433–463.

Scheper-Hughes, Nancy. 1992. *Death without Weeping: The Violence of Everyday Life in Brazil.* Berkeley: University of California Press.

———. 2000. "The Global Traffic in Human Organs." *Cultural Anthropology* 41(2): 191–211.

Scheper-Hughes, N., and M. Lock. 1987. "The Mindful Body: A Prolegomenon of Future Work in Medical Anthropology." *Medical Anthropology Quarterly* 1: 16–41.

Schiattarella, Roberto, and Paolo Piacentini. 2003. "Old and New Dualisms in the Italian Labour Market." In Matteo Di Matteo and Paolo Piacentini, eds., *The Italian Economy at the Dawn of the 21st Century.* Pp. 81–103. Farnham, England: Ashgate.

Schiebinger, Londa, ed. 2000. *Feminism and the Body.* Oxford: Oxford University Press.

Schild, Veronica. 1998. "New Subjects of Rights? Women's Movements and the Construction of Citizenship in the 'New Democracies.'" In Sonia Alvarez, Evelina Dagnino, and Arturo Escobar, eds., *Culture of Politics, Politics of Cultures: Revisioning Latin American Social Movements.* Pp. 93–117. Boulder, Colo.: Westview.

Schlesinger, Philip. 1992. "'Europeanness': A New Cultural Battlefield." *Innovation: The European Journal of Social Sciences* 5(2): 11–23.

Schneider, Jane. 1998. "Introduction: The Dynamics of Neo-Orientalism in Italy (1848–1995)." In Jane Schneider, ed. *Italy's "Southern Question": Orientalism in One Country.* Pp. 1–26. Oxford: Berg.

Schneider, Jane, ed. 1998. *Italy's "Southern Question": Orientalism in One Country.* Oxford: Berg.

Scott, James. 1985. *Weapons of the Weak: Everyday Forms of Peasant Resistance*. New Haven, Conn.: Yale University Press.

Sen, Gita. 1997. "Globalization, Justice, Equity: A Gender Perspective." *Development* 40(2): 21–26.

Sennett, Richard. 1998. *The Corrosion of Character: The Personal Consequences of Work in the New Capitalism*. New York: Norton.

Seremetakis, C. Nadia. 1999. "Toxic Beauties: Medicine, Information, and Body Consumption in Transnational Europe." *Social Text* 19(3): 115–129.

Serrao, Eugenia. 2005. "Mobbing e danno esistenziale." http://dirittolavoro.altervista.org/mobbing_dannoesistenziale_serrao.html (accessed November 5, 2010).

Servedio, Vincenzio. 2010. "Mobbing e bossing." http://knol.google.com/k/antonio- conte/mobbing-and-bossing (accessed July 5, 2010).

Setta, Monica. 2002. *Cuore di manager*. Milan: Sperling & Kupfer.

Sforzi, F. 1990. "The Quantitative Importance of Marshallian Industrial Districts in the Italian Economy." In F. Pyke, G. Becattini, and W. Sengenberger, eds., *Industrial Districts and Interfirm Cooperation in Italy*. Pp. 75–107. Geneva: IILS.

Sharma, Aradhana. 2006. "Crossbreeding Institutions, Breeding Struggle: Women's Empowerment, Neoliberal Governmentality, and State (Re)Formation in India." *Cultural Anthropology* 21(1): 60–95.

Sharma, A., and A. Gupta. 2006. "Introduction." In A. Sharma and A. Gupta, eds., *The Anthropology of the State: A Reader*. Oxford: Blackwell.

Shore, Cris. 1990. *Italian Communism: The Escape from Leninism: An Anthropological Perspective*. London: Pluto.

Shore, Cris, and Stephen Nugent, eds. 2002. *Elite Cultures: Anthropological Perspectives*. London: Routledge.

Silverman, Sydel. 1975. *Three Bells of Civilization*. New York: Columbia University Press.

Simon, J. 1987. "The Emergence of a Risk Society." *Socialist Review* 95: 61–89.

Sinclair, Upton. (1906). 2007. *The Jungle*. Raleigh, N.C.: Hayes Barton.

Slaughter, Anne-Marie. 2003. "Governing the Global Economy through Government Networks." In David Held and Anthony McGrew, eds., *The Global Transformations Reader: An Introduction to the Globalization Debate*. Pp. 189–203. Cambridge: Polity.

Smith, Jason. 2009. "Soul on Strike." In Franco "Bifo" Berardi, ed., *The Soul at Work: From Alienation to Autonomy*. Pp. 9–19. Los Angeles, Calif.: Semiotext(e).

Smith, Paul. 2004. "Precarious Politics." *Symploke* 12(1–2): 254–260.

Spackman, Barbara. 1996. *Fascist Virilities: Rhetoric, Ideology and Social Fantasy in Italy*. Minneapolis: University of Minnesota Press.

Spiller, Cristina Nardi. 2003. *The Dynamics of the Price Structure and the Business Cycle: The Italian Evidence from 1945–2000*. Heidelberg: Physica.

Spindel, Patricia. 2008. *Psychological Warfare at Work: How Harassers and Bullies Injure Individuals and Organizations*. Toronto: Spindel and Associates.

Spitulnik, Debra. 1998. "Mediating Unity and Diversity: The Production of Language Ideologies in Zambian Broadcasting." In B. Scheiffelin, K. Woolard, and P. Kroskrity, eds., *Language Ideologies: Practice and Theory*. Oxford: Oxford University Press.

———. 2001. "The Social Circulation of Media Discourse and the Mediation of Communities." In A. Duranti, ed., *Linguistic Anthropology: A Reader*. Oxford: Blackwell.

Stacul, Jaro. 2007. "Understanding Neoliberalism: Reflections on the 'End of Politics' in Northern Italy." *Journal of Modern Italian Studies* 12(4): 450–459.

Stanko, E. 1988. "Keeping Women In and Out of Line: Sexual Harassment." In S. Walby, ed., *Gender Segregation at Work*. Pp. 109–127. Milton Keynes, England: Open University Press.

Stearns, Peter. 1994. *American Cool: Constructing a Twentieth-Century Emotional Style*. New York: New York University Press.

———. 2006. *American Fear: The Causes and Consequences of High Anxiety*. London: Routledge.

Stein, Howard F. 2005. "Corporate Violence." In Conerly Casey and Robert B. Edgerton, eds., *A Companion to Psychological Anthropology: Modernity and Psychocultural Change*. Pp. 436–451. Oxford: Blackwell.

Steinmetz, George. 1999. "Introduction: Culture and the State." In George Steinmetz, ed., *State/Culture: State-Formation after the Cultural Turn*. Pp. 1–50. Ithaca, N.Y.: Cornell University Press.

Sternhall, Zeev, with Mario Sznajder and Maia Asheri. 1994. *The Birth of Fascist Ideology: From Cultural Rebellion to Political Revolution*. Translated by David Maisel. Princeton, N.J.: Princeton University Press.

Strange, Susan. 1996. *The Retreat of the State*. Cambridge: Cambridge University Press.

———. 2003. "The Declining Authority of States." In David Held and Anthony McGrew, eds., *The Global Transformations Reader: An Introduction to the Globalization Debate*. Pp. 121–126. Cambridge: Polity.

Strathern, Andrew. 1977. "Why Is Shame on the Skin?" In John Blacking, ed., *The Anthropology of the Body*. Pp. 99–115. New York: Academic.

Strathern, Marilyn. 2000a. "Introduction: New Accountabilities." In Marilyn Strathern, ed., *Audit Cultures*. Pp. 1–18. London: Routledge.

———. 2000b. "The Tyranny of Transparency." *British Educational Research Journal* 26(3): 309–321.

Tambini, Damian. 1996. "Padania's Virtual Nationalism." *Telos* 109: 159–165.

Taylor, Charles. 1989. *Sources of the Self: The Making of Modern Identity*. Cambridge, Mass.: Harvard University Press.

Taylor, Janelle S. 2004. "Big Ideas: Feminist Ethnographies of Reproduction." *American Ethnologist* 31(1): 123–130.

Terpolilli, Paolo. 2004. "Il fenomeno mobbing e la costrittività organizzativa." *L'Ispettore e la Societa* 23(6): 16–24.

Thompson, E. P. 1967. "Time, Work, Discipline and Industrial Capitalism." *Past and Present* 38: 56–97.

Thrift, Nigel. 2000. "Performing Cultures in the New Economy." *Annals of the Association of American Geographers* 90(4): 674–692.

Ticktin, Miriam. 2006. "Where Ethics and Politics Meet: The Violence of Humanitarianism in France." *American Ethnologist* 33(1): 33–49.

Toma, Andrea. 2003. "The Family and Social Networks in the Socio-Economic Development of Italy." In Matteo Di Matteo and Paolo Piacentini, eds., *The Italian Economy at the Dawn of the 21st Century*. Pp. 313–330. Farnham, England: Ashgate.

Toscano, Alberto. 2007. "Vital Strategies: Maurizio Lazzarato and the Metaphysics of Contemporary Capitalism." *Theory, Culture, and Society* 24(6): 71–91.

Tossutti, Livianna. 2001. "Globalization and the 'New Localism' in Northern Italy." *Mediterranean Politics* 6(1): 64–83.

Trouillot, Michel-Rolph. 2003. *Global Transformations: Anthropology and the Modern World*. New York: Palgrave Macmillan.

Tsing, Anna L. 2004. *Friction: An Ethnography of Global Connection*. Princeton, N.J.: Princeton University Press.

Turner, Bryan. 2001. "The Erosion of Citizenship." *British Journal of Sociology* 52(2): 189–209.

Turner, Terence. 1980. "The Social Skin." In Jeremy Cherfas and Roger Lewin, eds., *Not Work Alone: A Cross-Cultural View of Activities Superfluous to Survival*. Pp. 112–140. Beverly Hills, Calif.: Sage.

UIL (Unione Italiana del Lavoro). 2006. "Mobbing: Nuova proposta." www.uil.it/mobbing_nuova _proposta.html (accessed Dec. 10, 2006).

Urton, Gary. 1997. *The Social Life of Numbers*. Austin: University of Texas Press.

Van Apeldoorn, Bastiaan. 2002. *Transnational Capitalism and the Struggle over European Integration*. London: Routledge.

Van Cleave, Rachel A. 2005. "Sex, Lies and Honor in Italian Rape Law." *Suffolk University Law Review* 38: 427–454.

Varese News. 2004. "Dall'ufficio al day hospital, un'escalation di casi." *Varese News*, March 4. http://www.vareseweb.it/lavoro/articoli-lavoro/2004/marzo/5-3mobbing _clinica.htm (accessed December 3, 2006).

Veneto Lavoro. 2004. *Regione del Veneto: Il Mercato del lavoro nel Veneto tendenze e politiche rapporto 2004*. Milan: Francoangeli.

Vercelli, Alessandro, and Luciano Fiordoni. 2003. "The Italian Economy after the Bretton Woods Era (1971–2001)." In Matteo Di Matteo and Paolo Piacentini, eds., *The Italian Economy at the Dawn of the 21st Century*. Pp. 13–38. Farnham, England: Ashgate.

Verdery, Katherine. 2000. "Privatization as Transforming Persons." In Sorin Antohi and Vladimir Tismaneanu, eds., *The Revolutions of 1989 and Their Aftermath*. Pp. 175–197. Budapest: Central European University Press.

Vinay, Paolo. 2000. "Women in Health Professions and New Perspectives in Research." In Laura Corradi, ed., *Women's Health Network: State of Affairs, Concepts, Approaches, Organizations in the Health Movement: Country Report: Italy*. Pp. 23–26. Hanover, Germany: EWHNET.

Vita di Donna. 2006. "Copia di Vita." www.vitadidonnait/copia_di_vita_di_000070.htm (accessed December 2006).

Vološinov, V. N. 1973. *Marxism and the Philosophy of Language*. Cambridge, Mass.: Harvard University Press.

Von Barr, Christian. 2000. *The Common European Law of Torts*. Oxford: Oxford University Press.

Walkerdine, Valerie. 2006. "Workers in the New Economy: Transformation as Border Crossing." *Ethos* 34: 10–41.

Weber, Max. 2001. *The Protestant Ethic and the Spirit of Capitalism*. London: Routledge.

Weiss, David. 2005. "Constructing the Queer 'I': Performativity, Citationality and Desire in *Queer Eye for the Straight Guy*." *Popular Communication* 3(2): 73–95.

Weldes, Jutta, Mark Laffey, Hugh Gusterson, and Raymond Duvall, eds. 1999. *Cultures of Insecurity*. Minneapolis: University of Minnesota Press.

Westhues, Kenneth. 2008. *The Anatomy of an Academic Mobbing: Two Cases.* Lewiston, N.Y.: Mellen.

Whitaker, Elizabeth. 2003. "The Idea of Health: History, Medical Pluralism, and the Management of the Body in Emilia-Romagna, Italy." *Medical Anthropology Quarterly* 17(3): 348–375.

White, Geoffrey. 1990. "Moral Discourse and the Rhetoric of Emotions." In Catherine Lutz and Lila Abu-Lughod, eds., *Language and the Politics of Emotion.* Pp. 46–68. Cambridge: Cambridge University Press.

———. 2005. "Emotive Institutions." In Conerly Casey and Robert B. Edgerton, eds., *A Companion to Psychological Anthropology: Modernity and Psychocultural Change.* Pp. 241–253. Oxford: Blackwell.

Wilce, James M. 1998. *Eloquence in Trouble: The Poetics and Politics of Complaint in Rural Bangladesh.* New York: Oxford University Press.

———. 2003. "Speaking of Feelings." *American Anthropologist* 105(4): 852–855.

Williams, Megan K. 2004. "Mobbing: Italian Style." CBS Radio. www.cbc.ca/dispatches/sept03june04.html (accessed June 21, 2010).

Willis, Paul. 1977. *Learning to Labor: How Working Class Kids Get Working Class Jobs.* New York: Columbia University Press.

Willson, Perry. 1985. "'The Golden Factory': Industrial Health and Scientific Management in an Italian Light Engineering Firm: The Magneti Marelli in the Fascist Period." In Paul Weindling, ed., *The Social History of Occupational Health.* Pp. 240–258. London: Croom Helm.

Wilson, Ara. 2004. *The Intimate Economies of Bangkok: Tomboys, Tycoons and Avon Ladies in the Global City.* Berkeley: University of California Press.

Yanagisako, Sylvia J. 2002. *Producing Culture and Capital: Family Firms in Italy.* Princeton, N.J.: Princeton University Press.

Yelvington, Kevin A. 1995. *Producing Power: Ethnicity, Gender and Class in a Caribbean Workplace.* Philadelphia: Temple University Press.

———. 1996. "Flirting in the Factory." *Journal of the Royal Anthropological Institute* 2(2): 313–333.

Zippel, Kathrin S. 2006. *The Politics of Sexual Harassment: A Comparative Study of the United States, European Union, and Germany.* Cambridge: Cambridge University Press.

Index

industrialization, 3, 10, 19, 20, 28, 83, 88
INFAIL (National Fascist Institute for Insurance against Work-Related Accidents), 109
inflexibility, 83, 106, 124. *See also* flexibility; workers, inflexible
injury, 14, 16, 57–58, 64, 78, 80–81, 120, 139, 153, 155, 157
innuendo, sexual, 129, 134
insecurity, 4, 8, 53, 94, 104, 111, 156, 159, 169n3. *See also* security
insurance, 20–21, 105, 109, 120–121, 123, 127, 158, 174n10
integrity: moral, 136, 149; physical, 17, 62, 65, 109–110, 113, 126, 130, 134, 138–139, 142, 144, 149, 154–155, 160–161, 174n10; psychological, 57, 62, 134, 136, 139, 142, 154–155, 160, 174n10
internship, 23, 29, 31, 48
isolation, 1, 6, 7, 38, 51, 53, 57, 64–66, 68–69, 72, 86, 87, 89–90, 96, 103, 105, 112–113, 140, 144–145
ISPESL (Institute for Prevention and Work Safety), 112, 160, 173n4
Italian Labor Union, 159
Italian Movement of Associated Mobbees, 7
Italian Society of Occupational Health, 109
Italy, 1–9, 11–14, 16, 18, 21, 23, 27–29, 35–36, 41, 52, 55, 57–58, 62, 66, 67, 70, 77, 82, 84, 90, 92, 93, 96, 98, 100, 108, 110, 113–114, 118, 123, 125, 130–136, 138, 143, 148, 150–153, 156, 161, 164, 166, 170n2, 171n2:4, 174n3:1, 173n3; central, 19; northern, 5, 19, 28, 79, 85, 169n5; southern, 19, 65, 85, 97, 169n5. *See also* citizenship, Italian; Constitution, Italian; courts, Italian; demographics, Italian; economy, Italian; identity, Italian; society, Italian; state, Italian

Jain, Lochlann, 59, 81
jealousy, 82, 86, 145, 148

Kleinman, Arthur, 59
Krause, Elizabeth, 85

labor, 3–9, 13, 15, 17–20, 23–26, 29–31, 36–38, 40, 43, 45, 47, 49–50, 53, 56–57, 59, 61, 63–67, 78–79, 80–81, 86–87, 89–93, 97, 100–101, 104–105, 110, 117, 119, 127, 132, 134, 136, 140, 145–146, 152–153, 155, 157–158, 162–166, 169n5; 172n1; affective, 73, 77, 80, 146; casualized, 4, 8, 14, 67, 88; conceptualization of, 6, 9–10, 12, 18, 20, 27, 32, 41, 45,

53, 57, 61–62, 69, 89, 111, 125, 156; conditions, 125, 127; conflict, 2, 122, 159; costs, 11, 19, 82, 87; culture, 54, 160; devaluation of, 18, 119, 152; environment, 46, 63, 77, 94, 106, 107, 112, 114, 120, 126, 134, 140, 142, 151, 153, 156, 173n6; flexible, 65, 79, 82–83, 108; Fordist, 101; immaterial, 33, 57–58, 61–62, 64, 66–67, 77, 146, 169n6; industrial, 109, 125–126, 153; laws, 14, 55, 143, 170n10; manual, 62, 92; medicalization of, 57, 110; movements, 9, 14, 58; neoliberal, 14, 20, 35, 52, 55, 57, 68, 71, 88, 105, 108, 147, 149; organization of, 13, 17, 37, 113, 126–127, 151, 160; part-time, 22, 85; policies, 20–21, 41, 52, 55, 90; post-Fordist, 58, 61, 66, 77, 112, 126; post-industrial, 88, 119, 125, 153; practices, 17, 30, 40, 107–108, 110, 112, 125, 135, 151; privatization of, 8–9, 156; protection, 3–5, 9–10, 20, 21, 24, 27–29, 33–34, 48, 55, 62, 65, 89, 93, 108–109, 112, 126–127, 138, 148, 152, 154, 156, 158, 160; reforms, 3, 7; regimes, 5, 13, 21, 23, 30, 36, 38–39, 41, 52–53, 55, 57–58, 65–67, 70, 79–80, 83–84, 88, 92, 94, 98, 100, 108, 113–114, 125–126, 147, 149–151, 153, 169n4; relationships, 19, 30, 37, 53, 80, 114, 120–121, 126, 151; rights, 5, 26, 93, 118, 126, 148; risk, 4–5, 11, 17, 18, 20, 24–25, 34–36, 38, 45, 55, 59, 66–68, 79–80, 82, 85, 87–88, 100, 105, 110, 120, 126, 134, 148, 151, 153, 156–157, 159, 163–164, 166–167; stable, 18, 25–26, 28, 33, 35, 49, 58, 73, 100, 152, 166; value of, 29–30, 57, 161; volunteer, 62, 67, 80; women's, 34, 47, 83–87, 90, 172n1, 175n2. *See also* employers; labor force; markets, labor; medicalization, of labor; policy, labor; precariousness, of labor; protection, labor; reforms, labor; safeguards, of labor; workplace
labor force, 9, 15, 18–20, 25, 27–29, 33–34, 37–38, 46, 52, 82–85, 154–156, 158, 166–167
Law 196 (1997), 22, 156
Law 221 (1993), 156
Law 626 (1994), 154–155, 157–161, 163
lawyers, 14, 15, 50, 98, 104, 115, 139, 141, 145, 157
Lazzarato, Maurizio, 61, 172n3:3
Leymann, Heinz, 6
Lock, Margaret, 110

maladjustment, 120, 174n9
Marazzi, Christian, 61
marginalization, 6, 25, 41–42, 47, 65, 68, 72,

NEW ANTHROPOLOGIES OF EUROPE

Daphne Berdahl, Matti Bunzl, and Michael Herzfeld, founding editors

Noelle J. Molé is a political and medical anthropologist. She teaches in the Writing Program and Department of Anthropology at Princeton University.